Cohesion and Dissent in America

SUNY Series in American Literature
David R. Sewell, Editor

Cohesion and Dissent in America

Carol Colatrella
and
Joseph Alkana
Editors

STATE UNIVERSITY OF NEW YORK PRESS

Published by
State University of New York Press, Albany

Printed in the United States of America

For information, address State University of New York
Press, State University Plaza, Albany, N.Y., 12246

Production by E. Moore
Marketing by Fran Keneston

Library of Congress Cataloging-in-Publication Data

Cohesion and dissent in America / edited by Carol Colatrella and
Joseph Alkana.
p. cm. — (SUNY series in American literature)
ISBN 0-7914-1717-4 (alk. paper). — ISBN 0-7914-1718-2 (pbk. : alk. paper)
1. American literature—History and criticism—Theory, etc.
2. United States—Civilization—Historiography. 3. Literature and history. 4. Bercovitch, Sacvan. 5. Historicism. I. Colatrella, Carol. II. Alkana, Joseph, 1953– . III. Series.
PS25.C57 1993
810.9—dc20 92-45265
CIP

10 9 8 7 6 5 4 3 2 1

Contents

Acknowledgments

The contributors to this anthology have all been influenced by the work of Sacvan Bercovitch. Many of the chapters began as projects undertaken during a 1987 summer seminar on American dissent conducted by him at the School of Criticism and Theory (SCT) at Dartmouth College. The enthusiasm of SCT participants encouraged us as we gathered various essays that resulted from the seminar experience; we thank them collectively. We also thank the administration and faculty of Dartmouth for their support of the SCT, especially Marianne Hirsch, who served as faculty liaison, and we are grateful for the encouragement and advice of the school's administrators, Geoffrey Hartman and Michael Riffaterre.

A number of colleagues offered practical advice and professional support that assisted us; Mara Holt, Wayne Lesser, Peter Bellis, Robert F. Denton, June Deery, and Michael Halloran deserve special thanks. Our editor at SUNY Press, Carola Sautter, and the press's reviewers gave careful criticism that guided our editing; we thank them for their time and patience. We appreciate the support of our families and acknowledge the significant contribution of Kerry Alkana.

Our greatest debt of gratitude is owed to Sacvan Bercovitch, who graciously shared our burden by generously giving his advice and support on many occasions. His teaching and mentoring demonstrate a thoughtful concern that we appreciate and that we attempt to emulate in working with our own students.

We dedicate our work to David Alkana and Sascha Bercovitch, who are America's future.

Thanks are due to the following individuals and publishers for permission to quote from copyrighted works:

Valerie Eliot and Faber and Faber, for permission to reproduce excerpts from "Little Gidding," "The Dry Salvages," "Burnt Norton," and various letters by Eliot in Chapter 4, "T. S. Eliot's American Dissent/Descent," by Donald Childs.

Scofield Thayer, for permission to reproduce lines from "To Li T'ai Po," by Maxwell Bodenheim, and Houghton Mifflin Company, for permission to quote from "Guns as Keys," by Amy Lowell in Chapter 6, "The Orient as Pretext for Aesthetic and Cultural Revolution in Modern American Poetry," by Kathleen Flanagan.

The following chapters have appeared in other books or journals. Acknowledgment is made to the publishers for permission to reprint them here:

Chapter 1, "Discovering America: A Cross-Cultural Perspective," by Sacvan Bercovitch, is adapted from his introduction to *The Rites of Assent: Transformations in the Symbolic Construction of America* (New York and London: Routledge, 1993).

Chapter 2, "Jewish Critics and American Literature: The Case of Sacvan Bercovitch," by Rael Meyerowitz, originally appeared in *Studies in Puritan American Spirituality* 3 (1992).

Chapter 3, "Sacvan Bercovitch, Stanley Cavell, and the Romance Theory of American Fiction," by Emily Miller Budick, originally appeared in *PMLA* 107, no. 1 (January 1992).

Chapter 5, "Work on Truth in America: The Example of William James," by Barry Allen, originally appeared in *Studies in Puritan American Spirituality* 3 (1992).

Chapter 8, "The Hybridity of Culture in Arturo Islas's *The Rain God*, by José David Saldívar, is a version of an essay that originally appeared in *Dispositio* 16/41 (1991).

Chapter 10, "Problematizing American Dissent: The Subject of Phillis Wheatley," by Helen Burke, originally appeared in *Tulsa Studies in Women's Literature* 10, no. 1 (Spring 1991).

CAROL COLATRELLA
JOSEPH ALKANA

JOSEPH ALKANA

Introduction

Cohesion, Dissent, and the Aims of Criticism

Of recent theories about American culture and cultural studies, perhaps the most wide-ranging in their implications are Sacvan Bercovitch's ideas about cohesion and dissent. Bercovitch has developed these ideas throughout the course of his writings on American literature and culture. In these writings—most prominently, *The Puritan Origins of the American Self, The American Jeremiad,* and, more recently, *The Office of The Scarlet Letter*—Bercovitch has focused on texts central to the way Americans define themselves to themselves. His inquiries into these texts have disclosed patterns of American rhetoric and symbology that have been characteristic, enduring, and in many respects dominant. At the same time as he has examined these texts, Bercovitch repeatedly has questioned pervasive assumptions about method and interpretation in American literary and cultural studies.

One such assumption that has been central to American literary historians has to do with the relationship between the writer and society. American literary scholars frequently have shaped their work in the form of narratives of conflict, specifically conflict between individual writers and American society as a whole. Thus, for example, in two founding works of American literary studies, Vernon Parrington traces the development of "native liberalisms" in their struggles against traditional authority, and F. O. Matthiessen, in a similar vein, claims as the "one common denominator" of American Renaissance texts "their devotion to the possibilities of democracy."[1] Many influential studies that followed, even those that primarily concerned themselves with issues of aesthetics and consciousness, would rely on a similar characterization of American literature. In one such study, the consideration of form and style is enabled by a particular vision of American culture: "American literature is a struggle with already existing literary, social, and historical organizations for power over environment and over language itself."[2] From this perspective, American literary consciousness emerges through its struggles against convention. Notions such as this depend on a narrative of American culture, a narrative constituted by the tension between a conformist society and a series of individual voices more closely associated with an ideal of America.

The relationship of these individual voices to society, along with the ways in which scholars have narrated this story, have been subjected to a series of inquiries within the work of Sacvan Bercovitch. In *The Puritan Origins of the American Self,* the constituent terms of this narrative, "America" and the "self," are discussed. Bercovitch explores how these two concepts simultaneously have come to prominence in American culture—and, most significantly, how these terms work to sustain each other within a teleological vision of America. In this national vision, America is always in progress toward its ideal. The term "America" consequently conveys a sense of both promise and anxiety about the shortcomings of the present. As Bercovitch notes in the opening of *The Puritan Origins,* this vision has had immense power in American culture. Accordingly, he centers his analysis "on the interaction of language, myth, and society, in an effort to trace the sources of our obsessive concern with the meaning of America."[3]

The other term in this pair, the "self," has also had great power in our culture. Like America, the self operates proleptically as it continually refers to an anticipated ideal. To understand this term, it is necessary to examine something other than the typical claim made on its behalf. The self has routinely been granted a kind of epistemological priority over society as a whole. Truth first arises in the individual consciousness, and only then does the society have access to it. In those narratives of American literary history that promote this claim for the centrality of the self, a debased society rejects the individual revelations of truth. As Bercovitch suggests in *The Puritan Origins,* once one accepts the claim of the priority of the individual consciousness, one is then obliged to accept the entire narrative of the *opposition* of individual consciousness to society. An alternative to this understanding of the relationship between the self and society is implied in Bercovitch's opening statement of the importance of "the rhetoric of American identity." The focus on rhetoric and on "the interaction of language, myth, and society" signifies a departure from traditional ways of approaching American writings. From this perspective, the individual work is neither the expression of a transcendent consciousness nor is it the incarnation of an American essence. Instead, meaning arises in the exploration of the specifics of social interaction.

Bercovitch's rhetorical analysis in *The Puritan Origins,* which provides the methodological basis for his subsequent work, describes how the symbol of selfhood has been invested with significance. In *The American Jeremiad* he extends his analysis of American selfhood by calling for renewed attention to the relationship between the self and the community. Specifically, he demonstrates how individual criticism of American society and demands for change may operate as ritual activities. Bercovitch argues that because of its "prescribed ritual form . . . [c]onflict itself was rendered a mode of control: a means of facilitating process through which process became an aid to socialization." For an example of this process, we may look to Thoreau, whose "aversion to most aspects of American life is well documented, and nowhere more fully than in *Walden.*" What is questioned here by Bercovitch is the way critics have often accepted Thoreau's aversion on its own terms, without attention to the way his criticisms of American life, particularly those in *Walden,* have themselves been engaged within the rhetoric of an American national errand. As Bercovitch states, "What makes *Walden* part of the tradition of the jeremiad is that the act of mimesis enables Thoreau simultaneously to berate his neighbors and to safeguard the values that undergird their way of life." Thoreau may call for individual and social change, but because this call is based on a return to an ideal of America, it effectively functions as a ritualized jeremiad.[4]

The symbol of America necessarily plays a large role in the rhetoric of the jeremiad. Conventionally, during the course of the jeremiad, the community is called to task for falling short of the ideal of America. An imagined ideal American community, with which the audience is invited to identify, is then projected onto a fictional future. The corruptions of daily activity are symbolically purged, and the performance over, a renewed sense of community is affirmed. Thus, the jeremiad ratifies the social order through a ritual process reminiscent of the Aristotelian psychology of tragedy. Bercovitch's interpretation of such conflict as a ritualized social activity exposes the shortcomings of critical celebrations of individual consciousness. By showing how the energy of the marginal consciousness is redirected toward the service of a central, communal ideal, Bercovitch, in effect, deconstructs the spatial metaphor on which the individual-community dichotomy—and the concomitant allegiance to the individual consciousness—has rested. The logic of the American jeremiad demands that the centrality of the community routinely be reconceived by the marginalized individual consciousness. And the individual consciousness, authorized by the community, no longer appears as a detached and free point of origin for ethical action.

Bercovitch thus begins his analysis of cohesion and dissent in American culture by interrogating an American literary history that has often posited an opposition between the individual and society. By shifting away from an analysis of literature that stresses the individual consciousness as the source of truth, Bercovitch displaces the radical dichotomy between, on the one hand, the individual consciousness as a source of knowledge and, on the other hand, a conformist community that reserves for itself the authority to adjudicate claims of knowledge. Instead, he distinguishes between individual experience (or belief) and a desire for social cohesion that routinely subsumes the former category. No longer do we have a situation in which literary works are *either* expressions of individual consciousness (consequently worthy of canonical status) *or* debased expressions of conventional, conformist thought. Rather, we have a *dynamic* relationship between individual and community, one that accommodates individual protest by highlighting the quintessentially American function of protest.

In *The Office of The Scarlet Letter*, Bercovitch continues his inquiry into a selfhood that derives its significance from the symbology of America. Turning his attention to a work central to the nineteenth-century American canon, Bercovitch explores the link between Hawthorne's comment that "the scarlet letter had not done its office," and Hester Prynne's return and voluntary restoration of the scarlet letter at the novel's conclusion. The apparent discrepancy between Hester's protest against Puritan authority and her final return to the locus of this authority is a problem that has generated relatively little discussion among the novel's critics. This oversight is not especially surprising given the scholarly preoccupation with Hester's resistance against narrow-minded community authority and the implied potential for transcendence on the part of the individual imagination. To Bercovitch, however, Hester Prynne's ultimate accommodation of Puritan authority reveals a most important aspect of the story. As Bercovitch notes, "*The Scarlet Letter* is a story of socialization in which the point of socialization is not to conform, but to consent."[5]

Socialization might seem an unusual perspective from which to view *The Scarlet Letter.* After all, in the character of Hester Prynne, Hawthorne provides one of the strongest nineteenth-century literary images of an individual who struggles against stultifying social conventions. Yet it is important to recall the antebellum political and intellectual milieu to which Hawthorne was responding. Because of the pervasive fear of social breakdown in the antebellum United States, a focus on the issue of socialization rather than individual consciousness is germane to *The Scarlet Letter.* Threats of regional conflict were prominent, but perhaps more importantly, social cohesion was especially threatened by the ethos of the expanding market economy. Whereas at one time eighteenth-century ideas about compassion and sympathy could be taken for granted, such mechanisms for social good, though still mainstays of antebellum moral philosophy, decreased in importance during the course of the nineteenth century. And, although nativist sentiments were not yet at their late nineteenth-century level, contemporary attacks on immigration indicate a feared loss of social homogeneity. Moreover, as Bercovitch notes in *The Office of The Scarlet Letter,* the years immediately preceding the writing and publication of the novel were politically tumultuous: not only was 1848 a time of revolution in Europe, but it was also the year of the Women's Rights Convention at Seneca Falls.

Within this historical situation, Hawthorne's use of the symbol of the scarlet letter suggests the routine operation of consensus in American society. Bercovitch focuses on Hawthorne's silence about why Hester decides to return to New England and to resume wearing the scarlet letter. As Bercovitch remarks, "she has no choice but to resume the A. To make choices involves alternatives; it requires us to reject or exclude on the ground that certain meanings are wrong or incompatible or mutually contradictory" (*Office* 21–22). Her action in the final chapter describes the reciprocal operation of individual dissent and social cohesion. Hester validates her individualism with an act that simultaneously affirms individualism and social hegemony. And, as Bercovitch continues, the reader is implicated in the process through the need to interpret: "To have choice (in Hawthorne's fiction) is to keep open the prospect for interpretation on the grounds that reality never means either one thing or another but, rather, is Meaning fragmented by plural points of view." This "fragmentation" creates "an enriched sense of unity, provided we attend to the principles of liberal exegesis" (*Office* 22). Thus, Bercovitch tells us, in our attention to the ambiguities of *The Scarlet Letter,* we have been following Hawthorne's directions of how to interpret the novel according to the logic of American culture, that of "liberal exegesis." If, however, we do not follow Hawthorne's directions, we instead find ourselves confronted with an ideological question: How does liberalism work?

In response to this question, Bercovitch observes the insistence of the ending, the fact that although "process" prevails, it serves to obscure the operation of "telos" (*Office* 159). The "process" to which he refers amounts to the multiplicity of interpretations of the scarlet letter that Hawthorne repeatedly invokes, a multiplicity that has preoccupied critics interested in ambiguity. The "telos" has a more definite, albeit double significance: the return of Hester Prynne and the reassertion of normative social relations. This fulfillment of the office of the scarlet letter is inevitable, and it is the manifestation of cultural cohesion. Ironically, this operation of social cohesion is what we see at work in scholarly analyses that celebrate the ambiguities of *The Scarlet Letter.* Problematizing the feature that has so often been central to critics of Hawthorne's writings, Bercovitch defines ambiguity as "the absence of conflict" (*Office* 26). Hawthorne's literary strategy amounts to an enactment of liberal ideology: "His purpose is to rechannel indeterminacy into pluralism, conflict into correspondence, and relativism into consensus" (*Office* 24). The problem with many past scholarly interpretations of Hawthorne has been that in their celebrations of indeterminacy and ambiguity, they have participated in a tradition of liberal exegesis. By disclosing how the interpretive act is already inscribed within cultural bounds, Bercovitch reveals the manner in which this scholarly tradition of interpretation effectively displaces political difference with pluralistic interpretation.

The critique of pluralism that Bercovitch offers in *The Office of The Scarlet Letter* extends the account of cultural dynamics he has provided in his earlier works, and it also provides a subtle yet important shift of emphasis. Both *The Puritan Origins of the American Self* and *The American Jeremiad* discuss works in the literary canon, such as *Walden* and *Leaves of Grass,* alongside non-literary writings, such as early American sermons, in terms of their relationships to American culture. But in *The Office of The Scarlet Letter,* he describes his purpose as the attempt "to integrate ideological and aesthetic criticism" (xvii). And he elaborates on this proposed integration when he states that while his own approach attends to the workings of ideology, it does not preclude a concern with literary structure: "ideological analysis can be a richly aesthetic form of criticism. Properly conceived, it blends the appreciative and the cognitive" (*Office* 155). Having established in his earlier work the significance of rhetorical criticism, Bercovitch now turns to certain aspects of formal criticism in his analysis. As he states, his approach "blends the appreciative and the cognitive" with the goal of replacing "the reductive polarities of both old formalisms and new moralisms" (155). This methodological revision warrants attention. By highlighting the significance of aesthetic issues within a piece of explicitly ideological criticism, he seems to suggest an increasingly complex idea of the role of the critic. Certainly the critic in *The Office of The Scarlet Letter* has the obligation to read against the grain of the novel, to examine the significance of contexts to the text. But, in addition, the "aesthetic" and the "appreciative" cannot be ignored by the critic of American culture. Instead of evoking the image of the heroic reader who uncovers the hidden political and cultural significance of the text, Bercovitch assumes that the text does not necessarily fail to act on the critical reader.

Bercovitch's reassessment of the critic's work introduces the important issue of how scholars are to understand the discipline of literary studies. In recent years, scholars have discussed with increasing specificity how and why certain writings have been excluded from disciplinary concern, and they have undertaken the important work of reevaluating the literary canon and those critical works that have helped to shape this canon. The construction of these dominant discourses of American culture along with the ways in which a network of interlocking symbols have been invested with significance are especially salient issues in Bercovitch's work. His analyses of symbology have helped to open up literary and cultural studies in important ways. A potential problem arises, however. Like all systems of analysis that bring to light underlying processes, Bercovitch's has the capacity to generate a critical formalism, one that would advance a deterministic vision of American culture and pessimism about the possibility of change. Such a closed, deterministic analysis could seem the logical outcome of a theoretical opposition between individual will and social cohesion that inevitably resolves itself in a ritualized and mutually reinforcing manner.

Despite the appeal of this logic and the tough-minded critical posture it evokes, this manner of interpreting American culture would decidedly contradict the rhetorical tone and the inclination of Bercovitch's own work. As he notes, he neither advocates "a conspiracy theory of canon formation" nor the idea that "literature is a form of co-optation" (*Office* xx). His discussion of the way a work such as *The Scarlet Letter* both depicts and engages its readers in an enactment of a socialization process shows how criticism has perpetuated this process of mystification. But by removing the patina of the natural which has been associated with individualistic American dissent, Bercovitch implies the possibility of a social criticism that is not complicit in ritualized cooptation.[6] And, by announcing as his methodological goal the integration of "ideological and aesthetic criticism," Bercovitch offers the possibility of altering the terms of literary studies. He suggests how to avoid the problem created by dualistic figurations of the discipline that only offer as possibilities either endorsements of modernist conceptions of the individual imagination, or a style of historicist scholarship that threatens to obscure the distinctive qualities of literary studies.

Nevertheless, the possibility of interpreting Bercovitch's work as both pessimistic and deterministic remains as long as we do not directly acknowledge the cultural work of the critic's writing. Accordingly, it is necessary here to add—or, more properly, restore—the term *pedagogy* to the debate over Americanist criticism. The way pedagogy has been obscured becomes most apparent when we look at the way that scholars have distinguished between theory and practice. In the conventional way of conceiving this division, theory has amounted to the reading of certain types of texts, generally philosophical or metacritical commentaries. By contrast, practice has been the reading of certain other texts, those traditionally defined as more literary. With the advent of poststructuralistic notions of intertextuality and the argument that all texts may be examined in terms of literary structure, the distinction between different types of texts has seemed increasingly arbitrary. This distinction has largely appeared to be the result of those historical and institutional pressures that led to the formation of distinct disciplines. If we now are willing to understand the theoretical work of literary studies as the reading of all texts, we can acknowledge as the practical ends of scholarship the displaced act of pedagogy. Teaching is, after all, what most academics ostensibly get paid for. Should we not then—in the same spirit that motivates us to consider the cultural contexts of aesthetic works—restore to consideration the activity that fills the days of so many scholars?

By restoring pedagogy to the critical discussion, we can avoid both the despair that accompanies determinism and the grandiosity that situates literary and cultural analysis at the forefront of all human activity. The restoration of pedagogy is an important analytic move for those concerned about the potentially deterministic tendencies of the analysis of American cultural processes. By noting that academics will use Bercovitch's analyses to teach American literature and culture, we may find a counterbalance to the apparent logic of determinism. Indeed, a sensitivity to the urgency of Bercovitch's prose suggests that however difficult or improbable the possibilities of changing American culture, on some level such a possibility is sufficiently available to warrant a response other than a passive acceptance of the seemingly inevitable.

This collection of essays demonstrates the dissemination of Bercovitch's ideas through a generation of scholars who have found themselves constructively responding to his work. The essays that follow offer a variety of reconceptions of American literary and cultural dynamics, reconceptions that have arisen through engagements with Bercovitch's writings. These engagements, as one might expect, do not necessarily lead to new readings of formal structure in various works—although, as in the case of Bercovitch's reading of *The Scarlet Letter*, attention to such structures routinely plays an important part of analysis. What they do point toward are enhanced understandings of the cultural work literature has performed, the ways in which certain cultural tensions are inscribed in texts, and the ways these texts may perform cultural work of their own. The direction established by Bercovitch's model of cohesion and dissent in American culture guides the writers of these essays in their explorations of American cultural dynamics. Quite often, the discussion returns to potential difficulties within the analytic model itself when it is used to investigate a specific text or problem.

The first group of essays, in the section called "Cohesion and Dissent in the History of American Theory," presents three discussions of Bercovitch's ideas as they bear on the theories and activities of Americanist critics. Bercovitch himself offers a history of his own inquiry into American culture, an inquiry that began with a recognition of the symbology of American culture as "an open secret" to a Canadian. His cross-cultural investigation into the "institutionalization of dissent" reveals important problems, not only with respect to the analysis of literature but with regard to the stance of those critics who define themselves as oppositional. In "Jewish Critics and American Literature: The Case of Sacvan Bercovitch," Rael Meyerowitz discusses the ambiguities and difficulties attendant to Bercovitch's position as a Jewish commentator on the most sacred texts of American literature (be they Puritan or nineteenth-century). In addition, he raises a concern similar to that of Bercovitch: Meyerowitz asks whether theoretically sophisticated scholars are themselves implicated in the problematic ritualizing and containment of dissent. Emily Miller Budick's essay, "Sacvan Bercovitch, Stanley Cavell, and the Romance Theory of American Fiction," addresses the idea of the containment of dissent from the perspective of one interested in the function of the American romance. Using Stanley Cavell's ideas about speech as a way to explore Bercovitch's conception of American ideology, Budick turns to *The Scarlet Letter* and discusses the problems raised by the commitment to free and uncircumscribed speech on the part of writers of the romance.

The second section, "Establishing Modernist Traditions of Dissent," features discussions of writers whose work shortly preceded or coincided with the creation of American literary studies as an academic discipline. Donald Childs, in "T. S. Eliot's American Dissent/Descent," notes a series of recurrent tensions in Eliot's writings, particularly his prose. Childs suggests that by recognizing Eliot's reactions to Puritan rhetoric and ideology we can develop a fuller understanding of the kinds of concerns that motivated Eliot's literary criticism, his socio-political writings, and his early work in philosophy. The operation of cohesion and dissent in philosophy is discussed in Barry Allen's essay, "Works on Truth in America: The Example of William James." Allen argues that James's Pragmatism follows in the tradition of an Emersonian rhetoric of American newness, and, accordingly, it neglects its own roots in the western philosophical tradition of truth as that which leads to good. By ignoring these intellectual roots, James unwittingly reinvents in an American idiom the traditional bases for philosophical discourse. The apparently opposite action of translation of discourse *out* of an American idiom is treated in Kathleen Flanagan's "The Orient as Pretext for Aesthetic and Cultural Revolution in Modern American Poetry." Flanagan tells of how modernists such as Ezra Pound, Amy Lowell, and John Gould Fletcher maintained an idealized image of oriental aesthetics, an image divorced from all cultural and historical realities, to ground their own work. As Flanagan points out, these writers used this aesthetic to introduce apparent innovations that, in fact, left unchallenged central tenets of western poetics.

The third group of essays, "Cohesion, Dissent, and Contemporary Cultural Boundaries," offers discussions of the dynamics of dissent in more recent literary works. In "'Chaos Goes Uncourted': John Yau's Dis(-)Orienting Poetics," Priscilla Wald explores the relationship between aesthetic and political representation. This relationship forms one way in which cultural subjects "can be dialectically engaged with the processes of their creation and location—and with the epic task of founding a 'home.'" Specific cultural tasks are also evident in José David Saldívar's "The Hybridity of Culture in Arturo Islas's *The Rain God*." Saldívar, noting the tensions specific to Chicano identity, indicates how the dynamics of book publishing shapes the contemporary reception of ethnic literature and how in the work of Islas we may find a refutation of the narrow American sense of literary and cultural heritage. The relationship between the writer's work and the politics of literature forms the basis of Kathy Smith's inquiry, "Norman Mailer and the Radical Text." Smith discusses Mailer's recent work with PEN, the international writers' organization, and his *Armies of the Night* with respect to the logic of consensus. In these three essays we can see how challenges to cultural authority reveal the normalizing discourse of cohesion as it forces these writers to look back critically onto the construction of the dissenting subject.

The dissenting subject forms the focus of the final section, "Problems of Marginality in America." Helen Burke's essay, "Problematizing American Dissent: The Subject of Phillis Wheatley," raises difficult questions about the study of works that had been excluded from the modernist literary canon. Distinguishing between Wheatley as a rhetorical subject and Wheatley as a historical subject, Burke shows how Wheatley's identity as a writer "was achieved at the cost of reinscribing the very structure that oppressed her." Speech did not empower Wheatley, nor does it resolve the problems raised in Theron Britt's "Before the Law, after the Judgment: Schizophrenia in John Barth's *The Floating Opera*." Commenting on the link between law and schizophrenia in Barth's first novel, Britt argues that although the critique of the existential self undermines traditional authority, the cultural pattern of cohesion reasserts itself in the appearance of postmodern indeterminism. In the concluding essay, "Bercovitch's Paradox: Critical Dissent, Marginality, and the Example of Melville," Carol Colatrella returns to the issue of Bercovitch's cross-cultural criticism through a discussion of *Typee*. Melville's sailor protagonist, Tommo, serves as a kind of model of Bercovitch's cultural critic, one who is sufficiently engaged to feel a part of and apart from both American and Typee cultures.

Tommo's discomfort is reminiscent of the position of the critic of American culture. Insofar as criticism of American culture is all too easily understood to reinforce cultural cohesion, those who find themselves responding to Bercovitch's ideas can take no easy comfort in any simple notion of oppositional criticism. Through the act of teaching, critics of culture are transformed into disseminators of culture. This is not by any means meant to suggest that criticism is futile. Nevertheless, critics must recognize the cultural resources that have so often transformed dissent into cohesion. Close attention to these resources guides the writers of the following essays in their considerations of the specific historical and cultural situations that accompany the texts they discuss.

NOTES

1. Vernon L. Parrington, *Main Currents in American Thought* (New York: Harcourt, Brace, and Co., 1930), 1.vi. F.O. Matthiessen, *The American Renaissance* (New York: Oxford University Press, 1941), ix. Critics have recently reassessed Matthiessen's work, noting the conflicts between his stated political allegiances and his inattention to slavery and race relations among other problems. For an extensive treatment of these issues, see William E. Cain, *F. O. Matthiessen and the Politics of Criticism* (Madison: University of Wisconsin Press, 1988). Also of interest are Jonathan Arac, "F.O. Matthiessen: Authorizing an American Renaissance," in *The American Renaissance Reconsidered,* ed. Walter Benn Michaels and Donald E. Pease (Baltimore: Johns Hopkins University Press, 1984), 90–112, and Myra Jehlen's remarks about Matthiessen in her introduction to *Ideology and Classic American Literature,* ed. Sacvan Bercovitch and Myra Jehlen (New York: Cambridge University Press, 1986).

2. Richard Poirier, *A World Elsewhere: The Place of Style in American Literature* (New York: Oxford University Press, 1966), ix.

3. Sacvan Bercovitch, *The Puritan Origins of the American Self,* (New Haven: Yale University Press, 1975), ix.

4. Sacvan Bercovitch, *The American Jeremiad* (Madison: University of Wisconsin Press, 1978), 160, 185, 186.

5. Sacvan Bercovitch, *The Office of the Scarlet Letter* (Baltimore: Johns Hopkins University Press, 1991), xiii. Further references to *Office* will be made parenthetically in the text.

6. In the closing chapter of *The American Jeremiad*, "The Symbol of America," Bercovitch points out that any rhetorical power apparently gained by the cultural critic through the use of the term *America* is routinely redirected into a ritualized reaffirmation of American teleology. Accordingly, the purposes of the wary critic are best served by an avoidance of any visionary appeal to American potential.

Part I

Cohesion and Dissent in the History of American Theory

SACVAN BERCOVITCH

1

Discovering America: A Cross-Cultural Perspective

When I first came to the United States, I knew nothing about America. I attribute my immigrant naiveté to the peculiar insularity of my upbringing. I was nurtured in the rhetoric of denial. To begin with, I absorbed Canada's provincial attitudes toward "the States"—a provinciality deepened by the pressures of geographical proximity and economic dependence. Characteristically, this expressed itself through a mixture of hostility and amnesia, as though we were living next door to an invisible giant, whose invisibility could be interpreted as nonexistence. The interpretation was reflected in the virtual absence of "America" throughout my education, from elementary and high school, where U.S. history ended in 1776, to my fortuitous college training at the adult extension of the Montreal YMCA, where a few unavoidable U.S. authors

---

Reprinted from *The Rites of Assent* by Sacvan Bercovitch, 1993, by permission of the publisher, Routledge, Inc.

were taught as part of a course on Commonwealth literature. I learned certain hard facts, of course, mainly pejorative, and I knew the landmarks from Wall Street to Hollywood; but the symbology that connected them—the American dream that elsewhere (I later discovered) was an open secret, a mystery accredited by the world—remained hidden from me, like the spirit in the letter of the uninitiate's text.

A more important influence was the Yiddishist-left-wing world of my parents. I recall it as an outpost barricaded from the threat of assimilation by radical politics and belles lettres, an immigrant enclave locked into a romantic-Marxist utopianism long after its disillusionment with Stalin, and fortified by the alleged spiritual values of art in the face of utter cultural estrangement. It was there, far more than at school, that I learned the strategies of denial. Their object in this case was Canada. I cannot recall a single reference to national matters in serious conversation. Literary discussions ranged from Sholom Aleichem to Franz Kafka, with polemical excursions on Yiddish contemporaries published in the local newspaper, *Der Keneder Odler* ("The Canadian Eagle," a mixed metaphor, carrying cross-cultural ironies for me even then). Politics consisted in a conflict of imaginary options for world revolution, extending from Trotsky's lost cause to the visionary boundaries of anarchism. It seems appropriate that I should have graduated from high school not to college, but, for several years, to a socialist kibbutz in what used to be called "the Arabian desert."

The harvest of these experiences was an abiding suspicion of high rhetoric, especially as a blueprint of the future, and an abiding fascination with the redemptive promises of language, especially as a source of personal identity and social cohesion. Still, nothing in my background had prepared me for my encounter with a secular modern nation living in a dream. "I hear America singing," writes Whitman, who concludes: "The United States are themselves the greatest poem." So, too, Emerson: "America is a poem in our eyes." I arrived at a similar conclusion, but from a different perspective and to a different effect. My experience of the music of America (as I came to think of it) was closer to the epiphany of otherness recorded in Kafka's "Investigations of a Dog." The canine narrator of that story tells us that one day in his youth a group of seven dogs appeared before him, suddenly, "out of some place of darkness," to the accompaniment of "terrible" and ravishing sounds:

> At that time I still knew hardly anything of the creative gift with which the canine race alone is endowed . . . for though

> music had [always] surrounded me . . . my elders had [never] drawn my attention to it. . . . [A]ll the more astonishing, then . . . were those seven musical artists to me. They did not speak, they did not sing, they remained generally silent, almost determinedly silent; but from the empty air they conjured music. Everything was music, the lifting and setting of their feet, certain turns of the head, their running and standing still, the positions they took up in relation to one another, the symmetrical patterns which they produced. . . . [M]y mind could attend to nothing but this blast of music which seemed to come from all sides, from the heights, from the deeps, from everywhere, surrounding the listener, overwhelming him. . . . I longed to . . . beg [the musicians] to enlighten me, to ask them what they were doing. . . . [Their music] was incomprehensible to me, and also quite definitely beyond my capacities . . . I rushed about, told my story, made accusations and investigations. . . . I was resolved to pursue [the problem] indefatigably until I solved it.

The pursuit unfolds as a series of ingenious inferences, deductions, and explications extending to virtually every aspect of "dogdom," from the higher laws of "universal dog nature" to the specialized issue of "soaring dogs" (how do they "remain for the most part high up in the air, apparently doing nothing but simply resting there?") and the still-controversial "rules of science" for getting food: Should you bring it forth by "incantation" or "water the ground as much as you can"?[1] Nothing, it seems, escapes observation, except the presence of human beings.

Kafka's story is a great parable of interpretation as mystification—facts marshaled endlessly to build up contexts whose effect, if not intent, is to conceal or explain away. It is also a great parable of the limitations of cultural critique—*limitations*, not just illusions, for in fact the story conveys a good deal about the dog's world, in spite of the narrator's inability to transcend it; or rather, as a function of his nontranscending condition. In this double sense, negative and ambiguous, Kafka's "investigations" apply directly to my own as an Americanist. The general parallels may be drawn out through a Chinese box of skewed interpretive positions: dog vis-à-vis human, Russian-Jewish immigrant vis-à-vis French Canadian Montreal, Canada vis-à-vis the States, and eventually "America," as I came to understand it, vis-à-vis the cultural norms and structures it represents.

These are not precise symmetries; but they point to certain

common principles of exegesis. I begin with the negative implications. (1) To interpret is not to make sense of a mystery out there. It is to discover otherness as mystery (something "overwhelming," "incomprehensible"), and then to explain the mystery as the wonders of an invisible world, a realm of meaningful "silence," resonant with universals. (2) To investigate those wonders is not to come to terms with the new or unexpected. It is to domesticate the unknown by transferring the agency of meaning from the mystery out there to realities we recognize, and so to invest the familiar—ourselves, or our kind—with the powers of a higher reality: "universal laws," the view of eternity, the canine principles of music. (3) To establish the laws and rules of that higher reality is not to break through the limitations we experience. It is to deny our conditions of dependency by translating those limitations into metastructures of culture, history, and the mind. As for motives, we may infer from Kafka's parable that they are self-defensive or self-aggrandizing, and that in either case interpretation is a strategy for repressing the actual worlds around us, expressing itself through yearnings for a world elsewhere.

We might call this the "hermeneutics of transcendence." The possibilities it offers for self-aggrandizement (repressing otherness for purposes of control or incorporation) are not far to seek: One need only think of the manifold uses of *he* for God and/or humanity. But this is to interpret from the vantage point of dominance. From the dog's subordinate point of view, or the scholar's, to magnify the categories of our containment is to diminish our capacities for understanding.[2]

A negative prospect, as I said, especially since it is Kafka's *donné* that we have no choice but to interpret. However, it is complemented in the parable by the *enabling* ambiguities of limitation. As the title suggests, "Investigations of a Dog" points not only to the dog's attempts to describe Kafka's world, but, at the same time, to Kafka's attempts to describe dogdom. And the result, as I interpret it, is not a double impasse. It is a model of cross-cultural criticism. Its terms are reciprocity, as against dichotomy: not canine *or* human, but the contingencies of both, as revealed (in degree) through the re-cognition of limitation. We might call this the "hermeneutics of nontranscendence." It may be said to reverse traditional comparativist methods by its emphasis on the historicity of archetypes and essences. Its aim is not to harmonize "apparent" differences (in the manner of pluralist consensus), but on the contrary to highlight conflicting appearances, so as to explore the substantive differences they imply. This entails the recognition of universals as culture-specific barriers to understanding; it is grounded in the faith that barriers, so specified, may become (within limits) avenues of discovery; and its logic may be briefly stated. If dreams of transcendence are indices to the traps of culture, then inquiry into the trapping process may provide insight both into our own and into others' actual nontranscending condition. Such insight is problematic, provisional, and *nourished* by a frustrating sense of boundaries. It denies us access to apocalypse, but it helps make our surrounding worlds visible.

I would like to think that my own investigations as an Americanist show the benefits of this approach. For purposes of analysis, I review these thematically, rather than chronologically. My subject is the discovery of an other America, in the double sense of Kafka's parable: negatively, as cultural otherness, and ambiguously, as a set of cultural secrets, the other America hidden from view by interpretation. Emerson's American Scholar grows concentrically toward transcendence, in an expanding circle from nature to books to representative selfhood. My own unrepresentative (not to say eccentric) experience may be described as a series of increasingly particularized border crossings: first, into America proper; then, into the interdisciplinary field of American studies; and finally, into the special area of American literary scholarship.

I crossed into the States with a Canadian's commonsense view of the Americas: two continents, North and South, each of them a mosaic of nations—which is to say, a variety of European models of civilization—joined by the semitropical bush countries of Central America. How could I *not* see "America" as a cultural artifact? I knew that that sort of definition applied to all national identities—except Canada, which by consensus was "a country without a mythology."[3] But if Canada was an exception that proved the rule, America was its antithesis, the example par excellence of collective fantasy. Consider the claims of Puritan origins. By comparison, myths of other national beginnings were plausible at least. The mists of antiquity cover the claims of Siegfried and King Arthur and the exiled Trojan heroes who sired Virgil's Rome. Scripture itself authorizes Joshua's claims to Canaan. But we *know* that the Puritans did not found the United States. In fact, we know that by 1690, sixty years after the Great Migration and a century before independence, not even the colony of Massachusetts was Puritan. Nonetheless, the belief in America's Puritan ur-fathers was evident everywhere three centuries later, at every ritual occasion, from Thanksgiving Day to July Fourth, throughout the literature, from Harriet Beecher Stowe to Thomas Pynchon, and in every form of literature, including endless debates about whether or not the Puritan legacy was a good thing.

My study of Puritanism started out as an investigation of what appeared to me to be a cultural secret. I expected to discover the creation of a national past, the invention of a Puritan tradition commensurate with the needs of a modern republic. Instead, as I traced the act of creation back through the nineteenth into the eighteenth and seventeenth centuries, I found that its roots lay with the Puritans after all.[4] The tradition *had* been made up, as suspected, but it was built out of historical materials, selected for historical reasons. The fantasy of Puritan origins had worked because these Puritans represented (among other things) the movement toward modernity, because they associated that movement with their prospects in the New World, and because they developed a rhetoric that joined both these aspects of their venture, cultural and territorial, in a vision that was simultaneously distinctive, expansive, spiritual, and secular. Their major legacy was neither religious nor institutional. The Puritans are not particularly responsible for the Calvinist strain in the United States, or for civil religion, or for any particular democratic forms, not even the town meeting. They did not invent guilt, or the Protestant work ethic, or individualism, or contract society. All of these were in varying degrees part of the New England Way, and together they might be said to express its movement into modernity. But the distinctive contribution, it seemed to me, lay in the realm of symbology. The Puritans provided their heirs, in New England first and then in the United States, with a useful, flexible, durable, and compelling fantasy of American identity.

I mean "compelling" in a descriptive, not a celebratory, sense. My discovery pertained to the historicity of myth, and the secret it yielded applied as well to my Canadian geography of the New World: what I had considered to be my neutral, commonsense view of the territory out there as an extension of various European civilizations. To see America as myth was to historicize the Canadian identity—to see in it the contours of another, complementary myth. I refer to the dominant vision of Canada: a "loose scattering of enclaves or outposts of culture and civilization," protected from a "hostile bush-country" by the Royal Canadian Mounted Police.[5] The Mountie is a symbolic figure in this design, of course. But the design itself represents a distinctive national fantasy, which I now saw as a variation of the same myth of conquest that had shaped the growth of the United States.

"Canada" was the *colonial* version of the myth, a story told by invaders who claimed authority for conquest from abroad—from European royalty and civilizations centered in England and France.[6] "America" was the indigenous *imperialist* inversion. It relocated the seat of empire from the Old World to the New; it reversed the very meaning of "newness" from its colonial status of dependency to a declaration not just of independence but of superiority; and in this new sense it sanctified the "empty continent" as itself constituting the natural-divine patent for conquest. Gradually, the imperial counterpart to the bush-country police became the frontiersman, living in harmony with nature and yet the harbinger of civilization, a paradox explicable by the fact that the frontier itself had been transformed from its colonial sense of "barrier" into an imperial summons to expand.

The issue, then, was not a clash of opposites, Canadian facts versus American fantasies. It was a juxtaposition of myths, colonial vis-à-vis imperial, each of them a borderland of fantasy and fact. The colonial version had issued in "Canada," a country with a mythology elsewhere, systematically decentered and characterized, accordingly, by a rhetoric of absence: non-Indian, non-European, non-American, nonmythological. The other, imperial issue was America. As I followed its changing terms of identity (Puritan errand, national mission, manifest destiny, the dream), the windings of language turned out to be the matter of history. America, an act of symbolic appropriation, came alive to me as the twin dynamics of empire: on the one hand, a process of violence unparalleled (proportionately) by even the Spanish conquistadors and sustained into the twentieth century by a rhetoric of holy war against everything un-American; on the other hand, an unleashing of creative energies—enterprise, speculation, community building, personal initiative, industry, confidence, idealism, and hope—unsurpassed by any other modern nation.

It amounted to a demonstration from within of Walter Benjamin's thesis about barbarism and civilization. Polemicizing against the tradition of empathy in historical studies—which literary critics have inherited as the tradition of aesthetic appreciation[7]—Benjamin presents "the triumphal procession" of "cultural treasures" through a contrast between "the great minds and talents who created them" and "the anonymous toil of their contemporaries. There is no document of civilization," he concludes, "which is not at the same time a document of barbarism." To some extent, my view of America is a cross-cultural variation of that outlook, with certain differences in emphasis and approach. Benjamin was seeking to historicize art's claims to transcendence, but he tended not so much to challenge those claims as to insist on a complicity of opposites: "great minds" and "anonymous toil," cultural treasures and the inhumanity of power. My approach was geared to the dynamics of complicity, which in this case called the opposition itself into question. What I discovered in America was the simultaneity of violence and culture formation. America, as its meanings gradually unfolded to me, was interchangeably a cultural treasure of barbarism, a barbaric dream documented by a procession of "great minds and talents," and an interpretative process through which the worlds out there had been triumphantly repressed—first by myths of their inhabitants ("savage," "primitive") attended by facts of genocide, and then by symbols of the land ("virgin," "wilderness") attended by the creation of the United States as America.

So what began as English graduate studies in the United States became instead a trail into the myth-and-symbol thickets of American studies. I encountered in its foundational documents a scholarly achievement commensurate with the cultural creation of America: Perry Miller's intellectual construction of national origins out of the esoteric writings of forty Protestant sectarians; F. O. Matthiessen's aesthetic construction of a national literary tradition out of the masterpieces of five self-declared "isolatoes"; Frederick Jackson Turner's historical construction of the national character out of a frontier West that largely excluded its native inhabitants, not to speak of the nation's nonwestering immigrants. In all of these monumental works, as well as in their successors, an extraordinary capacity to analyze intricacies of thought, emotion, and imagination seemed bound up with an extraordinary unwillingness to extend analysis beyond the intricacies themselves. The America they revealed appeared out of nowhere—"out of some place of darkness," or rather a *spirit* of place,[8] variously labeled "nature," "the New England mind," "the Jeffersonian '76," "pioneer democracy"—like the seven musical performers in Kafka's story.

I registered the anomaly as a cultural secret of academia. American studies, as it had developed from the forties through the cold war decades, seemed a method designed *not* to explore its subject, somewhat as the dog's investigations, though conjured up by the music, are deliberately, exclusively, and astonishedly focused elsewhere—on the wonders of canine artistry ("the lifting and setting of their feet, certain turns of the head . . . the position they took up in relation to one another, the symmetrical patterns which they produced"). The analytic tools of American studies consisted of the same materials, the same patterns of thought and language, that Americanists had set out to investigate. This was empathic history with a vengeance. As in Kafka's story, analysis was the celebration of a mystery.

Nonetheless, their work had a compelling range and force, which I attributed to a daring act of transgression: the application of aesthetic criticism to what by tradition belonged to the province of cognitive criticism. I refer to the familiar distinction between art and artifact, *Kultur* and culture, that reaches back through German romanticism to the theological separation of sacred from secular. Theology, we know, had actually mandated separate methods of exegesis for that purpose: one method for unveiling the meanings of the Bible, proceeding from text to transcendent text, and from one divinely inspired (if perhaps anxiety-ridden) authority to the next; and another, profane method, an empirical approach suitable to ordinary books concerning the empirical truths of this world. The modern literary equivalent for that dichotomy, based on the sacralization of art, is the opposition between text and context. The latter is the arena of cognitive criticism, since "context" designates the world pro-fana, the "background" areas surrounding the temples of genius, a secondary reality illuminated by "secondary sources." Aesthetic criticism is designed to reveal the richness, the complexity, and the (unfathomable) depths of the "primary text" in its own "organic" terms. This so-called intrinsic method may draw on matters of context—psychology, sociology, philosophy, science—but only insofar as they serve the ends of appreciation. It may even reach outside of the strictly aesthetic to the realm of spirit (moral truths, universal values), provided that what it finds there is reincorporated, truth and beauty entwined, into the metacontextual pleasures of the text.

American studies seemed to have developed through a reverse strategy of incorporation. It drew methodically on contextual matters—it actively elicited cognitive analyses (of the American "mind," "heart," and "character")—but it required these to conform to the principles of aesthetic appreciation. If America was not literally a poem in these scholars' eyes, it was a literary canon that embodied the national promise. The Puritans had discovered America in the Bible; Jacksonians discovered the Bible in the Declaration of Independence and the Constitution; American studies added to this Biblia Americana the national literary classics. It may even be said to have concentrated upon them as the key to it all, somewhat as Christian typologists had discovered the secrets of Holy Scripture, Old and New, in stories of Christ. What followed was a series of investigations of the country's "exceptional" nature that was as rich, as complex, and as interdisciplinary as America itself—a pluralist enterprise armed with the instruments both of aesthetic and of cognitive analysis, all bent on the appreciation of a unique cultural artifact. Aesthetic instruments had a privileged place here because it was as art, by modern consensus, that the spirit most fully revealed itself. But the instruments of cognitive analysis were no less important. It was their task to reconstitute history itself as American; and, as we might expect, they did so most appreciatively when they repressed the adverse facts of American history, or else, more empathically still, represented these as a violation of the nation's promise and original intent.

The music that thus came, in Kafka's words, "from all sides, from the heights, from the deep, from everywhere," sounded to me like ideology. I sometimes thought of it as muzak, and I recognized in its strains a long series of scholarly ventures in culture formation, the nationalist project of modern literary history that had been baptized over a century before in the trinitarian faith of *Volksgeist*, World Spirit, and the sanctity of art. One extreme application, or distortion, of this genre was the aesthetics of fascism. Another extreme was the humanist enterprise (mingling chauvinism, utopianism, and social critique) of Georg Gottfried Gervinus, Francesco de Sanctis, and Desiré Nisard. American studies stood at the latter extreme, of course, and no doubt it was the humanist difference that allowed me to appreciate the insight it embodied into the dynamics of culture. Without quite articulating it as a principle of analysis, American studies taught by example, in practice, that rhetoric is not a surface coating, "mere metaphor," upon the deep structures of the real. It is substantially, fundamentally, what the real is, even (or especially) when the rhetoric serves to repress and deny. The dog's interpretations mask the rules of music, but they reveal the world he inhabits. Among other things, culture is how people interpret and what they believe.

A simple lesson, but it required time, observation, and participation to absorb. My outsider's view of American studies was that its America was a barbaric context made text, empathically, by Americanists. My American experience persuaded me that the poem was in some important sense an accurate representation of the way things worked. America was more than a figment of the imagination, an imperial wish-fulfillment dream brought to life in the assertion of nationhood. It was a way of imagining that expressed the mechanisms through which the made-up becomes the made-real. Like other modern nations, America was an imagined community. It was also a process of symbol making through which the norms and values of a modern culture were internalized, rationalized, spiritualized, and institutionalized—rendered the vehicle, as the American *Way*, both of conscience and of consensus.

The music of America still sounded to me like ideology, but it was ideology in a new key, requiring a blend of cognitive and appreciative analysis. Benjamin contrasts empathic understanding with historical materialism, an adversarial outlook of "cautious detachment" that, aware of the "origin" of culture, "cannot contemplate [its subject] without horror."[9] I sought a mode of mediation between horror and empathy. Accordingly, I turned to the more flexible, nonpejorative definitions of ideology available in anthropology: ideology as the web of ideas, practices, beliefs, and myths through which a society, any society, coheres and perpetuates itself. I hoped that ideological analysis, so conceived, would allow me both to exploit the insights of American studies and to revise its outlook. American studies had set out the interactions between symbol and fact, rhetoric and history, by synthesizing their different forms of discourse. I wanted to separate those forms (and their functions) in order to investigate the conditions of synthesis making. To that end, I hoped that ideological analysis would allow me to negotiate between the world and the word in such a way that the word, *America*, might be contexualized, recovered for purposes of cognitive criticism, while the world of America might be apprehended in its fantastic textuality, as the development of an empowering and (within limits) genuinely liberating rhetoric and vision.

Necessarily, this set me at odds with the dominant concepts of ideology in the field. I thought of these as three models of the hermeneutics of denial: (1) *The consensus model*, adopted by the leading schools of literary and historical scholarship during the cold-war decades. This denied that America had any ideology at all, since ideology meant dogma, bigotry, and repression; whereas Americans were open-minded, inclusive, and eclectic. (2) *The official Marxist model*, imported into academia during the depression and revived in the sixties. This denied that ideology had any truth value, since it was by definition false consciousness, the *camera obscura* of the ruling class. (3) *The multicultural model*, a medley of various indigenous themes, from the melting pot to the patchwork quilt, melded together or interlaced with various forms of neo-Marxism. This denied that America had an ideology, on the grounds that there were so many ideologies, all in flux: republicanism, agrarianism, free enterprise, consumerism, liberalism, working-class consciousness, corporate industrialism, and so on, to the point where it came to seem the other side of consensual open-endedness.

Against that background my concept of ideology was intended to insist on: (1) the ideological context of commonsense eclecticism; (2) the truth value of ideology, as a key not to the cosmos but to culture, which mediates our access to cosmic truth; and (3) the de facto coherence of American culture, as for example in the ideological symmetries underlying the models of multiculturalism and consensus. The symmetries seemed to me transparent in the relation I spoke of between the world and the word: the changing, conflictual, and yet continuously sustaining relation between the United States—in all its multifarious "realities" (pragmatic, agrarian, consumerist, etc.)—and the abstract, unifying meanings of America. Heterogeneity was not the antithesis to those abstractions; it was a function of hegemony. The open-ended inclusiveness of the United States was directly proportionate to America's capacity to incorporate *and exclude*, and more precisely to incorporate by exclusion. The culture seemed indefinite, infinitely processual, because as America it closed everything else out, as being either Old World and/or not-yet-America. And vice versa: The process by which it closed out everything un-American was also the spur toward an ideal of *liberal* inclusiveness, a vision of *representative* openness that eroded traditional barriers of nationality, territory, language, and ethnicity, and eventually, perhaps, would erode even the barriers of race and gender—which is to say, would open the prospects of liberalism to women and blacks as it had to the Irish, the Jews, and the far-flung regions of Alaska and Hawaii.

I am describing a broad, deeply ingrained symbolic strategy;

one need only think of the reciprocities between inclusive and exclusive representation in the concept of errand or of manifest destiny. But my concern here lay with a specific academic enterprise. It seemed to me that the process by which the United States had become America was nowhere more clearly displayed than in the bipolarities of American studies: on the one hand, a multiculturalism (or experiential pluralism) that rendered invisible the structures of national cohesion; on the other hand, a consensual identity, "American," that by definition transcended the "ideological limits" of class, region, generation, and race (i.e., redefined American identity, ideologically, as a process of transcending the boundaries of class, region, etc.). As this principle applied to American literary studies in particular, the relation between text and context opened into what I came to think of as a cultural symbology: a configuration or tangle of patterns of expression, interpretation, and belief common to all areas of society, including the aesthetic. So understood, "high literature" was neither an imitation of reality nor a Platonic (or Hegelian) ladder to a higher reality. It was a mediation between both, which I thought of in terms of ideological mimesis: a representation of the volatile relations between conceptual, imaginative, and social realities that was different from, often opposed to, and yet fundamentally reciprocal with the ways of the world in which it emerged. I intended my concept of ideological mimesis to convey not only literature's multivalence, but its capacities (in degree, within limits) for autonomy. Nonetheless, I again found myself at odds with the dominant models of analysis in the field, in this case the field of literary studies. I think here in particular of the New Criticism, which through the sixties and the seventies still reined in the area of textual analysis, and of oppositional criticism, which then as now comprised the most influential literary group in American studies.

My objections to the New Critics antedated my discovery of America. They thrived on the invisibility of context, somewhat as Kafka's narrator's ingenuities depend on his disembodiment of the music; or as the mystery he marvels at of "soaring dogs," floating on air, depends on the invisibility of whatever or whoever is holding them up. My own reading had convinced me, on the contrary, that literary texts were deeply embedded in issues of context; that this embeddedment was a central source of creative, moral, and intellectual vitality; and that to deny that source of empowerment on principle, or by professional reflex, was a form of aesthetic minimalism that drained literature of its richest meanings. It was also to instate certain cultural values under the cloak of invisibility, as embodying the transcendent unities of the text. And finally, under the guise of reverence, it was to evade the most challenging questions posed by the transhistorical qualities of literature, which center on the relation (not the dichotomy) between *trans* and *historical*. Criticism may aspire to judgments of eternity, but it takes place in history. As both Kafka and Benjamin remind us, the very forms of canonization are mediated by historical consciousness; we break through its limitations only in degree, and only by recognizing that we live in history, even if we live on literature.

But of course New Critics were ipso facto not Americanists. My direct engagement was with the oppositional critics. That term is a recent coinage, designating certain post-Marxist forms of cultural praxis. But in American studies it has a far broader import. I have in mind the adversarial stance of Americanist literary critics from the very inception of the field: the school of subversion (as it has been called) that constitutes the mainstream tradition of American studies from Vernon Parrington and Lewis Mumford through Matthiessen and Henry Nash Smith, and that has continued to provide many of its most distinguished figures. The principles of oppositionalism, so understood, center on an essentialist conflict between an always-oppressive society and an always-liberating literature—a sacred-secular library of America set against the ideologies in America of racism, imperialism, capitalism, and patriarchy. My objection to this particular text-context dichotomy was more complicated in application than that to the New Critics, but it was based on a similar premise. My reading of the classic American authors convinced me that they were imaginatively nourished by the culture, even when they were politically opposed to it. Melville's famous affirmation of the subversive imperative comes in an essay extolling America's destiny; and a similar dynamic informs the cultural work of Hawthorne and Emerson, as it also underlies the multiple connections between nay-saying and representative selfhood in the adventures of George Harris, Ruth Hall, Huckleberry Finn, Frederic Henry, the Invisible Man, Oedipa Maas, and Rutherford Calhoun.[10]

In all cases, the complementarity of text and context revealed a cultural symbology that not only tolerated but elicited resistance as a staple of social revitalization. This did not mean that the literature was not subversive in some sense. My disagreement with the oppositionalists lay not in particular interpretations of texts, but in their overall tendency toward allegory. I saw this as a sort of beatification of the subversive; as a denial against all historical evidence, from every field of art, of the continuously enriching reciprocity between dominant forms of art and forms of ideological domination; as a transfer of the powers of appreciative criticism to political agency; and as a confusion, accordingly, of literary analysis with social action. It was as though (in a mirror inversion of Kafka's parable) to deconstruct the musicians' patterns of performance—or to uncover adversarial tendencies within the symmetries they enacted, or to discover different groups of performers (the music, so to speak, of Benjamin's repressed world of "anonymous toil")—were to threaten the entire world of music, and potentially to undermine the moral and social structures within which the musicians functioned.

This romance quest for the subversive seemed to me to have its roots in a venerable (though "dark" and often mystical) branch of hermeneutics, the esoteric tradition that bridges gnosticism, kaballa, and the romantic vision of Satan as the secret hero of *Paradise Lost.* And in turn that visionary fusion of politics and art recalled the radical aesthetics of my youth. Here again literature was invested with the spiritual values of protest, and literary criticism, by extension, raised to the status of revolutionary activity. But the national emphasis in this case—the focus, positive and negative, on the American-ness of American literature—called attention to a cultural difference in the very concept of radicalism. I refer to a broad tradition of political dissent inspired by the figural America. Its connection to literary oppositionalism, as this unfolded from the Vietnam years through the Reagan eighties, was both theoretical and institutional. Briefly, the student rebels of one period became the academic authorities of the other. The continuities this transformation implies—beyond, or rather *within*, the profession of "generation gap," "rupture," and "politicization"—require me to return once more to my literal-metaphorical moment of border crossing, this time into the surprising radical America of the sixties.

It was not the radicalism that surprised me. Quite the contrary: I had expected to find the land of Sacco and Vanzetti, an unincorporated America of class contradictions, residual resistance, and emergent struggle. And so it was. But the protest rendered invisible the cultural limitations that these conflicts implied. The sources of conflict persisted—indeed, according to the protesters they had deepened—but they were described in terms that reinforced this society's values and myths. The counterculture swam into my view in a series of abstractions, two by two, like the procession of leviathans at the start of *Moby-Dick*, as the gates of Ishmael's wonder-world swing open: Freedom versus Tyranny, Opportunity versus Oppression, Progress versus Chaos; and mid-most of them all, like a Janus-faced phantom in the air, America, real and ideal. The real faced toward doomsday. The ideal, facing the millennium, appeared sometimes in the form of national representatives (Jefferson, Lincoln), sometimes as representative texts (the Mayflower Compact, the federal Constitution), sometimes in cultural key words (*equal rights, self realization*), or else in the appositional symbology of pluralism ("heterogeneity," "nation of nations").

My commonsense response was "co-optation." What else could this Americanization of utopia be but some long-ripened generational rite of passage, a ritual recycling of the energies of radical change into the structures of continuity? In this culture, I concluded, the conservatives were on the left; their characteristic strategy was to displace radical alternatives with an indigenous tradition of reform. Thus the alternative implicit in Nat Turner's revolt had been absorbed into the exemplary American protest embodied in *The Narrative of Frederick Douglass*; so, too, in the long run, were the alternatives offered by Paul Robeson and Malcolm X. The quintessentially liberal programs for change that linked Elizabeth Cady Stanton to Gloria Steinem encompassed, blurred, and eventually eliminated other feminist alternatives (those that did not focus on America), from the Grimké sisters to Emma Goldman and Angela Davis. It was the cultural work of Emerson and Emersonians, from (say) William James through Paul Goodman, to obviate socialist or communist alternatives to capitalism. This form of cultural work joined Jefferson to Thoreau and both to Martin Luther King, in an omnivorous oppositionalism that ingested all competing modes of radicalism—from the Fourierists to Herbert Marcuse and Noam Chomsky—in the course of redefining injustice as un-American, revolution as the legacy of '76, and inequities of class, race, and gender as disparities between the theory and the practice of American-ness.

These dissenters, it seemed clear, had miscalculated not just the power but the nature of rhetoric. They had thought to appropriate America as a trope of the spirit, and so to turn the national symbol, now freed of its base historical content, into a vehicle of moral and political renovation. In the event, however, the symbol had refigured the moral and political terms of renovation—had rendered freedom, opportunity, democracy, and radicalism itself part of the American Way.[11] But the results of their miscalculations, as I traced these back through the nineteen hundreds, had unexpected consequences. What I learned from that century-long lesson in co-optation altered my views both of American protest and of the radical outlook I had brought to it. The culture, I discovered, had indeed found ways of harnessing revolution for its own purposes; but the ways themselves were volatile, even (to a point) open-ended. They tended toward subversion even as they drew such tendencies into persistent, deeply conservative patterns of culture.

In short, the issue was not co-optation or dissent. It was varieties of co-optation, varieties of dissent, and above all varieties of co-optation/dissent. America was a symbolic *field*, continually influenced by extrinsic sources, and sometimes changing through those influences, but characteristically absorbing and adapting them to its own distinctive patterns. And in the course of adaptation, it was recurrently generating its own adversarial forms. The "alternative Americas" it spawned were (like the originating symbol) ideology and utopia combined. They opposed the system in ways that reaffirmed its ideals; but the process of reaffirmation constituted a radical tradition *of a certain kind*. Hence the ambiguities that linked Douglass to King, Thoreau to Goodman, Stanton to Steinem. In all these cases, dissent was demonstrably an appeal to, and through, the rhetoric and values of the dominant culture; and in every case, it issued in a fundamental challenge to the system: racism subverted in the story of a self-made man; patriarchy subverted through a revised version of the Declaration of Independence; the authority of government subverted by a July Fourth experiment in self-reliance.

The theory of co-optation, like Benjamin's attack on empathic history, assumes a basic dichotomy between radicalism and reform, as though one *could* be for or against an entire culture; as though not to be against a culture fundamentally (whatever that means) was to be fundamentally part of it; and as though one could hope to effect social change by advocating ideas or programs that were alien to whatever held together the society at large—which is to say, to its strategies of cohesion. The radical-reformist reciprocities I discovered pointed me in a different direction. They called for a reconsideration of the entire structure of dichotomies by which I had found American protest wanting. The European forms of radicalism I had inherited were indeed opposed to that tradition, but they, too,

I recognized, were couched in a rhetoric that expressed the cultures within which they had been generated. And they had given rise to forms of social action that were ambiguously liberating and/or restrictive, progressive and/or repressive, revolutionary and/or reformist.

The difference between the two traditions was not that of empirical analysis versus symbolic projection, activism versus acquiescence. It was an opposition between distinctive processes of culture formation, entailing, in each case, mixed forms of empirical (or detached) analysis and symbolic projection (or empathic understanding), and, as it happened, resulting in major differences both in modes of social cohesion and in prescriptions for social renovation. Insofar as this opposition, too, was a false one—insofar as (say) *Walden* resists *The Communist Manifesto* absolutely, denies altogether the theory of historical materialism, class identity, or the socialist state—it is because each rests on a hermeneutics of transcendence. Thoreau's appeal to self-reliance, like Karl Marx's to class struggle, implies a chiliastic solution ("the only true America," "the dictatorship of the proletariat"), built on apodictic either-or's: individualism or conformity, revolution or oppression. The result is not a contrast between true and false resistance to the barbarism of one's culture. It is a wholesale transfer of agency, as in Kafka's parable, from one's culture to the imputed higher laws of nature, history, and the mind.

What did seem to me distinctive in degree about the American instance was the cultural function of radicalism. It was a strategy of pluralism everywhere to compartmentalize dissent so as to absorb it, incrementally, *unus inter pares*, into a dominant liberal discourse. But American liberalism *privileged* dissent. One reason for the impact of the Puritans was their success in making a dissenting faith the cornerstone of community; and the continuities this suggests may be traced through the rhetoric of American Revolution and the Emersonian re-vision of individualism as the mandate both for permanent resistance and for American identity—a transcendental license to have your dissent and to make it too.

This was the context, as well, of oppositional criticism as I encountered it in the late sixties; and it remains the context of American literary studies in our time of dissensus. For although dissensus involves the disintegration of certain traditional structures of academic authority, nonetheless the *conditions* of dissensus do not transcend ideology. On the contrary: They are a purer expression of the liberal marketplace than the genteel modes they superseded, which offered at least some residual resistance to the pluralist incorporation of academia. In an earlier, more innocent time, upstart ethnics could make their way into the humanities on the condition that they re-formed themselves (in dress, manner, accent, and moral outlook) as custodians of Arnoldian Culture, the preservers of literature as a transcendent "criticism of life," meaning in their case the life of liberal capitalism. Their latter-day upstart heirs demand in effect that the humanities come down from that ivory tower, comply with the conditions of American free enterprise (equal opportunity, open competition, supply-and-demand specialization), and participate in the power structures of the state, including its structures of class, mass communication, and government.

This is not to disparage the work of oppositional critics, then and now.[12] They have raised important issues, exposed the constrictions of established theories and the injustice of established practices, and properly called attention to the pressures of history not only upon the literature we interpret but upon our categories of interpretation. In these and similar ways they have been right to call their criticism "subversive." But subversive in what sense, and to what ends, and for whom?

My misgiving first expressed itself in my sense of wonder at the scope and intensity of their political claims. Particular questions of interpretation apart, why were these Americanists so intent on demonstrating the subversiveness of authors who for the most part had either openly endorsed the American Way or else had lamented American corruption as the failure of the New Eden? Or, mutatis mutandis, why were they so intent on asserting the regenerative powers of literary studies (their own) that were not only inaccessible but unintelligible to society at large? I recall thinking in this regard of two Thurber cartoons, which might be considered examples by contrast of the advantages of cross-cultural perspective. One of these shows a copyist sitting before Rubens's "Rape of the Sabine Women" and carefully reproducing the flowers in a corner of the scene. The other cartoon shows a woman smiling like the *Mona Lisa*, while the perplexed man next to her asks: "What do you want to be enigmatic *for*, Monica?" What did these oppositionalists want Edith Wharton and William Faulkner—or more strangely still, their recondite readings of Wharton or Faulkner—to be radical *for*?

For an America, I believe, that rendered invisible the interpreter's complicity in the culture. I do not mean complicity as a synonym for moral (or even clerical) treason. One may be complicitous simultaneously in various aspects of culture: those that help people rationalize their greed, those that help naturalize existing or emergent networks of power, and those that open the way to fundamental moral and social improvements. In this case, however, complicity involved a strikingly uncritical stance (considering the professional self-reflexivity of these critics) toward precisely these sorts of ambiguities. In allegorizing the powers of opposition—and in effect transcendentalizing the subversive—these critics seemed almost willfully oblivious to their own cultural function. It was as though their method had somehow recast oppositionalism itself in the image of America; as though, to recall Benjamin's thesis, they had found at the origins of the errand not the barbarism of civilized progress but the redemptive wholeness of utopia; or, in the terms of Kafka's parable, as though they had appropriated to their academic performances the radical potential of the symbology they opposed. One general symptom is the alliance between radicalism and upward mobility in the profession at large—the rites of academia encoded in writings of dissent.[13] A more telling symptom, for my purposes, is the cultural function of American studies. Surely, it is no accident that, of all academic specialties, this field has been the most hospitable from the start to new waves of immigration from the other America into the profession. Nor is it by accident that, in spite of its very name, *American* studies (as in *United* States) has gravitated toward a *denial* of cohesion; that this *rhetoric* of denial has presented itself in protests against exclusion (i.e., *for integration*); that the protest has taken the form of hyphenated ethnicity—Italian-American, Irish-American, and Jewish-American hand in hand with African-American, Asian-American, and Native American—and that the result has been an adversarial form of interpretation that roots subversion in institutions of culture. It makes for a paradox that could obtain, in the old immigrant myth, only in America: a school of subversion geared toward the harmony of political activism and the good life, and directed (under the aegis of American literary studies) toward a fusion of personal, professional, and national identity.

I have found in this institutionalization of dissent still another boundary demarcating the problematics of cross-cultural criticism.[14]

Toward the end of Kafka's "Investigations of a Dog," the narrator is granted a visionary consolation. As he lies alone, near death, utterly exhausted by a long series of frustrations, suddenly, he tells us,

> a beautiful creature . . . stood before me. . . . My senses . . . seemed to see or to hear something about him [of which he himself was unaware]. . . . I thought I saw that the hound was already singing without knowing it, nay, more, that the melody, separated from him, was floating in the air in accordance with its own laws, and, as though he had no part in it, was moving toward me, toward me alone.

I suppose that an analogy might be drawn to those ineffable moments of wonder that light up the republic of American letters: Whitman's vision of America singing, that turns out to be an epic "Song of Myself"; the African slave Phillis Wheatley's first sight of what she later learned to call "the land of freedom's heaven-defended race"; the westward caravan at the start of *The Prairie*, face to face with Natty Bumppo, towering against the sunset; Mary Antin's Pisgah-view (from Ellis Island) of the new promised land; the uncut forests of Long Island at the end of *The Great Gatsby*, pandering in whispers to the last and greatest of human dreams; Perry Miller's vocational epiphany at the mouth of the Congo River, a calling (he reports) from the primal darkness to tell the story of a brave New World; John Boyle O'Reilly's immigrant vision, at Plymouth Rock, "Of light predestined" streaming from "The Mayflower's . . . chosen womb";[15] and before even those mythic Puritans, the discoverer Columbus, as Emerson identifies him, and with him, at the beginning of *his* career, in the opening pages of *Nature*:

> this beauty of Nature which is seen and felt as beauty, is the least part. . . .
>
> The presence of a higher, namely, of the spiritual element is essential to its perfection. The high and divine beauty which can be loved without effeminacy, is that which is found in combination with the human will. Beauty is the mark God sets upon virtue. . . . When a noble act is done . . . are not these heroes entitled to add the beauty of the scene to the beauty of the deed? When the bark of Columbus nears the shore of America;—before it, the beach lined with savages, fleeing out of their huts of cane; the sea behind; and the purple mountains of the Indian Archipelago around, can we separate the man

> from the living picture? Does not the New World clothe his form with her palm-groves and savannahs as fit drapery?[16]

I offer this emblem of discovery as an *ultimum* of the rhetoric of transcendence—an interpretation of origins and ends that appropriates the mysteries of gender, nature, and the Oversoul to the culturally transparent "I." And it is worth remarking that Emerson's American Scholar fits well into its "living picture." He, too, stands at the rhetorical "shore of America": a "New World" that he claims by naming, as being his by visionary right, simultaneously his and not-his, a hero's trophy of beauty, virtue, savagery, and representative selfhood. And the same is true of Emerson himself, standing in as the essential discoverer for Man Thinking and Columbus alike: "I do not make it; I arrive there, and behold what was there already. . . . And what a future it opens! . . . I am ready to die out of nature, and be born again into this new yet unapproachable America I have found in the West." That triumph of Culture is perhaps the richest instance in modern history of the dialectic Benjamin speaks of between barbarism and civilization; the fullest modern case against empathic history, as being the instrument of the victors:

> all rulers are the heirs of those who conquered before them. Hence, empathy with the victor invariably benefits the rulers. . . . Whoever has emerged victorious participates to this day in the triumphal procession in which the present rulers step over those who are lying prostrate. . . . According to traditional practice, the spoils are carried along in the procession. They are called cultural treasures.[17]

"The American Scholar" both mystifies the discourse of conquest and transfers its cultural spoils to the observer-interpreter (and those he represents). Even as he renders unto Caesar the things that are Caesar's, territory and inhabitants alike, Emerson renders them transcendentally unto God. "I arrive there, and behold what was there already": Emerson raises the victors' *veni-vidi-vici* into the music of the spheres by investing their "noble act" with the "presence of a higher, *namely*, of the spiritual element essential to its perfection." And he does so, like Columbus, draped in nature's purple, as the "savages" hasten in wonder toward his figural "bark," "fleeing out of their huts of cane," as once the Magi hastened from the East to witness the Nativity. Except that the drapery, for Columbus, was the "purple mountains of the Indian Archipelago"; in Emerson's case, the prospect extends indefinitely into and across the American interior, at once toward his own "inward mountains, with the tranquil eternal meadows spread at their base," and toward the Rockies of the "continental" West. And of course the "savages" are no longer visible in "The American Scholar." In their place, Emerson paints for us an awakening "our": "the sluggard intellect of this continent . . . look[ing] from under its iron lids" toward "the postponed expectation of the world . . . a new age, as the star in the constellation Harp, which now flames in our zenith, astronomers announce, shall one day be the pole-star for a thousand years."[18]

My own America, if I may call it so, elicited a different sense of wonder. To put this in its proper prosaic terms, it elicited a critical method designed to illuminate the conflicts implicit in border crossing, and to draw out their unresolved complementarities. I spoke of this method at the start as unrepresentative, thinking of the corporate American figured in Emerson's Scholar. But the contrast itself suggests another constituency: the other America hidden from view by that interpretation; or as I called it, appropriatively, the unincorporated country of my alien namesakes, Sacco and Vanzetti, a rhetorically United States of nonetheless mainly unresolved borders—between class and race, race and generation, generation and region, region and religion, religious and ethnic and national heritage—and a constantly shifting array of cultural crossings, including those between Jewish-Canadian marginality and Emersonian dissent.

The benefits of that method still seem pertinent to me, perhaps more now than ever, with the impending Americanization of what has been called, imprecisely, our "post-capitalist" world. I began this present investigation, after much hesitation about theme and focus, directly after a lecture I attended by a visiting Russian economist, Stanislav Shatalin. It was a dramatic occasion, since Shatalin was then directing the marketplace transformation under way in the USSR; and it had an added personal edge (I fancied) for me alone, since he happened to come from the same region from which my parents had emigrated at about the time of his birth. "We have been wandering in the wilderness for forty years," was Shatalin's summary of the Communist experience; "the time of ideology is over, and the time for truth has arrived"—by which, he explained, he meant free enterprise, individualism, and liberal democracy.[19] As he proceeded to outline his five-hundred-day truth plan, conjuring up transcendent things to come, I found my thoughts turning gradually elsewhere—drifting back, as though in accordance with a law of their own, to the process of my personal and professional discovery of New Canaan. I had had a different border-crossing experience, and I had a different, cross-cultural story to tell. My proper theme and focus, I realized, was the music of America.

NOTES

1. Walt Whitman, "I Hear America Singing," and Preface to *Leaves of Grass* (1855), in *Complete Poetry and Collected Prose*, ed. Justin Kaplan (New York: Library of America, 1982), 174, 5; Ralph Waldo Emerson, "The Poet," in *Essays and Lectures*, ed. Joel Porte (New York: Library of America, 1983), 465; Franz Kafka, "Investigations of a Dog," trans. Willa and Edwin Muir, in *The Complete Stories*, ed. Nahum N. Glatzer (New York: Schocken Books, 1971), 294, 280–81, 285–87, 315, 303.

2. This is repression in a familiar psychocultural sense: interpretation as a strategy for concealing our subjection to a master discourse. Again, the advantages are not far to seek—among these, evading the facts of subordination in ways that allow for compensatory modes of control—but the sense of reassurance this brings comes at the expense of critical awareness.

3. Douglas LePan, "A Country without a Mythology," cited in Northrop Frye, *The Bush Garden: Essays on the Canadian Imagination* (Toronto: Anansi, 1971), 164.

4. What I found has sometimes given me pause: Puritanism as a venture in utopia; a group of radical idealists whose insulated immigrant enclave was meant to provide a specimen of good things to come; a latter-day Zion at the vanguard of history, fired by a vision that fused nostalgia and progress, prophecy and political action. The analogies to the rhetoric of my own past seem so striking it still surprises me that they did not occur to me at once, and stop me in my tracks. I prefer to think of it in retrospect as a happy coincidence of history and subjectivity—an example of the nontranscendent process of scholarly intuition.

5. Frye, *Bush Garden*, 138; Margaret Atwood, *Survival: A Thematic Guide to Canadian Literature* (Toronto: Anansi, 1972), 31–33.

6. The dominant English Protestant influence allowed for the "mosaic" concept, as distinct from the monolithic Catholic versions of other colonial myths, from Mexico through Central and South America, and to some extent including Catholic Quebec.

7. I expand upon this connection later in the essay. Here it will suffice to quote Benjamin directly, since the affinities are obvious enough be-

tween the "cultural treasures" of the "victors" and the process of socialization (as we have come to understand it) embedded in the process of canon information:

> To historians who wish to relive an era, Fustel de Coulanges recommends that they blot out everything they know about the later course of history. There is no better way of characterizing the method with which historical materialism has broken. It is a process of empathy whose origin is the indolence of the heart, acedia, which despairs of grasping and holding the genuine historical image as it flares up briefly. Among medieval theologians it was regarded as the root cause of sadness. Flaubert, who was familiar with it, wrote: "Peu de gens devineront combien il a fallu etre triste pour ressusciter Carthage." [Cf. Matthew Arnold's melancholy touchstones of Culture.] The nature of this sadness stands out more clearly if one asks with whom the adherents of historicism actually empathize. The answer is inevitable: with the victor. . . . According to traditional practice, the spoils are carried along in the procession. They are called cultural treasures, and a historical materialist views them with cautious detachment. . . . He regards it as his task to brush history against the grain. (Walter Benjamin, "Theses on the Philosophy of History," in *Illuminations,* ed. Hannah Arendt, trans. Harry Zohn [New York: Schocken Books, 1968], 256–57).

Benjamin's contrast between empathic history and historical materialism applies in some measure to the contrast I suggest below between aesthetic and contextual criticism.

8. I adopt D. H. Lawrence's term deliberately, to suggest the limitations of even the most brilliant cross-cultural investigations. In this respect, *Studies in Classic American Literature* is itself a model subject for cultural study: a fascinating mixture of outsider's perspective, insider's mystifications (e.g., "spirit of place"), and common transatlantic myths, notably those rooted in romanticism. Equally suggestive is Alexis de Tocqueville's *Democracy in America,* with its extraordinary mixture of French aristocratic "foreignness," rehashed American myths (ranging from Puritan origins to the "empty continent"), and common "modern" assumptions, notably those stemming from the Enlightenment.

9. Benjamin, "Theses," 256.

10. I am partly indebted for this (more or less random) list to a column by George F. Will, "Beyond the Literature of Protest," *Washington Post,* 13 December 1990 (p. A23):

> Rutherford Calhoun is one of those rapscallions who have enlivened American Literature [ever] since Huck Finn

> decided civilization made him itch and lit out for the territories. . . . Calhoun is black.
>
> So is his creator Charles Johnson, who teaches at the University of Washington, and has written . . . an emancipation proclamation for black writers. It is his novel "Middle Passage," the winner of the National Book Award. It is an example of triumphant individualism on the part of both Calhoun and Johnson.
>
> Johnson noted that he is the first black male to win the award since Ralph Ellison won in 1953 for *Invisible Man*. Ellison's aim, says Johnson, was [the] creation of "a black American personality as complex, as multi-sided and synthetic as the American society that produced it. . . . Literature, he says . . . that is an extension of an ideology . . . lacks the power to change the reader's perceptions as the writer's perceptions change. . . . The novel is about—quietly about—patriotism."
>
> "If," Calhoun muses, "this weird, upside-down caricature of a country called America, if this land of refugees and former indentured servants, religious heretics and half-breeds, whoresons and fugitives—this cauldron of mongrels from all points of the compass—was all I could right call *home*, then aye: I was of it. . . ."
>
> Johnson anticipates in the 1990s a black fiction "of increasing intellectual and artistic generosity, one that enables us as a people—as a culture—to move from narrow complaint to broad celebration." I think he means celebration of the possibilities of American individualism. I know that his novel, and the award, are reasons for celebration.

A few notes may help situate Will's and Johnson's celebrations in relation to my own views. (1) Huckleberry Finn lights out for the territory in order to go "howling after the Indians" with Tom Sawyer, and he does so after a very long episode in which his "individualism," along with Tom's, is rather severely questioned. (2) Patriotism, even in its "quietest" manifestations, is not an example of thought freed of ideology, and neither, for that matter, is the concept of an art free of ideology. (3) Both Ellison's "synthetic" America and Calhoun's "upside-down caricature" of it are versions of a mainstream cultural ideal. (4) Will is wrong to identify Johnson's views specifically as a movement away from the sixties: see, for example, Coretta Scott King, "King's Dream . . . Is Really the American Dream," *Atlanta Journal and Constitution*, 5 Jan. 1986, 7.

11. A century before, southern leaders had learned that "America" could not be manipulated to mean the ideals of feudal hierarchy, because it already represented something else—a set of culture-specific ideals, among these representative individualism, pluralist democracy, and the rights of personal ascent. In the 1960s, as a century before, those ideals

functioned through the denial of their cultural specificity; but of course there were certain adjustments now to meet new circumstances. First, "America" served to exclude the ideals of radical, rather than feudal, collectivism: it denied class identity, as a century before it had denied racial hierarchy. Second, the protest leaders did not retreat into new havens of un-American resistance, as had the southern visionaries before them, from the inventors of the plantation myth to the literary Agrarians. Some radicals, of course, may be said to have seceded into the groves of academe (there is a poignant cultural emblem in this regard in the coexistence of southern Agrarians and neo-Marxists in New Haven during the late sixties). But by and large this new generation of rebels did not need to secede, because, unlike the southern Agrarians, they had already identified their ideals, the very terms of their dissent, with pluralist democracy, representative individualism, and the rights of personal ascent.

12. I should distinguish here between two kinds of oppositional criticism, one centered in the literature, the other in criticism itself. In what follows, my critique of the first group of critics—we might call them "authorial oppositionalists"—is more elaborate, because they have predominated from the beginning of American studies. The second group of critics—we might call these "self-reflexive oppositionalists"—represent a more recent development. They have come (in varying degrees) to acknowledge literature's cultural embeddedment, but they then proceed to transfer the source of opposition from aesthetics to praxis, from the object to the method of study.

13. Again, I should distinguish here between two kinds of oppositionalism: the critics who self-consciously "play the system" and those who (I claim) play into it. But the two are often aligned in fact, and they often tend to blur in effect—sometimes, indeed, to blur in a pluralist *concordia discors*, as in the recent spectacle of Stanley Fish, representing the various branches of political correctness and multiculturalism. I quote from an article on his defense of these "adversarial positions," in the *New York Times Magazine*, 3 May 1992, 50:

> And then there's his series of one-on-one debates with Dinesh D'Souza, the 30-year-old former Reagan White House policy analyst whose book about racial politics on campus graced the best-seller list for three months of last year. Prompted by D'Souza's lecture agent, Fish and D'Souza put themselves on the market—for a fee of $10,000 per debate. On five occasions in the last year the two men appeared before packed houses on college campuses to engage in orchestrated verbal fisticuffs.

The author, Adam Begley, quotes D'Souza as saying: "We can have a knockdown, drag-out debate and still have a drink afterward."

14. I do not claim this as a neutral territory of analysis. As I hope

this essay suggests, cross-cultural criticism is not a form of cultural relativism. Nontranscendence is also a realm of ideals, however subject to contingency; of the real, however vulnerable to interpretation; and of radical agency, within the limits imposed by the social and rhetorical construction of radicalisms.

15. Kafka, "Investigations," 312–14; Phillis Wheatley, "To His Excellency George Washington" (1775), in *Collected Works*, ed. John C. Shields (New York: Oxford University Press, 1988), 146; O'Reilley, "The Pilgrim Fathers," in *Old Colony Memorial: Plymouth Rock, Old Colony Sentinel*, 67, no. 31 (3 Aug. 1889): 3.

16. Emerson, *Nature*, in *Essays and Lectures*, 16, 17.

17. Emerson, "Experience," in *Essays and Lectures*, 485; Benjamin, "Theses," 256–57.

18. Emerson, "The American Scholar" and "Experience," in *Essays and Lectures*, 53, 485.

19. Shatalin delivered the talk on 2 October 1990 (summarized in *Meeting Report* [Kennan Institute for Advanced Russian Studies] 8, no. [1991], at the Woodrow Wilson International Center for Scholars.

RAEL MEYEROWITZ

2

Jewish Critics and American Literature: The Case of Sacvan Bercovitch

In the opening paragraph of his introduction to *The Unusable Past*, a distinctly usable, if perhaps overly programmatic and polemical, book on theory and its relation to American literature, Russell Reising says that his work "must admit of being tertiary."[1] He seems to mean that his contribution to the field of American letters is not primary or imaginative, nor is it a secondary critical or theoretical work of explication and interpretation, but has its locus, rather, at a further or second remove, in that he takes certain influential latter-day theories of American literature *themselves* as the objects of his critical scrutiny. What the rhetorical humility implicit in Reising's admission may mask, however, is that a "tertiary" position also functions as an empowering and compensatory *meta*-stance, a perspective *on* the very field, *in* which one might feel one's efforts to be less than central. This would also apply, of course, to the secondary activity of literary criticism or theory, and other intellectual pursuits; the point being that one tactic of coping with "horizontal" exclusion or marginalization is to get over or above it by resorting to another plane, climbing to a more "vertical" vantage point. If this ploy may not bring you any closer to the center, it may at least provide a better view of what is going on there.

I belabor this obvious point for reasons that will speak for themselves in due course. Suffice it for now to declare that my endeavor here must also admit of being tertiary, and that I hereby register an awareness of the fact that there may be something anomalous about putting the work of Sacvan Bercovitch under scrutiny in a volume that pays tribute to the ways in which his perspective has informed the critical work of a generation of newcomers to the academy. And yet this essay is perhaps not as out of place as it may seem, because, as I hope to show, it is in large measure *due* to Bercovitch's teaching and his literary and historical theories that I am at all able to formulate this analysis of Jewish critics and American literature and to apply it to Bercovitch as one in their number. And the paradoxical consequence is that, from the perspective of *this* tertiary critic, Bercovitch, the subject or creator of the theory also becomes its object, as he is himself enveloped in its embrace. This self-reflexive, self-containing effect is, I suspect, not peculiar to Bercovitch's work alone; it may indeed turn out to be a defining feature of, and a motivating factor for, various theories of American literature, in particular those authored by contemporary Jewish scholars.

Let us return to Reising's book, which is an ambitious leftist critique of the dozen or so acknowledged major theories of American literature produced since the Second World War and a select number of minor works from the genre and the period as well. Dividing these into three categories, namely, "Puritan origins theories," "cultural theories" and "self-reflexive theories," Reising goes about summarily describing and evaluating each of them. His rather reductive bottom line, however, is that *none* of these theories pays the requisite attention to the ways in which American literature is rooted in the realities of American political, economic, social, and historical life. Bercovitch is included in Reising's survey and is discussed under the "Puritan origins" rubric. What is surprising and ironic is that Bercovitch, whose own vigilance with regard to the insidious historical emptiness of so much of American cultural rhetoric has rendered his work essential for any historically responsible study of classic American literature, should be taken *so* to task for the alleged neglect of the sociopolitical dimension of these texts.

Referring first to Bercovitch's early book, *The Puritan Origins of the American Self*,[2] Reising criticizes Bercovitch for not being critical enough, for succumbing to Cotton Mather's subjectivist, mythic, and rhetorical biases, saying that "[e]ven if Mather blurs history into prophecy . . . Bercovitch's critical analysis of Mather's rhetorical method could better resist the centrifugal pull away from social history, perhaps replacing the historicism that Mather displaced" (*UP*, 76). Even if Reising is right—and there may be something in his claim—what he fails to deal with are the *reasons* for this apparent collusion between Mather and Bercovitch, for which history apparently suffers.

Reising is relatively more sympathetic to *The American Jeremiad*,[3] at least to its intentions. The book is seen as both an "extension of" and a "departure from" the earlier work, and Reising praises its foregrounding of "the political implications of jeremiadic rhetoric, as well as the complexity and resilience of that rhetoric's endurance" (*UP*, 82). However, Bercovitch is at fault here both for paying attention *only* to the canonically sanctioned classics of American literature, and, once again, for the sin of colluding with their neglect of historical and political responsibilities. He is seen to expose and oppose, but also to fall into and reinforce, the entrapping rituals of consensus that form "a dynamic and potent ideological brace for middle-class hegemony" in American literary culture, and thus to deny "the possibility of a truly adversary tradition within the American texts he discusses" (*UP*, 87).

One wonders whether there is *any* potential point of "progress" at which Bercovitch's work might arrive, where he would no longer be susceptible to this type of reprimand. How much extra credit would Reising grant, for instance, to the Bercovitch who in 1986 edited the canon-challenging book of essays *Reconstructing American Literary History*[4] as well as co-edited, and contributed a committed Afterword to, an equally iconoclastic volume entitled *Ideology and Classic American Literature*,[5] and who, in his teaching, always mounts devastating attacks on contemporary politics, demonstrating, *inter alia*, how the likes of Ronald Reagan could flagrantly but all-too-easily co-opt literary and rhetorical tropes for his own, hardly dissenting ends? Reising's agenda seems virtually to *require* that Bercovitch, "Puritan origins theorist" that he is, remain susceptible to critique.

Toward the end of his chapter on these Puritan theories, Reising asks a question that brings us closer to the agenda of this essay. Recalling a derogatory, covertly racist remark of Perry Miller's concerning the materialism and godlessness of so-called "settlers," Reising asks how it is that the latter, "and other elements of the American population—minorities, immigrants, women," allowed themselves to be "seduced by a rhetorical complex originally formulated as a defense against their threats to theocratic hegemony?" The question is a good one, but Reising himself makes no attempt to answer it. Instead he reverts immediately to a final assault on *Bercovitch's* failure "to forge a critical method capable of elucidating the adversarial elements that may not be compromised by the ambiguities of jeremiadic rhetoric" (*UP*, 88).

The ironies abound here. For, in the first place, Bercovitch has himself been the one to demonstrate how Puritan rhetoric had already begun to modify its orthodox "theocratic" origins almost as the *Arbella* (which, after all, transported one of the first immigrant minorities to these shores) was crossing the Atlantic, and continued from then on to adapt *its* errand to the rapidly changing conditions of American life. Secondly, it is precisely this adaptability, via the sophisticated and methodical exploitation of ambiguity (and other notoriously elusive and pervasive linguistic tropes), that has made it extremely difficult for "adversarial elements" to resist "the ambiguities of jeremiadic rhetoric." And it is surely none other than Bercovitch who has enabled us to see the latter at work and thereby given us the knowledge and awareness necessary for such resistance as might indeed be possible.

Bercovitch is quite explicit in his analysis and assessment of the persuasive potency of these forces, which have achieved their own very real historical, social, and political ends, however much one might abhor them. Here is a passage from the opening chapter of *The American Jeremiad:*

> Despite their allegiance to theocracy, the emigrant Puritans were part of the movement toward the future. Their rhetoric and vision facilitated the process of colonial growth. And in sustaining their rhetoric and vision, the latter-day Jeremiahs effectually forged a powerful vehicle of middle-class ideology: a ritual of progress through consensus, a system of sacred-secular symbols for a laissez-faire creed, a "civil religion" for a people chosen to spring fully formed into the modern world—America, the first-begotten daughter of democratic capitalism, the only country that developed, from the seventeenth through the nineteenth centuries, into a wholly middle-class culture. (*AJ*, 27–28)

Earlier, Bercovitch had spoken of "the affirmative energies through which the jeremiad survived the decline of Puritan New England" and shortly thereafter adds a sentiment of which Reising seems to lose sight every so often: "to describe those energies is not the same thing as to endorse them" (*AJ*, xv).

But let us grant that Reising is noticing something significant, that there is a modicum of truth to his claim that Bercovitch, perhaps despite his own statement, *did* end up endorsing what he set out merely to anatomize. What Reising fails to account for, or even to speculate on, is *why* it is that Bercovitch ends up falling prey to the very rhetorical traps that he exposes. And this brings me to what is perhaps most ironic about Bercovitch in this context, namely, that he is *himself* an immigrant and a member of the Jewish minority in the United States.

In fact, it is striking that quite a number of the critics of American literature who have produced influential theoretical works in the field have been Jewish. In Reising's book alone—and one might have expected him to pay some attention to this—fully *half* of the major theories that he deals with are the creation of Jewish scholars, of whom Bercovitch is only the most recent. In addition to him, Lionel Trilling, Leslie Fiedler, Leo Marx, and Charles Feidelson, Jr., are all Jewish, and I thus "name" them without necessarily knowing, or needing to know, anything about the degree or type of their allegiance to this inheritance. Indeed, it is precisely the implication in this last statement, that Jews, as opposed, perhaps, to certain other minorities, have something of a *choice* concerning their ethnic and/or cultural identity in America, that may be at issue here.

On the one hand, the basic freedom of an individual Jew to actually *opt* for any degree or type of Jewishness (without either being insistently typecast by others nevertheless, or placing his or her own right to full participation in American life in jeopardy) could not always be taken for granted in the United States. There is no need to rehearse the by-now well-documented general history of exclusions and quotas that some of this country's most prestigious institutions of higher education saw fit to impose on Jewish students and faculty during the early decades of this century. At the same time, it is well to recall the particular instance of Trilling, who was just enough of a "Jewish gentleman" to receive tenure in the English department at Columbia University after a lengthy and demeaning battle, and thus also ended up serving tenure as the testcase or thin edge of the wedge for other Jewish academics in the Ivy League.[6]

On the other hand, the United States is also the country that, during those selfsame decades, provided masses of immigrant Jews first with the chance of survival and shelter during extremely traumatic times, and then with the prospect, however conditional, of an economic, social, and cultural context within which to thrive and advance. The generation that came of age in time to live through the Second World War and the Holocaust must surely have experienced that turbulent era with a strong and unavoidable sense of Jewish self-awareness, but they must also have been thankful to be Americans at that time, at a relatively safe distance and under the reassuring aegis of the land of their birth.

This is not the place to enter into the complex and multivalent tale of the various interacting conflicts—between immigrant parents and native children, between religious ties and secular attractions, between the safety of parochial separatism and the freedom of cosmopolitan integration, between the reality of economic stability and the dream of universal justice and equality—that the Jewish community has had to undergo in America in the twentieth century. But even the implicit doubleness of attitude that I have attempted to outline above should give some idea of what may lie just below the textual surface, participating in the motivation of any Jewish author of a theory of American literature (or history, or society, or culture). I would be skeptical of even (or perhaps especially) the most vehement claims of contemporary Jewish American scholars that such issues are of no consequence whatsoever to their work.

It is certainly a grave mistake to conclude that ambiguous and uncomfortable questions concerning Jewish identity in America can now be dismissed as irrelevant because Jews may be thought already to have run their gauntlet of initiation into American life, and to have come through relatively unscathed. Jewish history teaches many lessons in the folly of such premature conclusions. While it *is* true that there are other groups on the American scene whose oppression and marginalization are being felt more acutely at the present time, and it is only as it should be that the literary establishment lends expression to and provides a context for their respective causes, there ought to be more than enough space in our politically resensitized academy for the perhaps more subtle, covert, and chronic issues affecting Jewish Americans today. Moreover, instead of competing for critical attention, such groups and their causes could themselves benefit from a careful look at the process whereby the Jewish intellectual minority gained or was granted such cultural access as it can be said to have today. The tale may yield valuable cautions that would enable such newer newcomers to avoid some of the pitfalls and unreasonably high prices of inclusion, while they wait on the establishment's pleasure for *their* turn to be waved in from the cultural margins.

While there are numerous historical and sociological studies that pay attention to the modern immigrant experience in America, there are very few that approach it from a primarily literary point of view. One notable exception is Marcus Klein's *Foreigners: The Making of American Literature, 1900–1940.* Klein's book is an important source for any project that would pay attention to the literary origins of not only Jewish but also other minority contributions to American cultural life. Klein begins by defining the situation of American literature during the early decades of the century as a conflict between modernism and what, with scathing irony, he calls "barbarism." The former, all its claims for radical literary innovation notwithstanding, is read as a last-ditch attempt of a fragmenting and dissolute white, Protestant, Anglo-Saxon hegemony to close ranks against the invading immigrant hordes in the name of transcendent, cosmopolitan cultural values. Thus, says Klein, "the modern movement as a whole offered an implication of a spiritual aristocracy being defined by an intellectual aristocracy."[7] Hereafter he shows how the "barbarians," the various "outsider" factions in American society (constituted by both actual and metaphorical "immigrants") had to forge a separate and oppositional literature and culture in order to establish themselves and survive. He draws together, into a loose radical alliance, various disparate literary and cultural movements and personalities with ostensibly little in common other than their struggle with a defensive establishment.

Though he leaves little doubt as to where his sympathies lie, perhaps Klein's most important point is not a partisan one. He suggests that the very notion of an *American* literature, the need to establish it, trace its roots, define it, and *belong* to it, gained impetus for *everyone* in the wake of the great social and historical upheavals at the beginning of the twentieth century. It became one way of reasserting one's Americanness, or of laying claim to it for the first time, to place oneself in a certain relation to America's literary heritage, by constructing or reconstructing it accordingly. Any ambitious literary American coming of age in this era could discover "motif and drama in his construction of a home place for himself, or of a tradition, and hence in his assertion of a cultural right and a cultural authority" (*F*, 288).

The disappointment of Klein's book is that it stops historically short; illuminating though his analysis is, one wishes that he had pursued it through the war years and into the latter half of the century. Klein, indeed, closes his book with a regretful coda acknowledging this lack—and with a particular mention of what he might have made of "the case of Lionel Trilling" (*F*, 290). For in this era there were again changes, though of a very different kind, to which Jewish intellectuals and writers were called upon to respond. One of the most important differences is that after World War II, Jewish access to the platform of the academy was made easier and smoother, and Jewish writers and critics were thereby invited, at least ostensibly, to participate in and contribute to mainstream American culture within institutions of higher learning. Thus postwar Jewish intellectuals were no longer called on to cope with flagrant cultural rejection, and adopting the literary tactics of a spurned and embattled minority became inappropriate. Now, an apparently reformed establishment was openly, if grudgingly, granting access to the selfsame "large numbers of free-thinking Jews" that T. S. Eliot had regarded as so "undesirable."[8]

If this created a more favorable atmosphere for intellectual and academic recognition, it also required a much more complex and delicate cultural exchange than that demanded by the clear-cut antipathy of the prewar period. Indeed, one way of interpreting the conscious or unconscious strategy of the American cultural elite at this juncture is precisely in Bercovitch's terms, as yet another instance of the co-optational embrace that smothers real opposition, the rhetorical gesture of inclusion whose purpose is to silence truly dissenting voices. To allow the "barbarians" (or, better still, their somewhat more civilized offspring) into that arena of sanctioned and sanitized critique called "the academy" is immediately to disarm and deflate them, to remove their sting, to defuse their explosive potential.

From this perspective, the fact that Jewish intellectuals were suddenly not only permitted but encouraged to have their public, academic say about whatever they chose, was at best an ambivalent blessing. It was surely one more nail in the coffin that the postwar era was preparing for any really thorough-going leftist critique of American culture, in which Jews had hitherto played a crucial and leading role (and which, of course, was already being eroded as the significance of Stalin's atrocities began to dawn and take their disillusioning effect). For even if no "magnanimous" opening of doors of this kind could be viewed without *some* suspicion (and without throwing previous exclusion into stark, indignant relief), one might well suppose that such license would eventually have the consequence of *curbing* the vehemence of certain critical practices, rather than fueling the determination to take them further.

But let us look at this situation differently and a little less negatively, from the point of view of the particular Jewish American critic who now had the opportunity to become a bona fide American scholar, who finally had the chance, that is, to devote intellectual energy to, and to take up residence within, the more traditional domain of American letters. Such scholars now had the *right* to turn their critical and theoretical attention on the very literary and cultural establishment to which they had gained access, but they did not do so primarily in order to voice their grievances and berate their once blameworthy, if now apparently contrite, hosts. It is surely understandable that they felt the need, on the contrary, if not exactly to express their gratitude, then at least to consolidate their new and hard-won "at-homeness" by more endearing, less combative means. Moreover, this greater freedom also carried a simultaneous bequest of other, perhaps unforeseen, responsibilities; for if, as institutional newcomers, they had to consider the necessity of polite, cautious negotiation, then how much more did having joined the ranks of the educators of America's youth oblige their critique to acquire the admixture of constructive guidance?

Summarizing these speculations, one could say that the labor of theorizing may give rise to a multipurpose product capable of simultaneously defiant or dissenting, and compliant or consenting, functions; it may have as much to do with "fitting in" and "adapting to," as with "accounting for" or "being critical of." At a time when a rapidly expanding academy was in any case becoming the arbiter of literary merit and the repository and guardian of American cultural values, an intelligent, persuasive theory of American literature could be a very useful, or usable, cultural artifact. Among other things, such a theory could serve, in Klein's terms, to make or remake American literature in a new image, and thus to place its author in an intimate (even where critical) relation to a literary heritage that it might otherwise have been difficult to draw near to. And herein, too, lies the motivation for giving initial consideration to the so-called canonical or classical works of American literature, for coming up with a new theory that might incorporate a certain reading or version of these texts, and to that extent lay claim to them as one's own.

For the fact is that, distanced as they are by one or two generations from Jewish orthodoxy and any strict religious adherence, many contemporary Jewish intellectuals in America must also find themselves in an uncomfortable limbo. They are, after all, relative outsiders with regard to at least two cultures, caught somewhere between a receding past and a yet looming future. Such dislocation may at times be invidious and certainly unenviable; its discontents, however, may be compensated for, not *only* by an empowering perspective, but *also* by a hopeful vision. If, as I indicated earlier, the former, clear-sighted, tertiary (or vertical) view is the dubious reward of the uninvolved individual, then the latter is a dream of promise, motivated by the desire to be a participant and to belong once more.

Therefore, it is not incidental (nor, indeed, intellectually inconvenient) that, as Jews and Americans, strangers and citizens, such scholars should find themselves compelled by their own generation's circumstances to become careful, engaged readers of, and perhaps also contributors to, the myths and metaphysics, the stories and histories, of America. They pursue, ostensibly on behalf of their disciplines but also on their own personal behalf, a vigorous, ongoing attempt to appropriate and speak for American culture, in order to earn specifically American honors and the blessing of an American name. And we may thus begin to see how and why it is that the Jewish American critic may at times achieve the effect of seeming to *belong* within, or to be *subject* to, his or her own theory of American literature, and to appear to be yielding to the very rhetorical, institutional, or cultural ploys that he or she scrutinizes and lays bare. To an as yet unappreciated degree, to yield to the specifications of American belonging and subjecthood (albeit while cocooned and insulated by the universal generalities of abstract theoretical speculation) is at least *part* of what this precariously poised scholar wants.

Though the extent to which this is true and the level of awareness at which it is being carried out may vary greatly, I am convinced that contemporary Jewish theorists of American literature are responding to a real existential and even political need. Regardless of how secondary or tertiary the *form* their work may take, its *function* is in part a primary one: They have discovered a culturally appropriate way of continuing the complex quest, begun by their predecessors, for integration and acculturation within

American society. Thus, they are still subject, perhaps residually, perhaps unconsciously, to simultaneous and paradoxical urges: on the one hand, to inscribe their doubts concerning the sincerity of their American welcome within radical textual critiques, and, on the other, to confirm, even celebrate, their "naturalization" by contributing to the cultural mainstream.

It remains for me to return briefly to the particular case of Sacvan Bercovitch, which, for a number of reasons, is a special one. His outsider's position, for instance, is dramatized or rendered more emphatic by certain other well-known biographical facts, in addition to his Jewishness: He is also an immigrant to the United States, from Canada; he carries the badge of a leftist heritage, not least in having been named for Sacco and Vanzetti; and his working-class background postponed the start of his academic career and certainly made him a relative latecomer to the Ivy League. The substantive effects of these circumstances, it might be argued, have been minimal. How, after all, has coming late interfered with a subsequently meteoric rise to prominence at Columbia and Harvard? "What's in a name?" And does being a Canadian in the United States today really make one any more marginal than, say, being Jewish does?

Such responses would to some extent miss the point, however, which is precisely not about scoring points for marginality. If their skepticism might be summed up in the question *"How much* of an outsider does all this make Bercovitch?" one answer would be, *"Just enough* of one!" Which is another way to say that the issue hinges precisely on that subtle and undecidable moment when what is quantifiable or factual shades into what is *rhetorical* or *symbolic,* and vice versa, the very pivot on which Bercovitch's theory of American literature and history turns. One may surmise that Bercovitch's theory is as convincing and fruitful as it is not least because his own place in America is somewhere between the absolute center and the far circumference (and by what criteria could one possibly plot it exactly?), and also because it is determined no less by conceptual, linguistic, textual, nominal phantasms than by social, economic, political, actual facts—if, indeed, such distinctions can any longer be made with any confidence.

Though Bercovitch may advocate an American reality that were not thus constituted, or that did not contain within it forces that would exploit such conjunctions and disjunctions unfairly, his diagnostic skills are nonetheless exercised in a cultural landscape in which rhetoric is *itself* a very powerful reality, as both his own work and his own experience in America attest. Is it any wonder, then, that the very theory that this critic produces would *focus* on the ambivalence of American cultural rhetoric and the highly complex relation to it of its authors, from Winthrop, Danforth, and Mather, through Edwards and Sherwood, to Emerson, Thoreau, Whitman, Hawthorne, Melville, and beyond?

Important though they are, these heady rhetorical self-reflections should not be allowed to obscure some of the rather more obvious but no less telling ironies pertaining to the fact that we have here a Jewish critic undertaking the most thorough and painstaking (dare one say, mishnaic or talmudic) commentary on the sacred primary and secondary texts of the Puritans! And given the significance for Puritanism of the Old Testament, especially in its new Promised Land, who better to do such exegesis than a scholar who, but for the accident of having been born into a predominantly secular world some half a century too late, would in all likelihood have been the pride of the yeshiva and a candidate for the rabbinate?

But speculative levity aside, and lest I be taken either too seriously *or* too lightly, let me add immediately that I intend only the loosest of analogies here and do not mean to imply that Bercovitch's readings of the Puritans and their heritage owe a direct debt to traditional Jewish scholarship. On the contrary; and this, precisely, is where more irony lies. Though *The American Jeremiad,* for instance, is suffused with biblical references and exegetical arguments connecting the fate of the Israelites with that of these new Americans, Bercovitch is almost completely faithful to the typological intent of the Christian clergymen whose spoken sermons and written tracts he analyzes. It is in fact a little chilling to find an entry in the book's index that reads: "Jews. *See* Conversion of the Jews" (*AJ,* 236), and Bercovitch devotes all of ten pages to placing this age-old Christian dream in its new rhetorical context, in a chapter aptly entitled "The Genetics of Salvation."

His take on the issue, however, does stress that aspect of seventeenth-century millennial thinking that links the Reformation, the Puritan experiment in the New World, and the eventual Second Coming with the concomitant relenting of God's anger toward the Chosen People and the restoration of Israel to former glory. It is here that Bercovitch even has occasion to mention some Jewish sources by name:

> The idea was a controversial one, but it gained authority from rabbinical and cabalistic tradition. From Akiba through Rashi

> and Maimonides to Menasseh ben Israel (who helped secure the immigration of Jews to Cromwell's England as "a condition precedent to their Redemption"), Jewish theologians emphasized the prophecies of Israel's restoration. In the decades before and after the planting of Massachusetts, their exegeses provoked a widespread messianic Zionism. The rabbis were particularly affected by the Reformation, in which many of them saw proof of the hastening fulfillment of scriptural promises, and, following the calculations of the Zohar, the Hebrew "Book of Mysteries," they fixed upon the year 1648 as the *annus mirabilis*. (*AJ*, 74–75).

This is, of course, an exceptional passage, but an intriguing one nevertheless. It is when the prevailing typological relationship between Jews and Puritans is suspended, even if only momentarily, and the *fact* of a contemporaneous Jewish opinion about these historical events is allowed to intrude, that one may surmise (if not quite detect) the oddness and ambivalence of the Jewish theorist's position here. The connection between what one might term the typological or metaphorical or rhetorical "Zionism" of the Puritan undertaking in America, and the original Jewish dream of the Return to Zion, inscribed in daily prayers, debated in religious scholarship, and either postponed or striven for over two millenia, *must* resonate in significant ways in the consciousness of a Jew who has strong connections with Jewish (particularly Yiddish) culture, and who not only witnessed the birth of the modern state of Israel in his own lifetime, but also makes no secret of having spent some personally relevant time there.[9]

There is, from this peculiar and interested angle, a rather gaping blind spot in the hyperbolic rhetorical exclusivism of certain statements within the opening paragraph of Bercovitch's otherwise very powerful and persuasive last chapter, "Epilogue: The Symbol of America." His intention here is to lend the emphasis of strong reiteration to the undoubtedly important differences between classical European conceptions of the separation of church and state and the unusual and all-pervasive marriage that the Puritan legacy leaves to the American polity:

> The ritual of the jeremiad bespeaks an ideological consensus—in moral, religious, economic, social, and intellectual matters—unmatched in any other modern culture. . . . Only America, of all national designations, has assumed the combined force

> of eschatology and chauvinism. . . . Of all symbols of identity, only *America* has united nationality and universality, civic and spiritual selfhood, secular and redemptive history, the country's past and paradise to be, in a single redemptive ideal. (*AJ*, 176)

But is there not at least *one* other, albeit non-Christian, "modern culture," "national designation," and "symbol of identity" to which these judgments might also apply? And does this combination of insistent tones with oversight or ellipsis not paradoxically reveal the site of ambivalence in Bercovitch's prose, and announce the recurrent issue of dual allegiance with which even so intellectually sophisticated a Jewish American, or American Jew, must still grapple?

Bercovitch's language seems to recover consciousness and to take an immediate step back in the direction of greater self-awareness when, in the very next paragraph, he analyzes a passage from Melville's *White-Jacket* that again makes the America-Israel connection explicit. A page later, moreover, one comes across a sentence that puts the matter beyond doubt: "The significance of 'holy land' depends on other lands not being holy; the chosenness of the chosen people implies their antagonism to the *goyim,* the profane 'nations of the earth.'" And finally, by way of drawing the chapter, and the book, to a close, Bercovitch speaks movingly of Hawthorne's Dimmesdale as "another Moses on Pisgah, overlooking the promised land that he will never enter," recalls the original Puritan hopes and prophecies, and takes the opportunity to quote the relevant biblical passages, from both Deuteronomy and the second book of Samuel, in which God's covenant with Israel is reconfirmed and a return to the land is assured (*AJ,* 178, 208–10).

What is one to make of this? And let me again say that I am not trying to imply that Bercovitch is a closet Zionist or even that his involvement with the specifically Puritan or American version of these matters is *merely* derivative and thus inauthentic. I do want tentatively to suggest that Bercovitch has a personally political and psychic stake in his Puritan scholarship, and that, in addition to everything else his work represents and achieves, it also manages to give expression to some of the anxieties of Jewish identity in America. What little we know of his background (and I really have no need or desire to intrude any further into private biography) provides some corroboration of this contention.

Reading *The American Jeremiad,* with its careful tracing of rhetorical Hebraic *topoi* through the original Puritan writings and the literary texts of the American authors who inherited and revised this tradition, one is alerted to the ironic fact that there are historically "real" Jews who have lived in America virtually throughout this period and who were always at least to some extent defined by their difference from some of their more thoroughly "indigenous" fellow Americans. One does not have to be a Jewish intellectual in America today to appreciate and understand, either metaphorically or literally, the legacy of Puritanism and its exclusions. But being a self-conscious member of the Jewish minority in America, as Bercovitch is, must almost certainly bring to such matters a double, if not multiple, perspective and a need to negotiate between what must at times feel like mutually exclusive experiences and interpretations.

But what have we gained by placing the work of Sacvan Bercovitch in this new and more complex context? And what is the benefit of his theory's apparently increasing capacity to extend to and account for the political and cultural circumstances of contemporary American life? It seems clear that its unfolding is particularly appropriate to an analysis of the way in which American public rhetoric continues consistently to incorporate dissenting voices (like those of Jews, women, African Americans, gays and lesbians, and others) by palliative, domesticating ploys that promise far more than they actually deliver, while serving the needs of the status quo.

Is it merely knee-jerk cynicism to suspect that the present era of sophisticated theorizing and academic superstardom might provide the system with yet one more ingenious method of containing radical energy and of ensuring, if not the continued powerlessness of potentially dissenting factions, then at least the slowing and postponing of their access to real power? *Does* the academy only function as a secluded arena in which such factions are kept busy by being given the opportunity to construct academic theories of one kind or another, even of American literature, history, and culture? And does this serve merely to confirm Bercovitch's view that genuine opposition and unique difference are done away with in America by way of poor if tempting substitutes for real change—in this case rhetorical invitations to participate, not in soporific nostalgia for an idealized, unattainable American past or future, but rather in scholarly postmodern meditations on the demise of these same myths—while the corporate, consumerist, capitalist machine rolls inexorably on?

Where does this leave not only Bercovitch but any concerned academic, if not still on the margins, on the liminal outskirts, his or her voice that of an unheeded prophet, of a John crying in the wilderness, a ranting Cassandra or wailing Jeremiah whose warnings fall on deaf ears? There clearly *is* a danger that the academy itself, and the specialized, arcane writing that it fosters and produces, will ironically remain on the ineffectual edges of American cultural life and thus unwittingly relegate all its potentially dissenting voices to self-defeating marginalization. But is this necessarily a trend more palpably in the ascendancy, and will these critics and theorists ultimately forego their critical usefulness and cultural relevance altogether, through the cunning ploys and easy satisfactions with which the establishment hopes to tempt and distract them?

Or might it be possible to hypothesize about America's ethically and ideologically responsible literary critics, whether Jewish or otherwise, that, with a growth in conviction about their acceptance and importance in American cultural life, such purveyors and practitioners might come to feel secure enough to adopt a more openly critical and publicly accessible stance? Perhaps the writings and convictions of Sacvan Bercovitch, as they have developed through the recent decades of political reaction in America and now begin to indicate new and sustaining directions as we press on toward a dubious but as yet unwritten future, may serve to instantiate the latter hope as it manifests itself in the trajectory of a single academic career.

NOTES

1. Russell Reising, *The Unusable Past: Theory and the Study of American Literature* (New York: Methuen, 1986), 1; abbreviated hereafter as *UP*.

2. Sacvan Bercovitch, *The Puritan Origins of the American Self* (New Haven: Yale University Press, 1975).

3. Sacvan Bercovitch, *The American Jeremiad* (Madison: University of Wisconsin Press, 1978); abbreviated hereafter as *AJ*.

4. Sacvan Bercovitch, ed., *Reconstructing American Literary History* (Cambridge: Harvard University Press, 1986).

5. Sacvan Bercovitch, "Afterword," in *Ideology and Classic American Literature,* ed. Sacvan Bercovitch and Myra Jehlen (New York: Cambridge University Press, 1986), 418–42.

6. The importance of Trilling's career in this context cannot be overestimated; there are a number of studies that pay attention both to Trilling's own ambivalence about the *explicitness* of his Jewish identity and to the ways in which his Jewishness seriously hampered his academic progress. See Diana Trilling, "Lionel Trilling: A Jew at Columbia," *Commentary* 67 (March 1979): 40–46; Alexander Bloom, *Prodigal Sons: The New York Intellectuals and Their World* (New York: Oxford University Press, 1986), 3–42; Mark Krupnick, *Lionel Trilling and the Fate of Cultural Criticism* (Evanston: Northwestern University Press, 1986), 1–55; Mark Shechner, *After the Revolution: Studies in Contemporary Jewish-American Imagination* (Bloomington: Indiana University Press, 1987), 71–90.

7. Marcus Klein, *Foreigners: The Making of American Literature, 1900–1940* (Chicago: Chicago University Press, 1981), 11; abbreviated hereafter as *F*.

8. T. S. Eliot, *After Strange Gods: A Primer of Modern Heresy* (London: Faber & Faber, 1934), 20.

9. During the fifties, Bercovitch spent some four years in Israel living on Kibbutz Nachshon, a fact that says at least as much about his leftist or socialist affiliations as it does about his connection to Zionism.

EMILY MILLER BUDICK

3

Sacvan Bercovitch, Stanley Cavell, and the Romance Theory of American Fiction

Two questions posed by recent developments in literary criticism and theory are whether a tradition of distinctly romance fiction exists, and, if so, whether we want to continue to define it in the terms that have prevailed in literary criticism over the last thirty-five years. The critical conversation now provides a rare opportunity for rethinking fundamental assumptions about American fiction—in particular about the so-called romance writings of Poe, Hawthorne, Melville, James, and Faulkner. This chance arises because, paradoxically perhaps, the present mood of radical questioning permits us once again to experience one of the dominant features of the tradition: its own questioning of the authority often attached to language and literature and to the social institutions they promote. In some ways, contemporary critics of the Hawthorne tradition can be likened to the heroine of the book that stands at the head of that tradition, *The Scarlet Letter.* Hester Prynne confronts and challenges her society. She also chooses, at the end of the book, to return to New England and to lend her voice to the emerging nation. So, I suggest, it may be that many of the readers, critics, scholars who register their resistance to this text continue, even more powerfully, perhaps, than some previous critics, to reinscribe its stunning power. Why? The moment of Hester's return forms the center of Sacvan Bercovitch's powerful new reading of the novel. What is the special power of Hawthorne's romance that readers continue to return to it? What, perhaps, constitutes the force (ideological, teleological, or otherwise) of return in this novel?

SACVAN BERCOVITCH AND THE IDEOLOGICAL ORIGINS OF THE AMERICAN SELF

A discussion of contemporary Americanist thinking about the romance tradition might seem a somewhat circuitous route to rereading Hawthorne's masterpiece, let alone to attempting a redefinition of the tradition itself. Nonetheless, a major subject of this and other romance texts seems to me to be how and why and from where we speak. Therefore, only by taking seriously the conversation that the fiction itself has generated can we begin to comprehend the tradition's enormous energy. This conversation has to do with the way in which literature either does or does not enter into the dominant ideology of its age, and with the consequences, for the individual and his or her community, of the relationship thus established between society and the text. The major argument against the once dominant romance theory of American fiction has been that it silenced a goodly number of texts, not to mention a large number of critical voices. Is this charge, either against the romance definition of the tradition or against the tradition itself, justified? Or is there some way, which we can illuminate, in which romance fiction, and the discussion concerning it, actually encourages cultural conversation?

In 1957, building on earlier work in canon formation and literary theory, Richard Chase argued, quite persuasively, that nineteenth-century American fiction constituted a genre distinct from the novel. This genre, which he called "romance," was distinguished for Chase by an antimimetic, allegorical, and symbolic structure. This structure explicitly evaded the representation of sociopolitical reality. It also, in Chase's reading, escaped direct engagement with political and ideological issues.[1] Though some critics have actually called into question Chase's fundamental distinction between the novel and the romance,[2] most have been far more concerned to dispute the second implication of Chase's theory, that

American romance fiction created (in Richard Poirier's phrase) a "world elsewhere," "out of space—out of time" or between the "Actual and the Imaginary" (these last two phrases come from Poe's "Dream-Land" and Hawthorne's *Scarlet Letter*). According to the New Americanist critics (as Frederick Crews has dubbed them), the Chase tradition of American romance criticism seriously neglected the sociopolitical implications of American literature. Because these critics were themselves responding to the pressures of World War II and the cold war, they sought to disengage America from ideology and thus to realize in the American tradition the unassailable bases of democracy, individualism, and pluralism.[3] It was in this attempt to realize their own, unstated, ideological agenda, that the Old Americanists, so argue the New, failed to recognize the ideology concealed within the works they analyzed.

Obviously this move on the part of American literary critics in the 1950s and 1960s has to do with various patterns in literary criticism generally. I do not want to launch, here, a thoroughgoing analysis of this criticism, to which I will return later in this paper. For the moment, I only want to present the challenge to the old romance definition and to grant that, given recent arguments concerning the biases implicit in genre definition, and given the further evidence of the exclusion of many texts from the American tradition, the New Americanists do seem to have a case against the romance theory of American fiction. This theory does seem to have denied some significant ideological factor both in the texts it analyzed and in its own construction as critical discourse. And yet, the question still remains: If the fictions of Poe, Hawthorne, Melville, James, and Faulkner are ideological, what kind of ideology do they put into play? and what is the relation between this ideology and the *form* of romance writing, that is, its antimimetic, nonrealistic strategies of representation? The texts' formal features were Chase's primary concern. They are certainly among the most striking features of the tradition.

Of the New Americanist critics, Sacvan Bercovitch comes closest to penetrating the relation between ideological context and literary structure in the romance tradition. Bercovitch is probably the most influential of the New Americanists. Nonetheless, he is also, in important ways, atypical of them, since he insists on a certain unity (what he calls, at some points, a "teleology") in American culture.[4] Because of what Bercovitch conserves of an older way of looking at American fiction (a way that was much informed by his own earlier contributions to the field),[5] he both illuminates (even as he defines) the value of much of the New Americanist critique and also points toward the specific achievement of American romance fiction. What is compelling about the New Americanism generally is its realization of the political dimension of the romance tradition; the way in which the tradition staked its claim on nothing less than its power to authorize and consolidate a uniquely American consciousness. What is equally true of the tradition, however, is that, even though the creation of such a consciousness may represent an ideological intention on the part of the romance writers, nonetheless this consciousness itself may be constituted by a resistance to ideology. This resistance to ideology, I suggest, is what the antimimetic form of the fiction embodies. This is the dominant feature of the tradition, to which Bercovitch's work can help us to gain access.

The first element of Bercovitch's argument that is important here is his definition of ideology. As Bercovitch uses the term, ideology is not a particular political agenda. Rather, it has to do with the insidership of a culture's members, something akin to Stanley Fish's idea of interpretive community.[6] Ideology, writes Bercovitch, who follows fairly closely the thinking of Louis Althusser and others, is "the ground and texture of consensus . . . the system of interlinked ideas, symbols, and beliefs by which a culture—any culture—seeks to justify and perpetuate itself; the web of rhetoric, ritual, and assumption through which society coerces, persuades, and coheres" (*PI,* 635). Being inside a tradition, subject to its restrictions, is for Bercovitch in no way a hindrance to freedom. Instead, it is the condition without which interpretation cannot occur. For this reason, Bercovitch reenacts, in his text, the cultural conversation he interprets. By referring, for example, to a "true sight" of Hester (*A-P,* 638), a phrase that echoes Thomas Hooker (as Michael Colacurcio in his discussion of "The Minister's Black Veil" also echoes him),[7] or by describing a lack of freedom within moral choice that hints repeatedly of affinities with Jonathan Edward's "Freedom of the Will," or by recurring to ideas of "self-reliance" and "self-doubt" distinctly recalling Emerson (*A-P,* 630–31), Bercovitch anchors his argument in a recognizable, ideological context. And yet, while quoting the conversation he decodes and while acknowledging his antecedents in the American tradition, Bercovitch hardly merges with his forebears and cointerpreters. By disclosing the all-but-invisible workings of America's ideology, he also sets himself apart from the American myth. In this way he registers his resistance, not to the ideology, but to its concealment. This exposing, according to some critics, is one job of literature and criticism. Writers do not, because they cannot, break out of ideology or interpretive community. They can, however, interpret ideology by reformulating or recasting it, to make it self-conscious and explicit.

In so revealing the American myth, Bercovitch does more than simply expose the ideological underpinnings of his culture. According to Bercovitch, America's ideology is itself an ideology of interpretation. In other words, part of the ideology of America is an insistence that the American citizen/writer/reader interpret and consent to the American consensus, not merely accept it. This, in Bercovitch's view, is what the end of *The Scarlet Letter* dramatizes. Traditionally, Hawthorne's text has been understood as being about individualism and human aspiration, and as therefore apolitical. Like other New Americanists, Bercovitch enables us to see that the text takes place within a political environment that it does not explicitly acknowledge, aiming at goals that it does not fully confess. Like its heroine Hester Prynne, Bercovitch suggests, *The Scarlet Letter* may not be the embodiment of resistance or rebellion, as generations of readers have assumed. Rather, concealing its ideological function, whether intentionally or not, it serves instead as an "agent of socialization" (*A-P,* 628).[8] Neither open-ended nor decentered,[9] *The Scarlet Letter* socializes the reader to the dominant American ideology it incorporates. The book, writes Bercovitch, "is a novel of endless points of view which together conspire to deprive us of choice" (*A-P,* 640); it "returns to cultural origins in order both to acknowledge the fear [of a divided present; of the threat of Revolution] and to evade the conflict" (*A-P,* 648; see also *A-M*).[10] It compels our participation in the social compact: "For the silence surrounding Hester's conversion to the scarlet letter is clearly deliberate on Hawthorne's part. It serves to mystify Hester's choice by forcing us to present it for ourselves, by ourselves" (*A-P,* 650).

This would make Hawthorne a very troubling writer, were it not for the fact that the act of representing for ourselves, by ourselves, transfers the interpretive activity from the text to the reader. To force representation, Bercovitch insists, is not to impose meaning: "Having given ample directives about how to understand the ways in which the letter had not done its office, Hawthorne now depends on us to recognize, freely and voluntarily—for he would not *impose* meaning upon us—the need for Hester's return. In effect, he invites us to participate in a liberal democracy of symbol-making. He elicits our interpretation in order to make our very search for meaning the vehicle of our accommodation to society" (*A-P,* 650). The key terms in Bercovitch's reading are *plurality, process,* and *interpretation,* that is, *both/and,* a formula that he consistently develops from his *American Jeremiad* (p. 12, for example) to the more recent essays (*A-P,* 635–37). These terms imply relationship. They suggest that American consensus consists as much of a dynamics of meaning-making as of shared beliefs. America's ideology of interpretation demands and requires of its citizens their active and willing consent (through interpretation) to the consensus of which they are already a part. This, in Bercovitch's view, is what the end of *The Scarlet Letter* dramatizes.

But the question Bercovitch's procedure forces us to ask (and it is part of Bercovitch's considerable achievement that he gets us to this question), is: What does it mean to consent to a consensus of which one is already a part? How can an ideology of interpretation not become, finally, a contradiction in terms, interpretation ultimately reduced, under the pressure of ideology, to a process of merely reformulating or allegorizing social or political events and beliefs? Of course, *interpretation,* as Bercovitch uses the term, can mean two different things. It can simply mean explaining something, restating an idea in different, perhaps easier and more readily accessible, language or concepts—thus reconstituting the problem of repetition and unity. Or the term can indicate a more personal and creative act, construing according to one's beliefs, realizing (as in a dramatic performance or a work of art) a private vision. By emphasizing words like *process* and *plurality,* Bercovitch seems to move interpretation in the direction of creative perception. Yet by linking interpretation to ideology—to "process as closure" (*A-P,* 649, 651)—he retreats from this more open conception. Interpretation so linked, for all its show of freedom, seems incapable of escaping from the tautological conditions of ideology.

Bercovitch provides a powerful reading of Hawthorne's romance, to which many readers will readily consent. Is our consent also forced, like Hester's in relation to New England (as Bercovitch's reading of Hawthorne claims), or like our own in relation to Hawthorne's novel, by a carefully wrought illusion of interpretive freedom? Something, I suggest, is going on in Bercovitch's writing, as in *The Scarlet Letter,* that is neither ideological coercion nor an escape from ideological engagement and that does afford the possibility of what we would want to call interpretive freedom and consent. Therefore, even though we might want to conclude that

Bercovitch, carrying on the tradition in which he participates, silently mystifies us, conjoining our consent, it is more than possible, I think, to explain, in somewhat less deterministic terms (at least partially), the power of Bercovitch's interpretation, as of Hawthorne's novel.

AVERSION, CONSENT, AND STANLEY CAVELL

Bercovitch perceives in American culture and writing "a cultural dialectic, attuned to the power of language no less than the language of power" (*PI,* 639). The Americanist philosopher Stanley Cavell can help us locate this power, to understand how language, even if it functions within an ideologically or consensually defined world, such as Bercovitch describes, can become an instrument of consent, predicated on personally interpretive vision.[11] In so doing, Cavell moves us closer to understanding the form of American romance fiction, its distinctively antimimetic, nonsociopolitical system of reference. This is the feature to which Bercovitch also responds, and that occasions what might seem the mystification of his argument as of the tradition itself. By evading sociopolitical, mimetic representation, the romance writers, I suggest, express their commitment, not to a process that ends in closure, but to free and uncircumscribed individual speaking. This speaking always entertains the possibility of social fracture, a potential that Hawthorne's book encodes in the event that parallels Hester's return: Pearl's departure. It also, however, because of what it registers about the conditions of speaking in society, promotes avenues of reconciliation, through which genuine consent may be voiced.

Since at some moment in the forthcoming discussion Bercovitch and Cavell will seem to occupy opposite and irreconcilable poles in the contemporary conversation on literary meaning and value—Bercovitch insisting on the closed, ideologically informed text where Cavell seems to see open-ended philosophical and linguistic inquiry—it is useful to demonstrate, from the beginning, and if only through something as apparently superficial as a lexicon of terms, how strikingly similar to each other these two Americanists sound. Many of Bercovitch's key terms and concepts—*self-doubt* (*A-P,* 630), *partiality* (*A-P,* 634, 635), *both/and* (*A-P,* 634, 635), *perspectives* (*A-P,* 635), and *points of view* (*A-P,* 640)—also figure prominently in Cavell's work. Since Bercovitch and Cavell come at these terms through reading the same texts but from within different disciplines, with different objectives and conclusions, one might use the coincidence of terminology as evidence of the view that an irresistible American consensus exists.

The agreement between Cavell and Bercovitch has even a further implication. For it is in their apparently very different, even mutually exclusive, interpretations of two key figures in the tradition—Hawthorne and Emerson—that Bercovitch and Cavell most profoundly concur on American culture. Both for Cavell and for Bercovitch, American consensus exists in a "dissensual" mode. Bercovitch and Cavell disagree, however, as to whether this "dissensus" (*PI,* 633–35) serves primarily to stifle dissent (in the service of promoting ideological and teleological continuity) or whether, by permitting real dissent, American culture (as it is defined and set into motion by writers like Emerson and Hawthorne) makes it possible for acts of genuine consent to define such consensus as Americans achieve. In other words, Bercovitch and Cavell differ sharply in their understanding of dissent in America.

If Bercovitch suggests why reading must take place within a commonsense understanding of how ideology affects interpretation, and, therefore, why even American romance fiction must be understood in a sociopolitical context, Cavell indicates why reading, which is also, especially in the romance tradition, as much a philosophical and psychological activity as it is a political one,[12] must also take place within a commonsense understanding of language. Since, for Bercovitch, ideology in America is rooted in language, Cavell's ordinary-language philosophy may help reveal how Bercovitch's ideology of interpretation allows individuals to move beyond consensus to active consent. By helping us to locate what in Hester's and Hawthorne's speaking (or in Bercovitch's, for that matter) remains free, despite their participation in the consensuses of their eras, Cavell may assist in (re)opening what Bercovitch sees as the closed ending of a text like *The Scarlet Letter*. And Cavell may help us to do this without delivering us to either an open-ended or a unified interpretation.

One must begin by noting that Cavell's idea of openness contains its own elements of closure. Language, in Cavell's view, enjoys specificities of meaning; it achieves meaning because it exists within a sociopolitical context of human relations. For Cavell, language has to do with accepting that "there is such a thing as language" and

> (1) that every mark of a language means something in the language, one thing rather than another; that a language is totally,

> systematically meaningful; (2) that words and their orderings are meant by human beings, that they contain (or conceal) their beliefs, express (or deny) their convictions; and (3) that the saying of something when and as it is said is as significant as the meaning and ordering of the words said. . . . Words come to us from a distance; they were there before we were; we are born into them. Meaning them is accepting that fact of their condition. To discover what is being said to us, as to discover what we are saying, is to discover the precise location from which it is said; to understand why it is said from just there, and at that time." (*SW*, 33, 63)

Therefore, a key concept in Cavell's philosophy of language is assuming "responsibility" for words (*OE*, 135; *SW*, 33). Such responsibility does not represent one's emplacement within a status quo to which one cannot help consenting. Rather responsibility is the consequence of a choice and a decision made available to us by language's indeterminacies and imprecisions.

Informing Cavell's work throughout is his concern to keep "philosophy," hence thinking and writing, "open to the threat or temptation to skepticism" (*AT*, 35). By "skepticism" Cavell means, most generally, the doubt, associated in the history of philosophy with Descartes, whether the world and persons other than oneself exist. This is the philosophical system that, in Cavell's view, Emerson sets out actively to inherit, in a specially American way, in "Self-Reliance," when he says, for example, "Man is timid and apologetic; he is no longer upright; he dares not say 'I think,' 'I am,' but quotes some saint or sage."[13] For Cavell the "pivot on which skepticisms turns" is not in the potential answers that such skepticism may seem to invite, but in the fact that an answer "is not up for decision" (*OE*, 135). Responsibility is the powerful response human beings can make to the "ineluctable fact that we cannot know." This responsibility extends to words as well as to deeds; and it results in a relationship to the world defined, not by knowing, but rather by what Cavell calls "acknowledgment."[14]

Therefore, unlike some recent critics,[15] Cavell does not view Emerson as a radical disseminator of social disharmony, a veritable deconstructor of American culture. Rather, he finds him, as Bercovitch finds Hawthorne, to be a formative figure in the continuity of American pluralism. This is Cavell on Emerson:

> The relation of Emerson's writing (the expression of his self-reliance) to his society (the realm of what he calls conformity)

> is one, as "Self-Reliance" puts it, of mutual aversion: "Self-reliance is the aversion of conformity." Naturally Emerson's critics take this to mean roughly that he is disgusted with society and wants no more to do with it. But "Self-reliance is the aversion of conformity" figures each side in terms of the other, declares the issue between them as always joined, never settled. But then this is to say that Emerson's writing and his society are in an unending argument with one another—that is to say, he writes in such a way as to *place* his writing in his unending argument (such is his loyal opposition)—an unending turning away from one another, hence endlessly a turning *toward* one another. So that, Emerson's aversion is like, and unlike, religious conversion. (*HH,* 138)

Cavell's Emerson, I claim, does not differ greatly from Bercovitch's Hawthorne. Bercovitch sets against Hawthorne another picture of Emerson. This is the "current proto-Nietzschean, neopragmatist Emerson . . . the genius of process as 'perpetual inchoation,' an 'opposition party' of one, 'avoid[ing] all pledges,' 'indifferent to social identifications' . . . whose office is 'resistance in itself,' as *conversely* it is the office of the A to persuade Hester against abandonment, and (after her return) to enclose her still-resisting self in history and community" (*A-P,* 642; Bercovitch quotes from Richard Poirier's *Renewal of Literature*).[16] Bercovitch's italicization of *conversely* could not be more meaningful for my purposes, since it recalls the major focus of Cavell's discussion: Emerson's word *aversion.* This word echoes related words, throughout Cavell's writings, such as *converse, conversation,* and *conversion.*

At times Cavell does seem to advocate the Emerson of perpetual inchoation, the apparent opposite of Bercovitch's Hawthorne (and of his Emerson). Nowhere is this genius-of-process Emerson more evident than in Cavell's play, in the above passage, with the word *aversion,* on which his revision of Emerson depends (Emerson's original sentence reads, "Self-reliance is its [conformity's] aversion").[17] Cavell's radical reinterpretation of Emerson's statement, hinging on the self-contradictory meanings of the word *aversion* (as of the word *con-form*), opens up the possibility of multiple opposing meanings, both of the words and of the sentence in which they appear. Indeed, the possibilities for parsing Emerson's sentence, once Cavell has taken up his challenge and set the game in motion, are endless, and endlessly dizzying. Drawn out, the game might proceed as follows: self-reliance averts conformity; self-reliance hates conformity; self-reliance is the constant attentiveness to averting it and casting it aside. *Self-reliance* (self-reliance) is to return to a position of dependence on the self, thus averting conformity; self-reliance is to return to a position of dependence, but this time on the self, suggesting that previously one depended on something else, namely society (this would be conformity), so that self-reliance is, finally, the turn away from what one used to turn toward. *Conformity* (con-form) is to share form with or to make form with; self-reliance as its aversion may then be subversive, if one drops out of the sharing and building process; but if aversion is *of* conformity, that is, belonging to it ("its"), then conformity contains self-reliance as a feature of its making, and to conform in American society would be to express one's self-reliance (an idea wholly consonant with Bercovitch's reading of *The Scarlet Letter*). The array of readings Cavell's interpretation opens up is so vast as to make one recall Bercovitch's claim about Hawthorne's multiple points of view: that they are so numerous as to deprive us of choice, insuring our consent. Since the word game toward which Cavell's words point responds to what Emerson seems to demand of him, it may only serve further to reenforce the idea of a consensus, suggesting the attunement of writer and reader that we call "ideology" or, in the case of literary history, "tradition." Whereas Bercovitch seems to imitate Hawthorne's silent mystification, Cavell seems to imitate Emerson's (not to mention Thoreau's) deconstruction of language.

By playing with Emerson's language (as, in *Senses of Walden*, he plays with Thoreau's), Cavell reveals the depths of these writers' capacity for the radical decomposition of linguistic meanings. In this way he demonstrates how self-reliance can issue in a withdrawal from social relations, out of this world into a self-contained and essentially linguistic "world elsewhere," to once again employ Richard Poirier's phrase. But the question Cavell moves us to ask, the question, he insists, Emerson pushes us to ask, is, *Why* this word, in this place and at this time? What interests Cavell, as it interests Bercovitch, is the difference, within an explicitly articulated commitment to society, between conformity and consent. This difference has to do, for both of them, with what Cavell cites as the aversive possibilities of consent, the fact that individuals can turn equally as much away from as toward each other. But whereas Bercovitch then goes on to read Hawthorne in terms of the ways in which dissent is constrained in the American context by a force of ideological, even teleological, commitment, Cavell tries to discover how and why Emerson, while reaffirming his total freedom to turn away, chooses nonetheless to return to society and reengage it. Human beings, we begin to realize, express their consent through language and not simply through social or political acts. Well in advance of speech-act theory, Emerson (in Cavell's reading) understands that the decision to consent cannot be separated from a decision to speak. Speaking itself constitutes an act of consent. But speaking cannot but enter into the conditions of language. These conditions include the indeterminacy of words, which enables individuals to express choices and assume responsibility. They also, however, imply the ideological and social (consensual) imperatives of the human world in which language exists and acts.

For Cavell, the freedom to turn away, which becomes the basis for a decision not to turn away, can be preserved only if it is unconditional, if its threat to the unity and continuity of culture remains undissipated. Dissent can issue in consent only if dissent can be taken all the way to disorder and disaffiliation, literally escaping consensus and destroying ideology and culture. By insisting on this unconditional freedom, Cavell releases us from the coerciveness or, at best, the qualified (because mystified) freedom of Bercovitch's ideology of interpretation. But by locating this freedom within language, Cavell also indicates why such freedom might well (as Bercovitch would have it) tend to reaffirm rather than destroy social relatedness. *Aversion* attests to Emerson's dissent in two distinct ways. The term affirms his resistance to American conformity. It also, however, dramatizes how words, because they are unstable, open up further, continuing pathways to interpretive freedom. The reader as well may turn away from Emerson as Emerson turns away from America. But by figuring each side in terms of the other, by declaring the issues between himself and America and between himself and his reader as always joined, and thus by placing his writing in an unending argument with America, Emerson also asserts the conditions of language that make our agreeing to meet upon the word (*SW*, 61–62), which is to say, our consent, possible, even probable.

Cavell's reading of Thoreau anticipates, and his work on Emerson directly addresses, issues in both deconstructionist criticism and the New Historicism.[18] Albeit in dramatically different ways, both deconstructionist and New Historicist criticism, Cavell realizes, like formalism before them, confront us with a kind of linguistic (and hence moral and political) determinism, difficult to dislodge. By decentering meaning, for example, and by relocating words within an infinite and infinitely interrelated linguistic environment in which words endlessly circulate, deconstructionist thinking makes all language to some significant extent the allegorical replication of other linguistic structures and their allegories. In so doing, deconstructionist criticism may reproduce the idea and function of ideology. If ideology overspecifies the meaning of words, so that interpretation can never free itself from the sociopolitical contexts language imports into every uttered word, free interpretation (deconstruction or word play), we may well feel, may simply undermine the meanings of words so severely that words can never convey anything but the deconstructionist idea itself. Ironically, then, the consequence of deconstructionist word play may be the same as ideological overspecification. Both phenomena may obliterate the space between ideology and interpretation.

Cavell breaks the impasse of the linguistic determinism, with which both the New Historicism and deconstruction—in reaction against formalism—are concerned, and to which each of them in its own way returns us, by shifting the interpretive question. The question is not, What do a writer's words mean? (That is a question of interpretation, in either of the two meanings considered.) Instead it is, What does a writer mean by using these words? (This is a question that gets outside the words.) The question Cavell poses to the text (the question that, in his view, both Thoreau and Emerson force us to ask) is *why* a writer uses these words, in this place, and at this time. The point of Cavell's engagement with the word *aversion,* therefore, is not to show the impossibility of deciding what the word means. Rather it is to get at the word's meaning by contemplating why Emerson chooses to express his aversion in this particular word, in this particular way.

By accepting the conditions of speech, the frame (call it "ideology," "consensus," "tautology," "allegory," "history" or, simply, "grammar") in which language takes place, Cavell mediates against the deconstruction of meaning. Cavell then, like the New Historicists, replaces the deconstructionist move, which sets ideology against itself. He recasts the question of meaning. But instead of asking "what" a word means or "what" meaning it conceals, he asks "why" a word means. By insisting on acknowledging language and accepting the conditions of speech—despite their slipperiness—Cavell makes language a manner of assuming responsibility, for both the speaking and the hearing of words. This responsibility does not mean dissipating our doubts as to whether or not a particular word means what we think it means or whether or not it means what it seems to be trying to avoid meaning. Aversive thinking, by preserving the force of Derridean insights, which is to say by preserving doubt, both linguistically and metaphysically, forces readers and writers, listeners and speakers, to take responsibility for their words. The doubt released by a word like *aversion* invites us to look for meaning in the placement of words, in the why and wherefore of a writer's decision to choose one word over another.

HESTER'S RETURN AND THE AVERSION OF IDEOLOGY

In his analysis of *The Scarlet Letter,* Bercovitch relocates the climax of the novel from its scenes of familial reconciliation—in the forest and on the scaffold—to the moment of Hester's solitary and silent(?) return to New England. For Bercovitch, and several other critics, this moment packs irresistible ideological power.[19] Is there a way of understanding Hester's return, when she takes up the letter "of her own free will, for not the sternest magistrate of that iron period would have imposed it" on her (*Scarlet Letter,* 274), in an Emersonian, Cavellian mode?[20] Can we understand it, in other words, as the aversion of conformity, in which, turning away from society, Hester returns to it once more, in order to reestablish a broken intimacy and to assume the responsibilities both of speaking and of listening?

The questions that Hester's return poses are why Hester chooses to return, and why, having so chosen, she also chooses to resume the letter and to speak through it. For even though the text does not tell us exactly why Hester chooses to return, nonetheless Hester and the letter are anything but silent at the end of the book. The letter, therefore, while it does not figure Hester's withdrawal from society (her rebellion or resistance), also does not signify her subordination to Puritan speaking (her silent consent). Rather, the letter figures Hester's own, free and uncircumscribed, aversive speaking. At the end of the book, Hester is exactly not silent in the way that she was earlier in the book, when, according to Hawthorne, the scarlet letter did *not* do its office (*Scarlet Letter,* 166). Hester's return to speech is twofold. In the first place, she speaks literally. She returns to New England, Hawthorne tells us, as a counselor and an articulator of American values. By way of further acknowledging this, Hawthorne attributes the final words of the story to Hester: "So said Hester Prynne, and glanced her sad eyes downward at the scarlet letter" (264). Having learned to speak for herself, Hester becomes the voice of the text itself. In order to emphasize that this speaking is free and uncoerced, Hawthorne positions Hester's return in relation to her daughter's decision not to return to New England. Therefore, while Hester's earlier decision to remain in New England also represents a choice (itself affirming the possibility of consent), choosing to remain and choosing to return emerge as two different orders of choice, not merely two different choices. Hawthorne is explicit that Hester is "kept by no restrictive clause of her condemnation within the limits of the Puritan settlement." She is "free to return to her birthplace, or to any other European land" (79). Staying is distinguished from leaving and returning by the force of return itself. It produces a special kind of speaking.

When Hester returns to New England and chooses to speak, the text emphasizes that her speaking is not only vocal, direct to her audience, but also oblique and cryptic, through the letter. As important as Hester's decision to return to her community and to language is where she places her words in relation to her audience. From the beginning of the story, the community's eyes are on Hester. Her placement of the *A* on her breast directs the public gaze there and acknowledges her shame in the eyes of the settlement's inhabitants. In glancing downward to her breast, she confesses that she sees herself as they do. But by placing the *A* there, Hester also accuses and resists the public. She exposes the community's shamelessness, when it refuses to avert its gaze from her body. Hester, then, will teach the community members a form of aversive seeing. By averting her own glance from them, she both sees herself as they see her and confesses to them that she so sees herself. But as her seeing is upside down, her viewers also see that she mirrors their accusatory glances. She reverses what they see and reflects or turns it back to them. Furthermore, in averting her eyes from her audience (creating a line of obliqueness that replicates the letter's own diagonals), Hester does not focus attention on the meanings that her words directly or indirectly convey or conceal. Rather, she establishes through her words an aversive relation to her audience. In this way Hester's *A* establishes that the "issue" between her and the Puritans is, as Cavell says about Emerson, "always joined, never settled," in an "unending argument" between them. The ideological power that Hester's letter packs serves the purposes of consent (and not of conformity) when individuals, recognizing that they will never settle the issues between them, nonetheless choose to meet upon the word, to turn, simultaneously, away from and toward each other, allowing themselves to catch and deflect, brave and be embarrassed by, each other's gaze. This aversive seeing eschews the direct articulation of any sociopolitical ideology. But its indirection is turned as much toward as away from community, and it issues in a kind of speaking that does not simply define or inform but establishes relations of commitment and acknowledgement. This speaking participates in and encourages listening.

Hester's final condition as the letter's author is not at all like the silence that characterizes both her and the letter throughout most of the story. Earlier, Hester is almost literally silent; she does not speak (not meaningfully, in any event) either to the community or to her daughter. Indeed, the destructive power of her silence is exhibited most clearly in what she does not say to Pearl.[21] In failing to speak to Pearl, Hester condemns her daughter to an ignorance of her social and biological origins so absolute that she cannot even begin to grasp the building blocks of speech. Tell me what the letter means, Pearl repeatedly asks her mother. Ask me one more time, her mother finally responds, and I will shut you in a dark closet. End of conversation.

Hester's literal silence is reflected in what her letter will and will not say. For the largest part of the story, Hester's letter also does not "speak," in the sense that it does not issue in meaningful communication or relationship with its audience. This is so despite the fact that, from the beginning, Hester attempts to make the *A* speak for her. The letter, as text, fails for two reasons. Insofar as it represents a quotation of the public consensus, with whatever flourishes of embroidery, it serves only to reiterate the status quo. The Puritans' letter, of course, is ideological in the narrowest sense of the word. Such ideological speaking is, for Hawthorne, a kind of silence. Hester's embroidery echoes this silence; it does not address it. But even as a radical assault against the Puritans' *A*, Hester's letter fails to speak. This is so because as a celebration of open-ended ambiguity, the letter produces a cacophony of opposing meanings, which drown out all possibility of personal voice. Hester's withdrawal of her literal voice reinforces our sense that, rendering the *A* ambiguous, Hester makes it as silent as the Puritans' *A* and her reiteration of that *A*. During the larger part of the book Hester's scarlet letter is a text inadequate to the task of communication, because, alternately closing and expanding the space between meaning and interpretation, it baffles conversation.

Hester's letter at the end of the book declares itself communally serviceable in the way it converts the silence of her resistance into a way of speaking, a way of speaking that, conserving the force of that resistance, also engages society. For Hawthorne, consent is no simple statement of affirmation, like a pledge of allegiance or a declaration of independence or the recitation of a catechism. It is also, however, *not* an unwritten or unspoken law, with (as Hester puts it) a consecration all its own (*Scarlet Letter*, 195). It is not a secret, not even in the sense of the secret workings of something like an ideology or teleology. Instead, it is a decidedly public event, much in the way that children (like Pearl, the scarlet letter incarnate) are public events. The relationship between consent and the acceptance of one's responsibility for one's children is not incidental to the novel. Consent conveys wholly intimate, private feelings, even doubts and uncertainties, into the social arena. There, despite the fact that such expressions of consent inevitably deviate from their internal, intrinsic meanings (such as they are), they are nevertheless owned. A consenting adult, like a parent, assumes personal responsibility, despite doubt. Consent, then, voices a relationship between radical doubt and the necessities of public commitment.

The coherence of American culture, in the view of this novel, its consensus within dissent (its "dissensus," in Bercovitch's idea), is the consequence of the fact that dissent in America is already identified as writing/speaking, which is itself understood as already negotiating between extremes of indeterminacy and specificity, and in which words themselves are the public medium of exchange between individuals (with their private subjectivities) and society. For Hawthorne, America's ideology is the negotiation that the text initiates, through its language, between a writer and a reader. This is the negotiation that is figured forth in Hester's decision to return to New England and, from that place, to speak. It is the negotiation conducted by the novel itself, nowhere more emphatically than in its closing words:

> on this simple slab of slate—as the curious investigator may still discern, and perplex himself with the purport—there appeared the semblance of an engraved escutcheon. It bore a device, a herald's wording of which might serve for a motto and brief description of our now concluded legend; so sombre is it, and relieved only by one ever-glowing point of light gloomier than the shadow:—"ON A FIELD, SABLE, THE LETTER A, GULES."

Reading Hawthorne's text as itself a kind of tombstone is not inconsistent with one way of understanding Hawthorne's reading of America.[22] America, some critics have felt, represented for Hawthorne the sinister triumph of repression, symbolized from first to last by the Puritans' *A*. The novel's conclusion might well seem to nail shut the coffin of this repetition and redundancy, which throughout the book has menaced its reading of human history. The legend on the stone repeats the legend contained in Hawthorne's story; the simple letter *a* is none other than the Puritan's *A*, which is also Hester's *A*, which is the legend on the stone, the legend that also drifts across the ocean like "a shapeless piece of driftwood . . . with the initials of a name upon it" (261), which is now the legend on Hawthorne's page ("our now concluded legend," he calls the book [264]). The final words of Hawthorne's text, furthermore, seem to turn a picture (the tombstone) into words as earlier Hester and the Puritans had converted words into a picture (the letter *A*). Thus this brief description identifies a tension felt throughout the text between the scarlet letter as reductive sign (a pictograph or hieroglyph) and the letter as symbol or language. It seems to be both, to the mutual annihilation of word and world. To top the death blow that the words seem to serve to Hawthorne's text, the motto is represented as a quotation, a "herald's wording," set off in capital letters and quotation marks. There seem to be no words, in other words, that escape the repetitiveness of language. We begin and end with the *A*, no more sure now than then what the *A* means, no more certain we can escape its tug back into the lack of articulation that the letter *a* by itself, outside the context of other letters, might signify.

By reading Hester's tombstone, as earlier he read her letter, Hawthorne seems to reveal reading to be repetition, quotation in one form or another. Interpretation, then, seems nothing more than a substitution of one set of words for another, words for pictures and pictures for words. The way in which language calls attention to itself at the conclusion to the novel (as, through the device of the *A*, it calls attention to itself throughout Hawthorne's romance) further enhances our sense of being trapped in a linguistic prison-house. But the situation is not nearly this simple. For despite what Hawthorne's reading of the tombstone (as of Puritan history) seems to be telling us, Hawthorne claims, and his book, in the view of most readers, affirms, that reading in this story (Hawthorne's reading of Hester's story, our reading of Hawthorne's) does provide some kind of relief. This is what the final words say: that the gloom is "relieved" by "one ever-glowing point of light," which, however more singular, and more gloomy, than anything else, still exists to shine its relief. This point of light is the sentence: *"ON A FIELD, SABLE, THE LETTER A, GULES."* Why? Is this relief just a matter of self-clarification, self-illumination? Or does the book's culminating phrase wrestle with a genuine insight and make it its own?

In the first instance, the final words reveal how the pattern of redundancy or quotation is by no means perfect. Quite simply, the series of letter *A's* or legends do not fall into place as neatly as one might imagine. The phrase is as much a misquotation as a quotation, and it crosses national boundaries, going outside of the American context into another. The quotation approximates the final line of Marvell's "The Unfortunate Lover," a poem that has more than a little in common with Hawthorne's novel.[23] Insofar as Marvell's line itself quotes and hence interprets a herald's wording, the rewording going on in Hawthorne's text, right at its conclusion, initiates a whole new series of interpretive endeavors. The sentence, for all its doubling and redoubling back and back again on the text, describing what has already been described, interpreting from picture to language and back again, and again, does achieve something, even if this something is not everything we might hope from language. It goes outside the text, outside the consensus it summarizes, to link the issue of how words mean with other people's raising the same issue in different but related ways.

But then the text goes on to achieve even more. Because the quotation, which Hawthorne takes from a "herald's wording," is placed at the end of the book, in the context of a narrative (and not within a book of emblems), it no longer remains a simple phrase designating the relative positions of objects and colors (a red letter on a black background). Rather, with the word *gules* sitting uncomfortably at the end of the phrase (not to mention, the end of the book), the phrase metamorphoses, for the native English speaker, into a sentence that reads, "On a field sable, the letter *A* gules." The word *gules* is not, of course, grammatically an intransitive verb, as it appears to be in Hawthorne's sentence. It is most often an adjective, occasionally a noun, and sometimes a transitive verb. But as Hawthorne places the phrase, in a text governed as much by the sound of language as by any set of syntactical and grammatical rules, *gules* takes on a verbal power. In this way it becomes a "glowing point of light gloomier than the shadow," making that light happen, making it gule.[24]

Of course in order to bring light to the text, the word *gules* must also guile, and beguile; gild and gull—all of which suggest themselves as meanings of the word *gules*. Hawthorne would not have us miss any of the sham that words (including his own) play upon us. But for all the ambiguity of language, for all the shadow in which its light exists, the light of language does illuminate and relieve. By placing his words within the context of other words, Hawthorne forces a statement out of the stalemate of language. In this way he demonstrates how we may harness language's capacity for making sense out of nonsense, how we may induce language not simply to be but to act. Hawthorne's sentence makes language declare itself, enter into the meaning-making process, discovering in an adjective the possibility for action, wording the world (cf. Cavell, *SW*, 43). The letter gules. Whatever it does, it causes something to happen, something deceptive perhaps (as the meanings guile, gild, and gull suggest), but something potentially active and affirmative, as well.

The tombstone, which might well be only one more figure for the silent, either ideologically gagged or deconstructively evasive, text, is relieved only by this ever-glowing point of light gloomier than the shadow, this sentence. But this sentence is there to relieve it. Hawthorne does not create his sentence out of nothing. Rather, respectfully recording each and every different *A*, quoting it, trying it on for size (as he does the *A* in the "Custom-House"), he acknowledges each of these *A's* in such a way as, not to wrest it out of the control of others, but to make it his own *A* as well. Thus the letter *A* gules; it glows; it creates a point of light, much like the rose (another meaning of the word *gules*) that grows upon the threshhold of the prison of the book's opening.[25] Through the word *gules* (as rose), the book circles back on itself. It reads itself, remembering what it has said and making good on its promises. The text, like language, cannot avoid certain kinds of deathly repetitions. Hence the tombstone substitutes for the prison, one kind of death for another (Chillingworth, in the opening scene, already alludes to this tombstone with its guling *A*). At the same time, however, the book restores to the reader the flower it plucks for him or her at the beginning of the text. Thus it suggests that the text itself can "relieve [its own] darkening close of a tale of human frailty and sorrow" (48). The rose, which is still there at the end, guling and providing its relief, is Hawthorne's substitute for Hester's scarlet letter. It is all that he, like Hester and the Puritans before him, and like all of the human community who have spoken or written, has to offer. But it is more than enough.

Through the text's final sentence, which is no longer a quotation, either of a herald's wording, or of a line from Marvell, or of the *A*, Hawthorne, I maintain, expresses his consent. His text becomes the self-sentencing process of meaning-making (like Hester's glancing at her own letter), which places Hawthorne's words, his writing, in a never-ending relationship with America. For Hawthorne, letters and words are both the intractably obfuscating symbols and the building blocks of language.[26] They are at one and the same time artifacts, handed down from generation to generation, and private instruments of personal expression. One cannot separate out the functions and conditions of language, except through usage, through listening to the voice of other texts and through placing both its words and one's own in relation to each other.

Can one refuse such consent?

Like the Puritans, Hawthorne knows that the prison and the cemetery are essential features, even of as utopian a society as America. Hawthorne's final words, therefore, even as they speak, recall these institutions. Not to speak, which is to say, not to consent, is a choice. But it is a choice that carries with it heavy consequences. If there is, as Bercovitch claims, a teleological force to Hawthorne's novel, it is contained in the silence to which nonconsent (rather than consent) may deliver us. For what the prison and graveyard also represent are the deadly, stultifying alternatives to society and to life itself. In absolute defiance of its alternative, silence, which, like Hester's withdrawal from society at the beginning of the novel or like Pearl's departure at the end, the failure to speak can effect, Hawthorne speaks, both to protest and to consent.

Like Hester's letter, which is, of course, Hawthorne's as well, Hawthorne's words place him in a richly aversive relation to America. If we, as readers, take up these words, they place us in this same relation. They make us responsible to listen and to speak. We can refuse these words. But if we do so, if we refuse to voice our consent, then, the letter on the tombstone also warns us, we may render ourselves and our community as silent as a tomb. The decision, but also the responsibility, is ours.

NOTES

1. Richard Chase, *The American Novel and Its Tradition* (New York: Doubleday, 1957), 12–13. Chase was building on the work of F. O. Matthiesson, *American Renaissance: Art and Expression in the Age of*

Emerson and Whitman (London: Oxford University Press, 1941); Charles Feidelson, Jr., *Symbolism and American Literature* (Chicago: University of Chicago Press, 1953); R. W. B. Lewis, *The American Adam: Innocence, Tragedy, and Tradition in the Nineteenth Century* (Chicago: University of Chicago Press, 1955); and Lionel Trilling, *The Liberal Imagination: Essays on Literature and Society* (New York: Viking, 1950); he was responding directly to F. R. Leavis's *The Great Tradition* (New York: Anchor, 1954). However we choose to understand the reasons for Chase's description of American writing (I will describe some of those reasons in a moment), its consequences for literary theory and history in the United States have been dramatic. That this is so is made clear by a continuous stream of books published during the heyday of the New Criticism. The most important of these were Joel Porte's *The Romance in America: Studies in Cooper, Poe, Hawthorne, Melville, and James* (Middletown, Conn.: Weslyan University Press, 1969) and Richard Poirier's *A World Elsewhere: The Place of Style in American Literature* (New York: Oxford University Press, 1966); also notable were Perry Miller's *The Raven and the Whale: The War of Words and Wits in the Era of Poe and Melville* (New York:: Harcourt, Brace, 1956); Harry Levin's, *The Power of Blackness: Hawthorne, Poe, Melville* (London: Faber, 1958); and Marius Bewley's *The Eccentric Design: Form in the Classic American Novel* (New York: Columbia University Press, 1963). These books were succeeded, in the 1970s, 1980s, and 1990s by another series of like-minded works, most especially Michael Davitt Bell's *The Development of American Romance: The Sacrifice of Relation* (Chicago: Chicago University Press, 1980) and Evan Carton's *The Rhetoric of American Romance: Dialectic and Identity in Emerson, Dickinson, Poe, and Hawthorne* (Baltimore: Johns Hopkins University Press, 1985). Also relevant here are Michael Davitt Bell, *Hawthorne and the Historical Romance of New England* (Princeton: Princeton University Press, 1971); Richard Brodhead, *Hawthorne, Melville, and the Novel* (Chicago: University of Chicago Press, 1976); Emily Miller Budick, *Fiction and Historical Consciousness: The American Romance Tradition* (New Haven: Yale University Press, 1989); Samuel Chase Coale, *In Hawthorne's Shadow: American Romance from Melville to Mailer* (Lexington: University of Kentucky Press, 1985); Edgar Dryden, *The Form of American Romance* (Baltimore: Johns Hopkins University Press, 1988); Edwin M. Eigner, *The Metaphysical Novel in England and America: Dickens, Bulwer, Melville, and Hawthorne* (Berkeley: University of California Press, 1978); Michael T. Gilmore, *The Middle Way: Puritanism and Ideology in American Romantic Fiction* (New Brunswick, N.J.: Rutgers University Press, 1977); Sam B. Girgus, *The Law of the Heart: Individualism and the Modern Self in American Literature* (Austin: University of Texas Press, 1979); John T. Irwin, *American Hieroglyphics: The Symbol of the Egyptian Hieroglyphics in the American Renaissance* (New Haven: Yale University Press, 1980); Harold Peter Simonson, *Radical Discontinuities: American Romanticism and Christian Consciousness* (Rutherford, N.J.:

Fairleigh Dickinson University Press, 1983); and, most recently, Kenneth Dauber, *The Idea of Authorship in America: Democratic Poetics from Franklin to Melville* (Madison: University of Wisconsin Press, 1990). All of these studies, of course, differ from each other, in terms of their individual arguments and readings. Indeed, they often define the tradition according to different member texts—Poe, for example, is variously in and out of the canon. Nonetheless, they—and other studies too numerous to list—share enough features to constitute a meaningful pattern in American literary criticism. For a recent overview of this subject, see George Dekker, "The Genealogy of American Romance," *ESQ: A Journal of the American Renaissance* 35 (1989): 69–83.

2. See, for example, Nina Baym, "Concepts of the Romance in Hawthorne's America," *Nineteenth-Century Fiction* 38 (1984): 426–43, and George Dekker, *The American Historical Romance* (Cambridge: Cambridge University Press, 1987).

3. Frederick Crews, "Whose American Renaissance?" *The New York Review of Books,* 27 Oct. 1988, 68–81; Crews's review discusses seven recent works of New Americanist criticism: Sacvan Bercovitch and Myra Jehlen, eds., *Ideology and Classic American Literature* (Cambridge: Cambridge University Press, 1986); Walter Benn Michaels and Donald E. Pease, eds., *The American Renaissance Reconsidered: Selected Papers from the English Institute, 1982–83* (Baltimore: Johns Hopkins University Press, 1985); Philip Fisher, *Hard Facts: Setting and Form in the American Novel* (New York: Oxford University Press, 1985); Donald E. Pease, *Visionary Compacts: American Renaissance Writings in Cultural Context* (Madison: University of Wisconsin Press, 1987); Jane Tompkins, *Sensational Designs: The Cultural Work of American Fiction 1970–1860* (New York: Oxford University Press, 1985); David S. Reynolds, *Beneath the American Renaissance: The Subversive Imagination in the Age of Emerson and Melville* (New York: Knopf, 1988); Russell J. Reising, *The Unusable Past: Theory and the Study of American Literature* (New York: Methuen, 1986). One might well add to Crews's list several other forceful works of New Americanist revisionism, such as Sacvan Bercovitch, "Hawthorne's A-Morality of Compromise," *Representations* 24 (1988): 1–27; hereafter referred to in my text as *A-M;* idem,"The A-Politics of Ambiguity in *The Scarlet Letter,*" *New Literary History* 19 (1988): 629–54; hereafter in my text as *A-P;* idem, "The Problem of Ideology in American Literary History," *Critical Inquiry* 12 (1986): 631–53; hereafter *PI;* and idem, ed., *Reconstructing American Literary History* (Cambridge: Harvard University Press, 1986). Also, Richard Brodhead, *The School of Hawthorne* (New York: Oxford University Press, 1986); Sharon Cameron, *The Corporeal Self: Allegories of the Body in Melville and Hawthorne* (Baltimore: Johns Hopkins University Press, 1981); Robert Clark, *History and Myth in American Fiction, 1823–52* (New York: St. Martin's Press, 1984); Dekker, *The American Historical Romance;* Michael T. Gilmore, *American Ro-*

manticism and the Marketplace (Chicago: Chicago University Press, 1985); Myra Jehlen, *American Incarnation: The Individual, the Nation, and the Continent* (Cambridge: Harvard University Press, 1986); Annette Kolodny, *The Lay of the Land: Metaphor as Experience in American Life and Letters* (Chapel Hill: University of North Carolina Press, 1975); Robert S. Levine, *Conspiracy and Romance: Studies in Brockden Brown, Cooper, Hawthorne, and Melville* (Cambridge: Cambridge University Press, 1989); John McWilliams, *Hawthorne, Melville, and the American Character: A Looking-Glass Business* (Cambridge: Cambridge University Press, 1984); Larry J. Reynolds, *European Revolutions and the American Literary Renaissance* (New Haven: Yale University Press, 1988); Fred G. See, *Desire and the Sign: Nineteenth-Century American Fiction* (Baton Rouge: Louisiana State University Press, 1987); and Robert Weisbuch, *Atlantic Double-Cross: American Literature and British Influence in the Age of Emerson* (Chicago: Chicago University Press, 1986). Joining in the argument with romance theorists, after Crews's essay, and including responses to that essay, is a recent volume of *Boundary 2* 17 (1990), edited by Donald Pease, which contains two especially relevant essays, one by Pease himself—"New Americanists: Revisionist Interventions into the Canon," pp. 1–37—and one by John P. McWilliams, "The Rationale for 'The American Romance,'" 71–82. According to Donald Pease, "the animus informing [Crews's review] can be reduced to a single complaint: the New Americanists have returned ideology to a field previously organized by an end to ideology consensus" (2).

4. In this sense, Bercovitch's work is close to that of Donald Pease's *Visionary Compacts.*

5. Sacvan Bercovitch, *The Puritan Origins of the American Self* (New Haven: Yale University Press, 1975), and *The American Jeremiad* (Madison: Wisconsin University Press, 1978).

6. Fish discusses this in *Is There a Text in This Class? The Authority of Interpretive Communities* (Cambridge: Harvard University Press, 1980).

7. Michael J. Colacurcio, *The Province of Piety: Moral History in Hawthorne's Early Tales* (Cambridge: Harvard University Press, 1984), 314–85.

8. For a like-minded reading, see Pease, *Visionary Compacts,* 81–107.

9. For a good deconstructionist reading of the book, see Millicent Bell, "The Obliquity of Signs: *The Scarlet Letter,*" in *Critical Essays on Hawthorne's The Scarlet Letter,* ed. David B. Kesterton (Boston: G. K. Hall, 1988), 157–69.

10. See also Larry J. Reynolds, *European Revolutions and the American Literary Renaissance* (New Haven: Yale University Press, 1988).

11. I will discuss the following works by Cavell: *Conditions Handsome and Unhandsome* (Chicago: University of Chicago Press, 1990), esp.

the opening essay, "Aversive Thinking," which I will abbreviate *AT* (I will refer to the volume itself as *CHU*) and the essay reprinted in the Appendix, entitled "Hope Against Hope"—originally printed in *The American Poetry Review* (Jan./Feb. 1986): 9–13; hereafter *HH*; *In Quest of the Ordinary: Lines of Skepticism and Romanticism* (Chicago: University of Chicago Press, 1988), hereafter *QO*; esp. the essay entitled "Being Odd, Getting Even: Threats to Individuality," which originally appeared in *Reconstructing Individualism: Autonomy, Individuality, and the Self in Western Thought*,ed. T. C. Heller, M. Sosna, and D. E. Wellbery (Stanford: Stanford University Press, 1986), 278–312; hereafter *OE*; *The Senses of Walden* (New York: Viking Press, 1972), hereafter *SW*; *This New yet Unapproachable America: Lectures after Emerson after Wittoenstein* (Albuquerque: Living Batch Press, 1989), hereafter *NA*; and *The Claim of Reason: Wittgenstein, Skepticism, Morality and Tragedy* (Oxford: Oxford University Press, 1979), hereafter *C*.

12. See my own earlier discussion of romance fiction in *Fiction and Historical Consciousness*.

13. Emerson, *The Selected Writings of Ralph Waldo Emerson*, ed. Brooks Atkinson (New York: Modern Library, 1950), 157.

14. I have to some extent discussed this issue in *Fiction and Historical Consciousness*, 119–21, for example.

15. For a review of recent trends in Emerson criticism, see Michael Lopex, "De-Transcendentalizing Emerson," *ESQ: A Journal of the American Renaissance* 34 (1988): 77–139.

16. Richard Poirier, *The Renewal of Literature: Emersonian Reflections* (New York: Random House, 1987).

17. Emerson, "Self-Reliance," 148.

18. By "deconstructionist criticism" I mean not the writings of Derrida but the adaptation of Derrida's ideas in literary criticism. For a consideration of Cavell's relationship to deconstruction, see Michael Fischer, *Stanley Cavell and Literary Skepticism* (Chicago: University of Chicago Press, 1989).

19. See also Leland S. Person, Jr., "Hester's Revenge: The Power of Silence in *The Scarlet Letter*," *Nineteenth-Century Literature* 43 (1989): 465–83.

20. All references to *The Scarlet Letter* are to *The Centenary Edition of the Works of Nathaniel Hawthorne*, ed. William Charvat et al. (Columbus: Ohio State University Press, 1962), vol. 1, and appear in parentheses in the text.

21. On the problem of Hester's not speaking to her daughter, see Michael Ragussis, "Family Discourse and Fiction in *The Scarlet Letter*,"

English Literary History 49 (1982): 863–88, and my own essay, "Hester's Skepticism, Hawthorne's Faith; or, What does a Woman Doubt?" *New Literary History* 22 (1991): 199–211.

22. For a discussion of the tombstone as a potential figure for the closing down of meaning and how Hawthorne's text resists that possibility, see James Walter, "The Letter and the Spirit in Hawthorne's Allegory of American Experience," *ESQ: A Journal of the American Renaissance* 32 (1986): 35–54.

23. In Marvell the line reads: "In a Field, *Sable,* a Lover gules"—quoted by Hyatt H. Waggoner, *The Presence of Hawthorne* (Baton Rouge: Louisiana State University Press, 1979), 71. On the connection between Hawthorne's ending and Marvell's poem, see Robert L. Brant, "Hawthorne and Melville," *American Literature* 30 (1958): 366.

24. For another discussion of the dynamics of the end of the novel, see Viola Sachs, "The Gnosis of Hawthorne and Melville: An Interpretation of *The Scarlet Letter* and *Moby Dick,*" *American Quarterly* 32 (1980); 123–41, and Waggoner, *Presence,* 67–75.

25. Hyatt Waggoner is thus wrong to conclude that "a story in which the action has moved, metaphorically, between the points defined in the first chapter as the cemetery, the prison, and the rose, ends with one of its reference points, the rose, missing" (70).

26. Cf. Charles Feidelson, Jr.: "as a single letter, the most indeterminate of all symbols, and first letter of the alphabet, the beginning of all communication, Hawthorne's emblem represents a potential point of coherence within a manifold historical experience" "The Scarlet Letter," in *Hawthorne Centenary Essays,* ed. Roy Harvey Pearce (Columbus: Ohio State University Press, 1964), 36.

Part II

Establishing Modernist Traditions of Dissent

DONALD CHILDS

4

T. S. Eliot's American Dissent/Descent

The task of literary historians is not just to show how art transcends culture, but also to identify and explore the ideological limits of their time, and then to bring these to bear upon literary analysis in such a way as to make use of the categories of culture, rather than being used by them.
Sacvan Bercovitch, *Reconstructing American Literary History*

We shall not cease from exploration
And the end of all our exploring
Will be to arrive where we started
And know the place for the first time.
T. S. Eliot, *Little Gidding*

A continually evolving issue in Eliot studies over the years has been the question of Eliot's nationality: British or American? From the point of view of geography and citizenship, the matter is clear: He left the United States in 1914, becoming a member of the Church of England in 1927 and a British citizen later the same year. From the point of view of imagination, however, the matter is not quite so clear. Ezra Pound observed of Eliot's Americanness that Eliot "has it perhaps worse than I have—poor devil."[1] F. O. Matthiessen suggested in 1935 that "no more than Henry James can Eliot be understood without reckoning with the Puritan mind."[2] Studies by Herbert Howarth, Lyndall Gordon, and Eric Sigg have suggested the extent to which New England's culture came to inform Eliot's thinking and feeling. In the 1980s, articles appeared relating Eliot to Emerson, Thoreau, Hawthorne, Whitman, Twain, and Henry Adams.[3]

This essay contributes to the work of recognizing and *re-cognizing* Eliot as American. The tool I use in this effort is Sacvan Bercovitch's understanding of the role of the American jeremiad in the creation of the myth of America. That is, in attempting to use the categories of culture, instead of being used by them, I accept for the most part Bercovitch's definition of certain of these categories. My contention is that attention to Eliot's narrative strategies (I focus largely on his prose, and occasionally on his poetry) will reveal—in both his reaction against and his repetition of the pattern of rhetoric and ideology inherited from his Puritan ancestors—an implicit understanding of America very similar to the myth of America that Bercovitch defines by reference to colonial Puritan hermeneutics. I would urge by this reading of Eliot not so much that we regard Bercovitch's work as a template for new readings of works by American writers (a part of its function here) as that we follow his turn toward rhetoric and history as a strategy for complicating our understanding of such works.

The most stimulating of the recent studies of the American Eliot is Gregory Jay's *T. S. Eliot and the Poetics of Literary History.* Applying Harold Bloom's theory of poetic influence, Jay reads Eliot's literary development as a transumption of his "strong" American precursors:

> Eliot . . . chooses his canon of "representative men"—the critics, poets, and saints who become the figural exemplars or typological antecedents through whom the individual talent imagines his own identity. . . . Eliot's pantheon forms a history of timeless moments whose function is to transfigure the pandemonium of feelings in his American nature.[4]

In Jay's reading, Eliot is seen taking up another position *within* the American dilemmas he has inherited, positing his difference from his American precursors by articulating what they repressed and repressing what they articulated.

Conceiving Eliot as within the American tradition has not been easy. His national, literary, and spiritual pilgrimage does not *seem* to have been the typical American pilgrimage that Samuel

Sherwood describes as a "flight into the wilderness." Eliot, rather, made a self-conscious flight *from* the wilderness, apparently dissenting from the version of America he encountered in the early years of the century. Samuel Danforth writes of his fellow New England Puritans as being on an errand into the wilderness "withdrawing . . . from the envy and preposterous zeal of such as were addicted to their old traditions."[5] Sherwood celebrates the "howling wilderness" as a necessary experience during the journey from English "oppression and persecution" to what he calls "the good land of promise in Canaan."[6] Eliot, however, regarded America not as a promising wilderness where the City of God might be built, but as a wasteland—not as a place where modern poetry might develop apart from the English literary tradition that William Carlos Williams found so oppressive, but as a "complete blank" where most certainly such a city could not be built.[7] His departure from the United States was at least in part a search for what he later called in *The Dry Salvages* "the life of significant soil."[8]

But as Eliot himself confessed, he carried America within him throughout his life. Toward the end of that life, he wrote about his poetry as follows: It "wouldn't be what it is if I'd been born in England, and it wouldn't be what it is if I'd stayed in America. It's a combination of things. But in its sources, in its emotional springs, it comes from America."[9] Gordon, in her 1977 biography of Eliot's early years and again in her 1988 biography of his later years, emphasizes the extent to which Eliot's poetry can be read as a type of the New England Puritan spiritual autobiography—a distillation of "the inner life from its dross of biographic trivia" so that what emerges is "the obsessive introspection of the Revd Arthur Dimmesdale in *The Scarlet Letter* . . . the insistent agonizing of a sinner of high gifts, gazing absorbed into the mirror of election with its associated dangers of pride and despair."[10]

Furthermore, as Jay observes, "While Eliot often seems to have renounced his American patrimony, he continued to write in response to its contradictions and dilemmas. Even his exile was part of an American tradition, his work as much an interpretation of home as was that of Henry James." Jay locates the origin of American identity in general, of course, in the Puritans and Founding Fathers—in their "self-conscious attempts to make a difference." And he locates Eliot's identity in particular in the same place: "From his New England lineage Eliot inherits a profoundly divided attitude toward nature and his own body, a severe habit of examining his soul's worth, a keen need for a philosophy of history, and a Protestant theory of language." But after observing that "Eliot's construction of authorizing foreign traditions to legitimate his break with America follows this pattern and had its roots in the figural and typological thought of Puritan New England," Jay begins his study not with the Puritan fathers but with the writers of the American Renaissance.[11]

Eliot's Puritan fathers, however, deserve closer attention. As Eliot himself observed in 1923, he had "an inherited disposition to rhetoric" from innumerable Puritan ancestors, and later confessed that he had emerged from an experience of "American Calvinism" that he felt no English theologian could understand.[12] Eliot is speaking not just of his literary ancestors, but of his literal ancestors: He is speaking of Andrew Eliot who brought the Eliots to New England and sat with one of Hawthorne's ancestors as a juror during one of Salem's witch trials, and of the ancestor who is remembered in Springfield, Massachusetts, by a statue called "The Puritan"—a man "striding along vigorously with his huge Bible grasped under one arm and, in the other, a pilgrim's staff."[13] In the very year he left America, Eliot suggested, in his parody of an American Thanksgiving Day sermon, the very idea of America, and the very inherited rhetoric through which this idea came to him, that he simultaneously fled and carried within him: "And what are we, the young men of America, doing to help build the city of God? . . . (silence, followed by breathing)."[14] I suggest that Eliot, the "descendent of pioneers,"[15] the descendent of New England's Unitarian preachers, and the cousin of New England's established families (Harvard's president in 1906, the year Eliot enrolled, was Charles William Eliot, a third cousin once removed of T. S. Eliot's grandfather), had internalized Puritan America to such an extent that he carried within him the inherited narrative strategies of the American jeremiad—and thereby a good deal of the ideology that Bercovitch finds latent within this Puritan hermeneutic.

Bercovitch reads in the New England preachers' rhetoric of "errands" and "flights" into the wilderness an interpretation of America as process—a process leading to a simultaneously sacred and secular promised land. "The Puritans' concept of errand," he observes, "entailed a fusion of secular and sacred history. The purpose of their jeremiads was to direct an imperiled people of God toward the fulfillment of their destiny, to guide them individually toward salvation, and collectively toward the American city of God."[16] The Puritan jeremiad—of which the Thanksgiving Day sermon Eliot parodies is a part—noted constant ingratitude, folly, and backsliding, "but the progress itself, from one errand to the next, attested to a process of fulfillment" (Bercovitch, *American Jeremiad,* 8). The process that was America, in other words, was defined as a particular kind of process—that is, as progress, both sacred and secular. In the end, Bercovitch writes, the millennial promise incorporated into the symbol of America "forecloses all alternative avenues of reform and change, personal and collective. Process and essence merge in the symbol of the Revolution, teleology precludes dialectics, and progress and conformity stand revealed as the twin pillars of the American temple of freedom" (*American Jeremiad,* 149).

Of course Eliot's departure from America in 1914 suggests scant regard for his inherited errand. Not for him Danforth's errand into the wilderness or Sherwood's "flight into the wilderness." Eliot's was an errand into European civilization. He disliked the version of America he encountered in the early years of the century; his *idea* of America was certainly something he could not face. From Oxford in 1915, he wrote of his fear of returning to the country of his birth: "I dread returning to . . . the nausea of factory whistles at seven and twelve o'clock . . . and the college bell, and the people in Cambridge whom one fights against and who absorb one all the same. . . . I don't know . . . whether I want to get married, and have a family, and live in America all my life, and compromise and conceal my opinions and forfeit my independence for the sake of my children's future."[17] Eliot was reacting against what Kenneth Asher calls America's "post-Civil War industrial capitalism": "What evolved . . . was the Genteel Tradition, a studied refinement consisting largely of well-to-do Bostonians aping English manners while averting their glance from the ugliness that sustained their leisure."[18] But in refusing his inherited errand, Eliot was dissenting from more than New England materialism and from more than Puritan metaphor. Here in his letter from Oxford is his dissent from one of the twin pillars of America, the pillar Bercovitch calls "conformity"—in this case, conformity to an America in which Eliot no longer believed.

In fact, Eliot dissented from both of the twin pillars of the American temple of freedom. He encountered the other pillar—progress—as a still-vital remnant of the American jeremiad in his family's Unitarianism. In fact, it was the very thing he rejected on the eve of his departure from America in 1914, when speaking to the Harvard Philosophy Club (of which he was president):

> I do not plan to deprecate the alcoholic or stimulant value of the idea of Progress. I belong to a church of which one of the tenets refers to the Progress of mankind onward and upward forever. I do not understand what this phrase means, but I acknowledge its value for enthusiasm; and however we may distrust enthusiasm or enthusiasts, we must not fail to provide for them. So long as people use the concept of Progress simply as an incentive to endeavor, they enjoy a harmless stimulant. . . . But as soon as a man makes of Progress something independent of human need and human meaning, something upon which these rather are dependent—then he is losing his hold upon social reality, he is become an intellectual drunkard.[19]

Here is the same general wariness of the deceptions of capital letters and the same particular wariness of the nineteenth century's tendency to regard progress as God that Eliot would within two years find in his equally antiromantic contemporary, T. E. Hulme. "There must be one word in the language spelt in capital letters," Hulme explains. "For a long time, and still for some people, the word was God. Then one became bored with the letter G, and went on to R, and for a hundred years it was Reason, and now all the best people take off their hats and lower their voices when they speak of Life. . . . Why should the idea of a constant, continuous and endless progress be any more rational and satisfactory than the idea of constancy?"[20] One can read Eliot's desire to avoid his religion's enthusiasm for progress and his errand toward Hulme from 1916 onward as part of his flight from the symbol of America. Like Hulme's flight from progress (toward a capital letter resident in the City on a Hill) to the permanence and order of constancy, Eliot's flight from Progress is in part a flight from the democratic progress that is America (teleologically, the City on a Hill) to the order and authority of British tradition.

But geography aside (Eliot settled in Britain in 1914 and did not return to the United States until 1933), there are important respects in which Eliot never really left America. He is what Bercovitch, describing the writers of the American Renaissance, calls "the typical American writer"—a writer distinguished by "his *refusal* to abandon the national covenant. . . . His identification with

America as it ought to be impels the writer to withdraw from what is in America. When he retreats into his art, however, it is characteristically to create a haven for what Thoreau called 'the only true America'" (*American Jeremiad,* 181–82). Eliot does precisely this, continually recreating America in his writing—not just in his poetry's rewriting of his American Renaissance precursors (a rewriting that Jay has made clear), but also in his dissertation, his literary criticism, and his sociopolitical writing.

To begin with, the language by which Eliot describes important aspects of the postmetaphysical world he outlines in his dissertation is similar in interesting ways to the language we have encountered in his description of the America he fled. His reaction to the threat to selfhood in the one, for instance, is the same as his reaction to the same threat in the other. In the beginning, according to Eliot, is the finite center—a felt whole of immediate experience that is not yet a self. But "in social behaviour," he writes, "in the conflict and readjustment of finite centres," there is a fall away from unity.[21] Here is an echo of the dreaded loss of independence of which he writes in the almost exactly contemporaneous letter from Oxford cited above. We first encounter other finite centers, he writes, as "recognized resistances and felt divergences," and then, "in adjusting our behaviour to that of others and in cooperating with them[,] we come to intend an identical world" (*Knowledge and Experience,* 142–43).

Here is the dreaded absorption by the world, despite resistance to it, that he mentions in his Oxford letter—the compromise (epistemological, on the one hand, more explicitly social, on the other) that is the first step toward conformity. "[T]he life of a soul," he concludes, "does not consist in the contemplation of one consistent world but in the painful task of unifying . . . jarring and incompatible ones, and passing, when possible, from two or more discordent viewpoints to a higher which shall somehow include and transmute them" (*Knowledge and Experience,* 147–48). Talk of "conflict," of "divergence," of "resistance," of the painfulness of the task, of being jarred, of incompatibility, and of discordant viewpoints reminds us that, in addition to the philosophical dimension of passages like these, there is also the dread of which his letter speaks—the dread of being included in and transmuted by an ideology of conformity and progress.

We should note, however, that Eliot is far from rejecting progress—so far, in fact, that rather than grounding his 1916 dissertation's subsumption of self and world in an ideal Absolute, as F. H.

Bradley (the subject of his dissertation) had done, Eliot defines our human being as a radical process that we merely (but nonetheless *must) conceive* as a progress toward an Absolute: "The Absolute is neither real nor unreal nor imaginary. . . . A metaphysic may be accepted or rejected without our assuming from the practical point of view it is either true or false" (*Knowledge and Experience,* 169). "What we can do," he explains, "is to describe in a general way the process of transition and development which takes place when there is an organism which is part of the world and yet is capable to a certain degree of contemplating the world" (156). In the end, as Walter Benn Michaels has shown, "only the practical remains."[22] The important question, in short, is pragmatic: Does our conception of the Absolute *work?* Is it a useful way of coping practically with our age's moment in an endless process?[23]

That the rhetoric of the myth of America is an element in Eliot's dissertation is suggested by his concluding remarks. "The point," this "pioneer" from St. Louis claims, "is that the world of practical verification has no definite frontiers, and that it is the business of philosophy to keep the frontiers open. . . . [T]his emphasis on practice—upon the relativity and instrumentality of human knowledge—is what impels us toward the Absolute" (*Knowledge and Experience,* 169). We find here two of the most important elements that Bercovitch isolates in the rhetoric of the American jeremiad. First, we have the all-important metaphor of the frontier—serving, as it does in the myth of America, not to mark a boundary between countries, but as a summons to territorial expansion. Philosophy, it seems, is on a continual errand into the conceptual wilderness. (A similar point—this time with regard to literary criticism—is made years later with much the same rhetoric: "Literary criticism is an activity which must constantly define its own boundaries; also, it must constantly be going beyond them.")[24] Second, we also have, in the dissertation's location of the Absolute somewhere at the unspecified end of the continuing process of knowing, the jeremiad's deferral of the millennium to an equally unspecified point at the end of the errand. While I would not presume to argue that the dissertation's pragmatic and hermeneutic sense of philosophy as a succession of superseded conceptual frontiers or horizons is itself of Puritan origins (although such a line of inquiry is tantalizing), or that its understanding of philosophy as a deferred errand is uniquely Puritan, I do suggest that the myth of America, and the Puritan-derived rhetoric that goes with it, is an identifiable and informing aspect of the New England sensibility writing the dissertation.

Bercovitch observes that in the development of the American jeremiad the process that is America comes to be understood simultaneously as the process that is the American self:

> The concept of American revolution transformed self-reliance into a function not only of the common good but of the redemption of mankind. In virtually every area of life, the jeremiad became the official ritual form of continuing revolution. . . . In short, it wed self-interest to social perfection, and conferred on both the unique blessings of American destiny. (*American Jeremiad,* 141)

In other words, the Puritan enthusiasm, awakening, and revival deemed essential to individual spiritual salvation came to be rewritten as equally essential to political salvation: "For well over two centuries . . . the major spokesmen for a self-proclaimed people of God subsumed the facts of social pluralism . . . in a comprehensive national ideal, transferred the terms of conflict normally inherent in that ideal from history to rhetoric, and secured the triumph of that rhetoric by identifying it with the assertion of a representative American self."[25] Eliot does the same, I have suggested, by transforming his personal concern about loss of self in America into a philosophical discourse larger than himself. In short, according to Bercovitch, "The American Puritan jeremiads . . . [turn] liminality itself into a mode of socialization. . . . The ritual of errand enforces an identity that is at once transitional and representative" (*American Jeremiad,* 25–26). Similarly, Eliot understands as a condition of knowing a world the need for every individual "I" to inscribe a socially constructed self upon his or her chest, without which inscription an individual "I" cannot participate in a common world.

The disposition toward Puritan rhetoric that I have traced in Eliot's early work in philosophy is also evident in his literary criticism. For the Puritans, Bercovitch observes,"selfhood appears as a state to be overcome, obliterated; and identity is asserted through an act of submission to a transcendental absolute."[26] In the development of the American jeremiad in the eighteenth century, he argues, America itself comes to serve as this transcendental absolute: "All the fragmented aspects of thought, belief, and behavior in this pluralistic society flowed into *America,* the symbol of continuing revolution, and then, in a ritual fusion of process and control, outward again to each self-reliant unit of culture" (*American Jeremiad,* 168). A very similar process is described in "Tradition and the Individual Talent." Eliot's lines about the need for the artist to overcome selfhood for the sake of a larger and more important whole are famous: "What happens is a continual surrender of [the artist] as he is at the moment to something which is more valuable. The progress of an artist is a continual self-sacrifice, a continual extinction of personality."[27] Of course the Puritan transcendental absolute—that "something which is more valuable"—is in this case not God or America, but the literary tradition. Nonetheless, here again are the twin pillars of America—conformity and continual progress.

But there is more. In one of the most important strategies Bercovitch identifies in the American jeremiad, the self is continually recognized in the past—and therefore *re-cognized*—as part of the ideological strategy by which the self is identified with America. Danforth's reference to the pilgrim fathers and America's regular reference to the Founding Fathers are instances of this strategy—a looking back to the good old days so as to redefine the self and mobilize the community toward the future. Eliot's strategy in "Tradition and the Individual Talent" is similar:

> No poet, no artist of any art, has his complete meaning alone. His significance, his appreciation is the appreciation of his relation to the dead poets and artists. You cannot value him alone; you must set him, for contrast and comparison, among the dead. . . . [The poet] . . . must inevitably be judged by the standards of the past. I say judged, not amputated, by them; not judged to be as good as, or worse or better than, the dead; and certainly not judged by the canons of dead critics. It is a judgement, a comparison, in which two things are measured by each other.[28]

Once more we have the oscillation between self and society found in both the dissertation and the jeremiad: Writers oscillate between a literary individuality and a literary universe and universality. "We say," suggests Eliot, the work "appears to conform, and is perhaps individual, or it appears individual, and may conform; but we are hardly likely to find that it is one and not the other."[29] Conformity and process again.

This recourse to the past to mobilize the community toward the future is also found in Eliot's theory of the dissociation of sensibility. According to Eliot, the English literary mind once possessed a unified sensibility that it is the modern poet's duty, after the dissociation wrought by Milton and Dryden, to reassert. Eliot's strategy of looking back to the future—to a certain extent, the strategy of modernism itself, in so far as Eliot, Yeats, Joyce, and Pound are representative moderns—is the same route to the modern world Bercovitch finds in the jeremiad: "The legend of the fathers was an impetus to modernization," he writes, "a call for progress that enhanced the glories of the past; a nostalgia for a golden age that enforced the values of the present" (*American Jeremiad,* 170). The jeremiad's motivating "backward glance" actually becomes a part of Eliot's poetic. It seems equally a strategy of *The Waste Land* (by means of its allusions to past literary fathers) and a strategy of *East Coker* (by means of its allusion to Eliot's literal forefather, the East Coker native Andrew Eliot who emigrated to New England in the seventeenth century). The simultaneously backward and forward glance of both the jeremiad and modernism is evident in *Little Gidding:*

> We die with the dying:
> See, they depart, and we go with them.
> We are born with the dead:
> See, they return, and bring us with them. (197)

In short, what Eliot in "Tradition and the Individual Talent" calls the "historical sense"—"a perception, not only of the pastness of the past, but of its presence"—is a version of the historical sense so much a part of the American jeremiad.[30]

An aspect of this inherited historical sense, ironically, is Eliot's uneasiness about the initial rupture with the past created by Puritan revolutions. It is the charge of disowning the past that Eliot, the closet Puritan, levels against the English Puritans of the seventeenth century (echoing the same charge he lays against America by means of his emigration to Britain). In Eliot's account of the matter, it was the Puritans who brought about the dissociation of sensibility. As Asher observes of Eliot's attitude toward the Puritan revolution in England: "The notorious 'dissociation of sensibility' . . . runs parallel to the dissolution of the old monarchy, with the final poetic and political ruptures occurring simultaneously." In short, Eliot regards the prerevolutionary state of English letters as pre-lapsarian: "English literary history comes to be written after a French model," Asher writes, "in which 1688 corresponds to 1789 as the date of ejection from the Eden of authoritarian institutions."[31] But Eliot himself goes a long way toward explaining the tension between the impulses toward rupture and continuity within himself in particular and Puritanism in general, acknowledging that kinship and friction are both a part of his relationship with his ancestors: "The writers of the past . . . in one's own place and language may be valuable to the . . . writer simply as something to rebel against. He will recognize the common ancestors: but he needn't necessarily *like* his relatives."[32] In short, there is no contradiction between inheritance and antipathy. Friction, he recognizes, is natural: The poet may "obtain stimulus from the hope of doing something that his predecessors have not done; he may even be in revolt against them, as a promising adolescent may revolt against the beliefs, the habits and the manners of his parents."[33] Friction is part of the family dynamic: We can see that the writer or adolescent in revolt against parents "is also a continuer of their traditions, that he preserves essential family characteristics, and that his difference of behaviour is a difference in the circumstances of another age."[34] For Eliot, friction is what Bercovitch would call "American friction"—the friction that produces the representative self, the friction that produces in the dissertation the common world of our concern, and the friction among ideas that Eliot regards as necessary to any living culture. And so, as Jeffrey Perl observes, Eliot can neither eliminate dissenters nor deny that dissent exists.[35] But of course he need not deny it or eliminate it, for, like America, he keeps it all in the family.

Not surprisingly, then, far from contradicting his rhetorical heritage, Eliot's search for authority, after the Puritan disowning of the past, actually duplicates the New England Puritan search for authority, begun as early as Winthrop's sermon written on board the Arabella. The very title of the sermon, "A Modell of Christian Charity," announces the American Puritan's search for a model of nonconformity to which he or she might conform. Ironically, then, Eliot, the twentieth-century Puritan criticizing the seventeenth-century Puritan, is all the more a New England Puritan (his dissent/descent all the more categorically American) for this anxiety about the Puritan rupture with traditional authority.

That Eliot's relatively American strategy of writing society as self and self as society energizes not just his literary criticism and philosophy, but also his socio-political writing, is evident from *The Idea of a Christian Society,* published in 1939. The result of his version of Christian political ideology, Eliot believes, will be a unified Christian sensibility. Ideally, he writes, the individual's "specifically religious emotions must be a kind of extension and sanctification of the domestic and social emotions."[36] In other words, he hopes to find in the individual religious sensibility a continuum (like the continuum he finds in his dissertation and his literary criticism) between the individual, on the one hand, and society or the cultural tradition, on the other. Individual identity and ideology, he recognizes, proceed as much from society as from self: "I have tried to picture, not a society of saints, but of ordinary men, of men whose Christianity is communal before being individual" (59–60). In *The Idea of a Christian Society,* then, as in his poetry and literary criticism, Eliot's writing is a writing of self as society and a writing of society as self—a model of writing Bercovitch has traced to the American jeremiad.

The rhetoric of the jeremiad is pervasive. Fearing the threat of totalitarianism—"a state of affairs in which we shall have regimentation and conformity, without respect for the needs of the individual soul"—he argues that "the only possibility of control and balance is a religious control and balance" (*Idea of a Christian Society,* 21–22). He is aiming for a balance and control similar to the balance and control Bercovitch defines as peculiar to America—a country with a national ideology that controls the dissent of parties and individuals alike by making dissent necessary to the achievement of the millennial American telos. "You cannot expect continuity and coherence in politics," Eliot writes, "you cannot expect reliable behaviour on fixed principles persisting through changed situations, unless there is an underlying political philosophy: not of a party, but of the nation" (40–41). "What the rulers believed," he argues, "would be less important than the beliefs to which they would be obliged to conform" (26). The flight from conformity and process in 1915, it seems, has by 1939 become a conscious errand toward them. "It is only in a society with a religious basis," he writes "—which is not the same thing as an ecclesiastical despotism—that you can get the proper harmony and tension, for the individual or for the community" (42).

That the rhetoric of the American jeremiad is operative here is confirmed by his concluding warning: "It is very easy for speculation on a possible Christian order in the future to tend to come to rest in a kind of apocalyptic vision of a golden age of virtue. But we have to remember that the Kingdom of Christ on earth will never be realised, and also that it is always being realised" (*Idea of a Christian Society,* 60). Here is the pattern of rhetoric Bercovitch traces over two centuries: Eliot suggests we are on an errand, but he warns that there are perils in the process; he acknowledges the general wreck of earthly empires, but his tone is hopeful. In Bercovitch's terms, "Anxiety functions . . . to excite and fortify expectations. Divisions and conflicts serve as a prelude to the assertion of continuity. [The purpose] . . . is simultaneously to raise tension and dispel doubt" (*American Jeremiad,* 146). In short, Eliot's ideal Christian society is to a certain extent a rewriting of the America he had inherited in the rhetoric of his Puritan ancestors.

In the end, then, I argue that Eliot's lifelong sense of his cultural mission—evident in his poetry, philosophy, literary criticism, and sociopolitical theorizing—derives in large measure from his inherited disposition to Puritan rhetoric and the American ideology implicit in it. As Gordon suggests, the Eliot corpus adds up to something very like the New England Puritan spiritual autobiography. And for both the Puritan and the Transcendentalist, Bercovitch writes, "auto-American-biography meant simultaneously a total assertion of the self, a jeremiad against the misdirected 'dead' present, and an act of prophecy which guaranteed the future by celebrating the regenerate" self-as-type-of-America located here and now.[37] Eliot's literary career assumes this very shape. As Gordon and Jay have shown in their very different ways, the prose and the poetry are radically autobiographical and radically American. As has always been evident, they constitute a jeremiad against the dead present—whether in Eliot's diagnosis of the modern world as suffering from a dissociation of sensibility, *The Waste Land*'s grouse against the modern world, or *Burnt Norton*'s criticism of the modern world as an "Eructation of unhealthy souls / Into the faded air, the torpid / Driven on the wind that sweeps the gloomy hills of London" (174). And as I have argued, Eliot's prose and poetry celebrate the self-as-type-of-America. That is, they celebrate the self as the site of conformity and process, as the site of individual and social salvation—from his early essay that makes a single process of tradition and the individual talent to *Little Gidding*'s observation of the coincidence of selfhood and nationality:

> love of a country
> Begins as our attachment to our own field of action
> And comes to find that action of little importance
> Though never indifferent. History may be servitude,
> History may be freedom. See, now they vanish,
> The faces and places, with the self which, as it could, loved them,
> To become renewed, transfigured, in another pattern. (195)

It seems, then, that the nets of nation, church, and family affected Eliot's flight from America much as they affected James Joyce's flight from Ireland. There is a sense, that is, in which Eliot no more left America in 1914 than Joyce left Ireland in 1904. The end of their exploring, to quote Eliot, was to arrive where they started "And know the place for the first time" (*Little Gidding,* 197). In analyzing Eliot's recourse in his writing about philosophy, literature, and politics to the narrative strategies of the American jeremiad, then, I suggest that we will come to recognize the force of Bercovitch's observation that for Americans the Puritans will always be something to rebel against (just as the Catholic church was for Joyce), but that the rebellion must be by interpretation. Eliot's movement from New England to England, from Puritanism to Anglicanism, and from the Boston family to the East Coker ancestors is apparently an act of dissent from America. But his writing proves in many ways, I suggest, to be an assent/ascent to America as the "city on a hill" through his continuous reinterpretation and reinscription of his narratively American descent.

NOTES

1. Ezra Pound, Letter to William Carlos Williams (11 Sept. 1920), in *The Letters of Ezra Pound 1907–1941,* ed. D. D. Paige (London: Faber, 1941).

2. F. O. Matthiessen, *The Achievement of T. S. Eliot,* 3d ed. (New York: Oxford University Press, 1959), 9.

3. See Herbert Howarth, *Notes on Some Figures behind T. S. Eliot* (Boston: Houghton Mifflin, 1964); Lyndall Gordon, *Eliot's Early Years* (Oxford: Oxford University Press, 1977); Eric Sigg, *The American Eliot: A*

Study of the Early Writings (Cambridge: Cambridge University Press, 1989). See also Ronald Bush, "T. S. Eliot Singing the Emerson Blues," in *Emerson: Prospect and Retrospect,* ed. Joel Porte (Cambridge: Harvard University Press, 1982), 179–97; and idem, "Nathaniel Hawthorne and T. S. Eliot's American Connection," *The Southern Review* 21, no. 4 (Autumn 1985): 924–33. And see Sam S. Basketh, "T. S. Eliot as an American Poet," *The Centennial Review* 26, no. 2 (Spring 1982): 147–71; Denis Donoghue, "On 'Gerontion,'" *The Southern Review* 21, no. 4 (Autumn 1985): 934–46; and Donald Gallup, "Mr. Eliot at the Churchill Club," *The Southern Review* 21, no. 4 (Autumn 1985): 969–73.

4. Gregory Jay, *T. S. Eliot and the Poetics of Literary History* (Baton Rouge: Louisiana State University Press, 1983), 21.

5. Samuel Danforth, "A Brief Recognition of New England's Errand into the Wilderness," in *The Wall and the Garden,* ed. A. W. Plumstead (Minneapolis: University of Minnesota Press, 1968), 57–58.

6. Samuel Sherwood, *The Church's Flight into the Wilderness: An Address on the Times* (New York: Loudon, 1776), 17, 23.

7. T. S. Eliot, "Ezra Pound," *New English Weekly,* 31 Oct. 1946, 27–28.

8. T. S. Eliot, *The Dry Salvages,* in *The Complete Poems and Plays of T. S. Eliot* (London: Faber & Faber, 1979), 190. All quotations of Eliot's poetry derive from this edition and are indicated by page numbers within parentheses.

9. T. S. Eliot "The Art of Poetry, I: T. S. Eliot," *Paris Review* 21 (Spring/Summer 1959): 69–70.

10. Lyndall Gordon, *Eliot's New Life* (Oxford: Oxford University Press, 1988), 2, 234.

11. Jay, *T. S. Eliot,* 11, 12, 21.

12. Eliot to Richard Aldington and Paul Elmer More, respectively, cited in Gordon, *New Life,* 40, 20.

13. Gordon, *Eliot's Early Years,* 4–5.

14. T. S. Eliot, Letter to Eleanor Hinkley (27 Nov. 1914), in *The Letters of T. S. Eliot, volume 1, 1898–1922,* ed. Valerie Eliot (London: Faber, 1988).

15. T. S. Eliot, Preface, *This American World,* by Edgar Ansel Mowrer (London: Faber & Gwyer, 1928), xiii.

16. Sacvan Bercovitch, *The American Jeremiad* (Madison: University of Wisconsin Press, 1978), 9.

17. Eliot, Letter to Conrad Aiken (25 Feb. 1915), in *Letters.*

18. Kenneth Asher, "T. S. Eliot and Ideology," *English Literary History* 55, no. 4 (Winter 1988): 897. The same distaste for the genteel tradition can be seen in Eliot's poem contemporary with his letter, "Mr. Apollinax," in which Professor Channing-Cheetah and Mrs. Flaccus represent the well-to-do Bostonians aping English manners. See Donald J. Childs, "'Mr. Apollinax,' Professor Channing-Cheetah, and T. S. Eliot," *Journal of Modern Literature* 13, no. 1 (1986): 172–77.

19. T. S. Eliot, "Relation between Politics and Metaphysics," Eliot Collection, Houghton Library, Harvard University, 11–12.

20. T. E. Hulme, "Programme," in *The Life and Opinions of T. E. Hulme,* by Alun R. Jones (London: Gollancz, 1960), 199–200.

21. T. S. Eliot, *Knowledge and Experience in the Philosophy of F. H. Bradley* (London: Faber & Faber, 1964), 24–25.

22. Walter Benn Michaels, "Philosophy in Kinkanja," in *Glyph 8* (Baltimore: Johns Hopkins University Press, 1981), 200.

23. On the pragmatic, hermeneutic, and poststructural dimensions of Eliot's work in philosophy, see Michaels, "Philosophy in Kinkanja"; Harriet Davidson, *T. S. Eliot and Hermeneutics* (Baton Rouge: Louisiana State University Press, 1985); and Michael Beehler, *T. S. Eliot, Wallace Stevens, and the Discourse of Difference* (Baton Rouge: Louisiana State University Press, 1987).

24. T. S. Eliot, *On Poetry and Poets* (London: Faber & Faber, 1957), 215.

25. Sacvan Bercovitch, *The Puritan Origins of the American Self* (London: Yale University Press, 1975), 186.

26. Bercovitch, *Puritan Origins,* 13.

27. T. S. Eliot, *Selected Essays,* 3d ed. enlarged (London: Faber & Faber, 1951), 17.

28. Eliot, *Selected Essays,* 15.

29. Eliot, *Selected Essays,* 15–16.

30. Eliot, *Selected Essays,* 14.

31. Asher, "Eliot and Ideology," 900, 901.

32. T. S. Eliot, *To Criticize the Critic* (London: Faber & Faber, 1965), 56.

33. Eliot, *On Poetry and Poets,* 58.

34. Eliot, *On Poetry and Poets,* 58.

35. Jeffrey M. Perl, "The Law of the Excluded Middle," *Renascense* 20. 3 (Spring 1988): 167.

36. T. S. Eliot, *The Idea of a Christian Society* (New York: Harcourt, Brace Co., 1940), 29.

37. Bercovitch, *Puritan Origins*, 184.

BARRY ALLEN

5

Work on Truth in America: The Example of William James

. . . a kind of new dawn is breaking among us philosophers.
William James

It is perhaps a surprising claim that dissent can inspire community. But history has given the United States a tradition and culture of dissent, which, as Bercovitch observes, "has made the very exposure of social flaws part of a ritual of socialization—a sort of liminal interior dialogue that in effect reinforces the mainstream culture."[1]

Puritan emigration raised the problem of authority in a company of radical nonconformists, and their first social crisis (the episode with Anne Hutchinson) revealed the limits of their success at containing dissent, as they tried to, by public consensus in the interpretation of sacred texts.[2] From these beginnings, "American" dissent is marked as such by its obligatory passage through what Bercovitch calls a symbology or historical vocabulary of rhetorical turns and sacred references, elaborated and revised over three centuries, and constantly proving its resources in what passes for public discourse in America.

Consider the example of William James.

At the fifth annual meeting of the New England Anti-Imperialist League in Boston in 1903, James delivered an "Address on the Philippine Question."[3] As a result of war with Spain (in 1898), the United States had assumed military control of the Philippines, while the army had more recently succeeded in crushing a Filipino insurrection. For the first time in its history, the United States was an imperial power.

James denounces the nation's "wayward spree of power." All "the anti-imperialist prophecies were right."

> One by one we have seen them punctually fulfilled:—The material ruin of the Islands; the transformation of native friendliness to execration; the demoralization of our army . . . forgery decorated, torture whitewashed, massacre condoned . . . these things, I say, or things like them, were things which anyone with any breadth of understanding clearly foretold. (*W*, 1131)

The act of empire exposes the falsity of American ideals:

> We used to believe . . . that we were of a different clay from other nations, that there was something deep in the American heart that answered to our happy birth, free from that hereditary burden which the nations of Europe bear, and which obliges them to grow by preying on their neighbours. Idle dream! pure Fourth of July fancy, scattered in five minutes by the first temptation. (*W*, 1134)

Calling upon the country "to return to the principles which it was suckled in" avails not. "American memories no longer serve a catchwords."

> The country has once for all regurgitated the Declaration of Independence and the Farewell Address . . . It has come to a hiatus. It has deliberately pushed itself into the circle of international hatreds, and joined the common pack of wolves. (*W*, 135)

The action of the present government

> makes of the old liberalism and the new liberalism of our country two discontinuous things. The older liberalism was

> in office, the new is in the opposition. Inwardly it is the same spirit, but outwardly the tactics, the questions, the reasons, and the phrases have to change. (*W,* 1135)

James thus frames his dissent in terms of sacred American images and texts, and he represents the opposition he calls for as a return to the truth of the Revolution.

Considering the whole performance, one recognizes what Bercovitch has called an "American jeremiad." Bercovitch explains that in traditional European preaching a jeremiad "was a lament over the ways of the world. It decried the sins of 'the people'—a community, a nation, a civilization, mankind in general—and warned of God's wrath to follow." The Puritans brought this sermon form with them to Massachusetts, "but from the start they sounded a different note." Unlike the European preacher, New England's clergy "were not simply castigating."

> The purpose of their jeremiads was to direct an imperiled people of God toward the fulfillment of their destiny, to guide them individually toward salvation, and collectively toward the American city of God . . . In explicit opposition to the traditional mode, [an American jeremiad] inverts the doctrine of vengeance into a promise of ultimate success, affirming to the world, and despite the world, the inviolability of the colonial cause. (*AJ,* 6–9)

The vision outlasted that lost local cause. The rhetoric of the jeremiad, elaborated, revised, and extended, served the interpretive needs of generations from colony to republic and beyond. For three centuries it has "nourished the imagination, inspired ever grander flights of self-justification, and so continued to provide a source of social cohesion and continuity" (*AJ,* 17).

Consider again the example of William James. His address confirms dismal prophecies "one by one . . . punctually fulfilled," Washington's Farewell Address unheeded, Jefferson's Declaration "regurgitated." But we must not abandon the errand, "the long, long campaign for truth and fair dealing," not until "the end of time." James closes with these words:

> Let us cheerfully settle into our interminable task. Everywhere it is the same struggle under various names,—light against darkness, right against might, love against hate. The

Lord of life is with us, and we cannot permanently fail. (*W*, 1135)

That William James should preach an American jeremiad indicates an investment in the symbolism with which Americans have imagined America since the beginning of the idea in the seventeenth century. Nor are these rhetorical resources and imaginary commitments discreetly set aside when James turns from an explicitly political text like the "Address on the Philippine Question." Max Weber described James's psychology of religion as "a true child of the world of ideas of [his] Puritan home."[4] The same may be said of the philosophy he called "pragmatism."

James imagines nature as a wilderness, rough and dangerous, but unburdened by history—a place where something new can always begin, including a new philosophy. "We condemn all noble, clean-cut, fixed, eternal, rational, temple-like systems of philosophy," he says. "These contradict the *dramatic temperament* of nature . . . We turn from them to the great unpent and unstayed wilderness of truth as we feel it to be constituted" (*M*, 49). There is an errand to be undertaken in this wilderness of truth. The New World experience of nature is a challenge to reconstruct the philosophy of the Old World, to make it new and truer. "A kind of new dawn is breaking among us philosophers," James says in *Pragmatism* (1907). It "reminds one almost of the protestant reformation" (*P*, 10, 62).

This newness was the New England Puritans' seminal contribution to the American imagination. On election day, May 1670, the Reverend Samuel Danforth exhorted the Massachusetts colonists to remember that "John began his ministry not in Jerusalem, nor in any famous city of Judea, but in the wilderness, i.e., in a woody, retired, and solitary place, thereby withdrawing himself from the envy and preposterous zeal of such as were addicted to their old traditions."[5] More than a century and a half later, Emerson still denounces "this worship of the past." "The centuries are conspirators against the sanity and authority of the soul . . . history is an impertinence and an injury, if it be anything more than a cheerful apologue or parable of my being and becoming." Emerson's America "is the country of the Future . . . it is a country of beginnings, of projects, of designs, and expectations."

"We have listened too long to the courtly muses of Europe." "All literature is yet to be written"—likewise all philosophy, history, science, religion. Emerson foresees "an American genius," as new and different as California. "Luckily for us, now that steam has narrowed the Atlantic to a strait, the nervous, rocky West is introducing a new and continental element into the national mind, and we shall yet have an American genius."[6]

A half century later (in 1911), speaking amid the redwoods and Sierras of California, Santayana declared the late William James the fulfiller of Emerson's prophecy. James, he says, "may be regarded as representing the genuine, the long silent American mind." His "way of thinking and feeling represented the true America . . . a new philosophical vista . . . a conception never before presented."[7]

It is curious to see this notorious critic of the "genteel" (i.e., Puritan) tradition praise James with the Puritans' own rhetoric of newness and errand. Yet it must be said that James offers little resistance to such a reading. He situates the coming of pragmatism in a series of historical events of exemplary newness, comparing it to "the changes from aristocracy to democracy, from classic to romantic, from theistic to pantheistic, from static to evolutionary ways of understanding life" (*M*, 39). He allows there were "forerunners of pragmatism," but "they were preluders only. Not until our time has it generalized itself, become conscious of a universal mission, pretended to a conquering destiny. I believe in that destiny," James says to a public audience at Boston's Lowell Institute, "and I hope I may end by inspiring you with my belief" (*P*, 30).[8]

James thinks philosophy has a kind of significance for life that is ill-served by academic professionalism. "Philosophy's results concern us all most vitally"; "no one of us can get along without the far-flashing beams of light it sends over the world's perspectives," and this "give[s] to what it says an interest that is much more than professional" (*P*, 10–11). Yet the philosophical alternatives of the present are inadequate to our deepest needs. James regrets the plight of "the seriously inquiring amateur in philosophy who turns to the philosophy-professors for the wherewithal to satisfy the fullness of his nature's needs" (*P*, 22); and says, "I offer this oddly-named thing pragmatism as a philosophy that can . . . remain religious like the rationalisms, but at the same time, like the empiricisms, it can preserve the richest intimacy with facts" (*P*, 23). For James, textbook predicates like *empiricism* and *rationalism* stand for living options to be struggled over with something not very different from religious emotion. "Within religion," he remarks, "emotion is apt to be tyrannical; but philosophy must favor the emotion that allies itself best with the whole body and drift of all the truths in sight. I conceive this to be the more strenuous type of emotion" (*M*, 125). Philosophy must be reconstructed, all its old and curious problems recentered, brought into true with that "great . . . wilderness of truth as we feel it to be constituted."

That is why pragmatism is first of all a method, "primarily a method of settling metaphysical disputes that might otherwise be interminable."

> The pragmatic method in such cases is to try to interpret each notion by tracing its respective practical consequences. What difference would it practically make to anyone if this notion rather than that notion were true? If no practical difference whatever can be traced, then the alternatives mean practically the same thing, and all dispute is idle. Wherever a dispute is serious, we ought to be able to show some practical difference that must follow from one side or the other's being right. (*P*, 28)

In a point to which I shall return, James observes how this method promises to situate truth, and philosophy, squarely in practice. "There can be . . . no difference in abstract truth that doesn't express itself in a difference in concrete fact and in conduct consequent upon that fact, imposed on somebody, somehow, somewhere and some when." This defines the office of philosophy: "The whole function of philosophy ought to be to find out what definite difference it will make to you and me, at definite instances of our life, if this world-formula or that world-formula be the true one" (*P*, 30). Philosophy ought not to be a thing of the schools; it has a public vocation, and speaks (or should speak) of high and final things to each and every individual. "—See, I say, how pragmatism shifts the emphasis":

> The centre of gravity of philosophy must therefore alter its place . . . It will be an alteration in the "seat of authority" that reminds one almost of the protestant reformation. And as, to papal minds, protestantism has often seemed a mere mess of anarchy and confusion, such, no doubt, will pragmatism often seem to ultrarationalistic minds in philosophy. It will seem so much sheer trash, philosophically. But life wags on, all the

> same, and compasses its ends, in protestant countries. I venture to think that philosophic protestantism will compass a not dissimilar prosperity. (*P*, 62)

James dramatizes pragmatism's newness by contrasting it with the "rationalism" of European metaphysics: "The essential contrast is that for rationalism reality is ready-made and complete from all eternity, while for pragmatism it is still in the making, and awaits part of its complexion from the future." Almost proudly, James declares "the alternative between pragmatism and rationalism . . . concerns the structure of the universe itself . . . On the one side the universe is absolutely secure, on the other it is still pursuing its adventures . . . really malleable, waiting to receive its final touches at our hands." Yet in philosophy, as in life, everything is finally a question of temperament, and what began as cosmology resolves into moral psychology. Pragmatism's is "a tramp and vagrant world, adrift in space, with neither elephant nor tortoise to plant the sole of its foot upon."

> Now the idea of this loose universe affects your typical rationalists in much the same way as "freedom of the press" might affect a veteran official in the russian bureau of censorship; or as "simplified spelling" might affect an elderly schoolmistress. It affects him as the swarm of protestant sects affects a papist onlooker. It appears as backboneless and devoid of principle as "opportunism" in politics appears to an old-fashioned french legitimist, or to a fanatical believer in the divine right of the people.
> . . . it is impossible not to see a temperamental difference at work in the choice of sides. The rationalist mind . . . is of a doctrinaire and authoritative complexion: the phrase *"must be"* is ever on its lips. The belly-band of its universe must be tight. A radical pragmatist on the other hand is a happy-go-lucky anarchistic sort of creature. (*P*, 123–25)

James's imaginative and rhetorical debt to Emerson is evident. "Men resist the conclusion in the morning," the latter writes, "but adopt it as the evening wears on, that temper prevails over everything of time, place, and condition."[9] For James, "temperaments with their cravings and refusals do determine men in their philosophies, and always will . . . Not only Walt Whitman could write 'who touches this book touches a man.'

The books of all the great philosophers are like so many men." History disappears as a significant difference; differences of class, race, gender, or historical experience among people or the symbolic artifacts they produce are reduced to purely psychological phenomena, subjective articulations of a rich and presumably universal human nature.

Anyone who can stand its loose and chancy sort of universe, a "drastic kind of universe from which the element of 'seriousness' is not to be expelled," is, James thinks, "a genuine pragmatist." In other words, pragmatism "has to fall back on a certain ultimate hardihood, a certain willingness to live without assurances or guarantees." It is therefore "bound to disappoint many sick souls." Pragmatism "has no saving message for incurably sick souls," no reassurance for those who are "simply afraid, afraid of more experience, afraid of life." A pragmatist has to find the radical absence of metaphysical foundations and predestined finality an energizing, liberating, wholesome thought. For the pragmatist (as for A. R. Ammons), "Firm ground is not available ground."[10]

Pragmatism gives rise to a new philosophy of truth when its method is brought to bear upon the language with which European philosophy has endeavored to define truth's essence. "Truth, as any dictionary will tell you, is a property of certain of our ideas. It means their 'agreement,' as falsity means their disagreement, with 'reality.'" James says that pragmatists and antipragmatists "both accept this definition as a matter of course. They begin to quarrel only after the question is raised as to what may precisely be meant by the term 'agreement,' and what by the term 'reality,' when reality is taken as something for our ideas to agree with" (*P*, 96). The pragmatic method, recall, is a method of interpretation: "You must bring out of each word its practical cash-value, [and] set it at work within the stream of your experience" (*P*, 31–32). Truth is agreement with reality, of course; in the language of the schools, *veritas est adaequatio intellectus ad rem.* But let us be pragmatic, and ask what this language comes to in practice. What practical difference does it make to us to have true rather than false ideas? "The moment pragmatism asks this question, it sees the answer: True ideas are those we can assimilate, validate, corroborate and verify. False ideas are those we cannot" (*P*, 97). What then is the pragmatic meaning of the "agreement with reality" that makes an idea true? "To 'agree' in the widest sense with a reality," James says,

> can only mean to be guided either straight up to it or into its surroundings, or to be put into such working touch with it or something connected with it better than if we disagreed. Better either intellectually or practically! . . . Any idea that helps us *deal,* whether practically or intellectually, with either the reality or its belongings, that doesn't entangle our progress in frustrations, that *fits,* in fact, and adapts our life to the reality's whole setting, will agree sufficiently to meet the requirement. It will hold true of that reality. (*P,* 102)

James considers this interpretation of truth to present "a momentous philosophical alternative" (*P,* 104), one that "involves much restatement of traditional notions" (*M,* 38); indeed, "the whole scene of the philosophic stage will change in some degree if [it] prevails" (*M,* 236). To dramatize its newness he again contrasts his pragmatist with an antipragmatic alter ego, a rationalist whose "one great assumption" is that "when you've got your true idea of anything, there's an end of the matter. You're in possession; you *know;* you have fulfilled your thinking destiny. You are where you ought to be mentally; you have obeyed your categorical imperative; and nothing more need to follow on that climax of your rational destiny. Epistemologically you are in stable equilibrium" (*P,* 96). Nietzsche called this a "Buddhism for Europeans." For James, it "seems, if you look at it coldly, to be an almost preposterous ideal" (*M,* 57). It should be left behind with all those fixed, eternal, rational, temple-like systems of Old World philosophy. Reinterpreted pragmatically, the agreement essential to truth is not a static, formal *adaequatio;* it is nothing but the agreeable practical consequences that attend actions guided by some ideas but not others, which ideas we then call "true." "This function of agreeable leading is what we mean by an idea's verification . . . just such consequences being what we have in mind whenever we say that our ideas 'agree' with reality" (*P,* 97).

So we should not think of the relation between ideas or beliefs and the reality with which they are concerned in anything like the way Greek and Scholastic philosophers did, as the mimetic assimilation of thinking and being. But James's point is not just to deflate this metaphysical interpretation of truth. If he dissents from the European tradition in the philosophy of truth, it is because his further aim is to *reconstruct* truth's relationship to nature or reality and to the good. In Plato's allegory we begin life as prisoners chained to the walls of a cave where we see only shadows and, knowing nothing better, take them for realities, until our contentment is unsettled by a glimpse outside and a vision of True Being. Hans Blumenberg describes Plato's story of escape from the cave "as the elementary typification of all processes of 'enlightenment,'" and he observes that "the allegory leaves unclear and unstated what motive it is that leads to the accomplishment of liberation and undeceiving—the first event is the return of the one 'undeceived' person into the cave, in order to disenchant the others." The value of this, the superior good of having the truth, seems to go without saying. Not until the contemporary work of Nietzsche and William James would this curious lacuna become problematic for philosophy.[11]

For James, the good of true ideas, the value for the sake of which one prefers true over false beliefs, is "essentially bound up with the way in which one moment in our experience may lead us toward other moments which it will be worth while to have been led to." *Truth* names the good we admire in any "process of conduction from a present idea to a future terminus, provided only it run prosperously." That "is the practical difference it makes to us to have true ideas." That, therefore, is "the only intelligible practical *meaning* to that difference in our beliefs which our habit of calling them true or false comports" (*P*, 97–98; *M*, 147). Where, for Plato, "we find fixity, purity, truth, and . . . perfect clarity . . . in those things that are always, unchanged, unaltered," while to accede to the truth is to "find surcease from one's travail of soul," for James such surcease is not truth but death. Truth lies with life, and life with power, which "ceases in the instant of repose; it resides in the moment of transition from a past to a new state, in the shooting of the gulf, in the darting to a new aim."[12]

Nietzsche also posed the question of truth's value to philosophy, and sought an answer in terms of *life* (*will*) and *power*. "Consider both the earliest and most recent philosophers: they are all oblivious of how much the will to truth itself first requires justification; here there is a lacuna in every philosophy . . . truth [is] not *permitted* to be a problem at all." There have long been skeptics who doubt we could *have* the truth, possessing it securely as knowledge. But philosophers have been strangely silent about truth's claim to preference. Yet to think that the problem around truth is an epistemological one evades what for Nietzsche is the more basic question of its value. Why assume truth is—if not unconditionally, then general—to be preferred over its many opposites (error, lie, myth, etc.)? Why the peculiar privilege of having the truth *despite* opinion, *despite* appearances, *despite* the utility or pleasure or security one may be obliged to forego in the name of truth? "Here," Nietzsche says, "I touch on my problem, on our problem, my unknown friends (for as yet I *know* of no friend): What meaning would *our* whole being possess if it were not this, that in us the will to truth becomes conscious of itself as a *problem*?"[13]

For Nietzsche, as for James, the traditional evaluation of truth's value has lost all of its former self-evidence. For both, there is no impressive difference between truth "itself" and what passes for true in practice; for both, what passes for true has nothing to do with "adequation" to a transcendent order of Being, fixed and closed forever. What James and Nietzsche make of these conclusions, however, is very different indeed. Schematically, where Nietzsche *reverses* truth's value "experimentally," as part of a projected revaluation of the highest values,[14] James *reserves* the word *true* as a name for the proper good for belief, which he then analyzes in pragmatic terms, as "essentially an affair of leading—leading that is useful because it is into quarters that contain objects that are important" (*P*, 103). If, therefore, James raises a new and radical question concerning the value of truth, his aim is by no means skeptical or deconstructive; far from it. He never seriously doubts truth's claim to the highest value. The point is not to upset the conviction that it must always be good to live in the truth, but to *revise* the terms of this evaluation in response to "the great . . . wilderness of truth as we feel it to be constituted."

This is an important difference. A philosophy that reverses the highest values presupposes Nietzsche's aristocratic solitude; it cannot be the philosophy of a democratically inclusive political community. Yet James envisions pragmatism as a public philosophy, and in this he is, I think, Emersonian. Bercovitch makes an important point concerning the difference between Emerson and European anti-nomianism from Carlyle to Nietzsche:

> Perhaps the most misleading commonplace of recent criticism is that our major [American] literature through Emerson is Antinomian. The Puritans banished Anne Hutchinson, we recall, because she set her private revelation above the common errand. The controversy foreshadows the fundamentally opposed

> concepts of greatness in Emerson and Carlyle. Emerson's hero . . . derives his greatness from the enterprise he represents . . . Carlyle's hero gathers strength precisely in proportion to his alienation. He stands sufficient in himself, a titan born to master the multitude . . . he finds his place in a latter-day Antinomian brotherhood that includes Shaw's Superman and Ibsen's Master Builder; Nietzsche's Zarathustra, that "terrible teacher of great contempt;" Byron's banished saint, whose immortal mind "makes itself/Requital for its good or evil thoughts." In contrast to all of these, Emerson . . . reminded himself in his journals to "beware of Antinomianism."[15]

Emerson's self-reliance is a nonconformism that defies, but does not threaten, public life: "The populace think that your rejection of popular standards is a rejection of all standard, and mere antinomianism." Where Zarathustra hopes and longs "to redeem all 'it was' into a 'thus I willed it,'" Emerson's self-reliance is a mode of self-trust that calls upon the individual to "accept the place the divine providence has found for you, the society of your contemporaries, the connection of events." Where Nietzsche speaks in the far-future tense, addressing unknown, future friends, rare free spirits and immoralists, wherever they may be (it is never where Nietzsche is), Emerson uses the strong present tense: "We must not harbor such disconsolate consciences, borrowed too much from the consciences of other nations. We must set up the strong present tense against all the rumours of wrath, past or to come." Were there a question where this "we" is situated, Bercovitch supplies the answer: "The natural habitat of the *Übermensch* is the sublime, anywhere; Emerson's is America."[16]

> Anne Hutchinson's self-reliance, like Wordsworth's, Byron's, Carlyle's and Nietzsche's, may hold out grand prospects for mankind, but it locates the divine center in the individual. The self-reliant American may declare his whim superior to the entire legal code, but he remains by definition the hero as guide and national benefactor.[17]

Nietzsche may have admired Emerson, but he did not need to appropriate or revise him, while James, who is perhaps too much of a democrat for both Nietzsche and Emerson, did. Addressing a public audience of "philosophic amateurs" in his Lowell Lectures, he says:

> We philosophers have to reckon with [your] feelings . . . In the last resort, I repeat, it will be by them that all our philosophies shall be judged. The finally victorious way of looking at things will be the most completely *impressive* way to the normal run of minds. (*P*, 25)

Was it Emerson or Nietzsche who said, "One must shed the bad taste of wanting to agree with the many"? Yet, after Emerson, James speaks in the strong present tense, of new things now under way, and he makes a visible effort (unimaginable from Nietzsche) to enlist his public in the undertaking and on terms of full equality:

> I wish to fill you with sympathy with a contemporaneous tendency in which I profoundly believe, and yet I have to talk like a professor to you who are not students . . . I know that you, ladies and gentlemen, have a philosophy, each and all of you, and that the most interesting and important thing about you is the way in which it determines the perspective in your several worlds . . . Believing in philosophy myself devoutly, and believing also that a kind of new dawn is breaking upon us philosophers, I feel impelled . . . to try to impart to you some news of the situation. (*P*, 9–11)

Like Thoreau, like Whitman, James speaks as a neighbor and exemplary democrat. His style of address ("to you . . . each and all of you") is simultaneously personal and general, individualizing and integrating. These are, not coincidentally, also the values James discovers at the heart of truth: "True ideas . . . lead to consistency, stability and flowing human intercourse. They lead away from eccentricity and isolation, from foiled and barren thinking" (*P*, 103). We are in the truth just so long as "the connexions and transitions come to us from point to point as being progressive, harmonious, satisfactory" (*P*, 47). Truth is certainly good. Unlike Nietzsche (but like Emerson, for whom "Truth, and goodness, and beauty, are but different faces of the same All"),[18] James is not interested in posing a fundamental challenge to the Platonic evaluation of truth. His aim is not to *displace* truth from the center of the moral universe, but to *recenter* it by grounding its claim to superior value in terms of an (imaginary) American experience of Nature.

Harold Bloom also contrasts Emerson and Nietzsche:

> Nietzsche, who could tolerate so few of his own contemporaries, delighted in Emerson, and seems to have understood Emerson very well. And I think Nietzsche particularly understood that Emerson had come to prophesy not a de-centering, as Nietzsche had, and as Derrida and De Man are brilliantly accomplishing, but a peculiarly American *re-centering,* and with it an American mode of interpretation, one that we have begun—but only begun—to develop, from Whitman and Peirce down to Stevens and Kenneth Burke; a mode that *is* intra-textual, but that stubbornly remains logocentric, and that still follows Emerson in valorizing eloquence, the inspired voice, *over* the scene of writing.[19]

This holds as well for the difference between James and Nietzsche, or pragmatism and deconstruction. James himself described pragmatism as an alteration in "the centre of gravity of philosophy." For him, it is a question of a *new* center, *recentering* philosophy, and not an eccentric or deconstructive decentering of its traditional problematic. Yet Bercovitch advances the question a step further when he shows how this privilege of the voice *contains* dissent in its own rhetoric. "I mean *containment* in its double sense," he explains, "as sustenance and restriction." Not, of course, that American writers "lacked courage or radical commitment, but that they had invested these in a vision designed to contain self-assertion . . . The symbol of America . . . set free titanic creative energies in our classic writers, and it confined their freedom to the terms of the American myth" (*AJ,* 180).

Consider again the example of William James. His pragmatism is a study in this confinement: sustained, in being able to take seriously the idea of something new and different in the work on truth in America; yet restricted, limited as philosophy, by mythical assumptions about the social formation that embeds the pursuit of truth in modern Western societies, including the United States, already in James's time.

For pragmatism, the valuable difference between true and false belief is the difference of value between good and bad consequences. "The truer idea is the one that pushes farther" (*M,* 255). That, and not mimetic fealty, is the reason to prefer the truth. But if we are consistent pragmatists, we should not assume straightaway that we understand what "pushing farther" comes to practically. How is this distance measured? How is truth determined in practice? It is important that the difference between beliefs that "work" and those that do not cannot be determined by the subject's say-so or acquiescence in their consequences. In that case there would be no difference between having a belief and having a true belief, while the whole point of the pragmatic philosophy of truth is that there *is* a difference, a valuable, practical difference, between true and false belief. There must then be some means of evaluating ideas and rules for action independently of the subject's naive sense of what works for her.

Indeed, James allows that "truth supposes a standard outside of the thinker to which he must conform."[20] But how are we to understand this pragmatically? And where or what is "outside"?—James once named it:

> I begin with the abstract notion of an objective reality. I postulate it, and ask on my own account, I vouching for this reality, what would make anyone else's idea of it true for me as well as for him.
>
> . . . If the other man's idea leads him, not only to believe that the reality is there, but to use it [the idea] as the reality's temporary substitute, by letting it evoke *adaptive thoughts and acts similar to those which the reality itself would provoke,* then it is true in the only intelligible sense, true through its particular consequences, and true for me [i.e., objective reality] as well as for the man. (*M*, 33, emphasis added)

This remarkable argument is said to anticipate "the results of the general truth-processes of mankind," as if at the "end of inquiry" the difference between good and bad beliefs or mental habits would be perfectly obvious to anybody. Perhaps it would be. But in the meantime, life goes on, conduct is evaluated, decisions reached, powers of intervention in the name of truth and knowledge exercised and expanded. Two questions remain: First, how is the "adaptivity" of a mental habit, and thus the "objectivity" of a belief, evaluated in practice? By what criterion, procedure or authority? Second, what assures the connection between such criteria (or the practice of their application) and the prosperity that James anticipates from having the truth?

It is not impossible to answer the first question, but it is difficult to do so and remain sanguine about the answer to the second. In a large and expanding range of cases, the difference between true and false is determined by one or another professional expert, whose office and license and position in the social economy of knowledge gives her or his judgment a certain truth power in practice. A power to determine—not without qualification or finally, but in the first instance and with the balance of presumption—what from case to case *passes for truth.* For instance, to take a case that is obviously important for James, the power to determine the difference between adaptive and maladaptive mental habits is invested in our physicians, psychiatrists, forensic psychologists, and others working in an ensemble of professional knowledges that intersect at the hospital, the school, and the penitentiary.[21]

This makes me skeptical of the unity of truth and the good, although for James it does nothing of the kind. He has no doubt that "the possession of true thoughts means everywhere the possession of valuable instruments of action" or that "our duty to gain truth . . . can account for itself by excellent practical reasons" (*P*, 97). This is known without having to take any closer look at what actually circulates as "the truth" or to what effect. If it weren't good, it just wouldn't be truth. In this way James mystifies the social context of asymmetrical power relations apart from which truth and knowledge do not exist. Despite his rhetoric about the need for concreteness in philosophy and his condemnation of "vicious abstractionism," he himself operates with an untenably abstract conception of *practice* and of the *subject* of practice. He thinks of truth as an ideal instrument for coping with a universal plight like "experience" or "nature." In other words, he assumes that the more particularly differentiated social identity (female? disabled? indigent?) of the subject who has or, more likely, wants or is said to need the truth, is never an issue so far as concerns the value of what, in any case that touches them, passes for true. In the end, James seems less interested in situating truth squarely in social practice than in rhetorically representing that practice as if it were happily situated in a "community" where what passes for the truth cannot fail to be empowering. James's dissent from European philosophy is limited, as Nietzsche's was not, by his, as it were, temperamental determination never seriously to question the Platonic-Christian idea that it is always good to have the truth, the more truth the better—in James's New World variation, the more truth, the more adaptive and prosperous "our" (anybody's) experience.

In this, I suggest, he shares the fate Bercovitch descries in the poets of American difference: "The defiant act that might have posed fundamental social alternatives became instead a fundamental force against social change . . . the radical energies he celebrated served to sustain the culture, because the same ideal that released those energies transformed itself into a mode of cultural cohesion and continuity" (*AJ*, 204–5).

NOTES

1. Sacvan Bercovitch, *The American Jeremiad* (Madison: Wisconsin University Press, 1978), 205; hereafter abbreviated as *AJ*. Also see Bercovitch, "The Rites of Assent: Rhetoric, Ritual, and the Ideology of American Consensus," in *The American Self: Myth, Ideology, and Popular Culture*, ed. S. B. Girgus (Albuquerque: University of New Mexico Press, 1981).

2. See E. S. Morgan, *The Puritan Dilemma* (Boston: Little, Brown, 1958), esp. chap. 10 (on Anne Hutchinson); and Perry Miller, *Orthodoxy in Massachusetts* (Cambridge: Harvard University Press, 1933).

3. William James, *Writings 1902–1910* (New York: Library of America, 1987), 1130–35; hereafter abbreviated as *W*.

4. Max Weber, *The Protestant Ethic and the Spirit of Capitalism* (New York: Charles Scribner's Sons, 1958), 232–33. Also see H. M. Feinstein, *Becoming William James* (Ithaca: Cornell University Press, 1984). There are two chief sources for James's pragmatic philosophy: *Pragmatism: A New Name for Some Old Ways of Thinking* (1907) (Cambridge: Harvard University Press, 1978), hereafter abbreviated as *P*; and *The Meaning of Truth: A Sequel to "Pragmatism"* (1909) (Cambridge: Harvard University Press, 1978), hereafter abbreviated as *M*. For a concise and accurate introduction to pragmatic philosophy, see J. P. Murphy, *Pragmatism from Peirce to Davidson* (Boulder: Westview Press, 1990).

5. Samuel Danforth, *A Brief Recognition of New England's Errand into the Wilderness* (Cambridge, 1671). I owe this reference to Sacvan Bercovitch and the 1987 School of Criticism and Theory seminar on American dissent.

6. Emerson, *Essays and Lectures* (New York: Library of America, 1983), 270 ("Self-Reliance"), 71 ("American Scholar"), 216–17 ("The Young American"), 101 ("Literary Ethics").

7. George Santayana, "The Genteel Tradition in American Philosophy," in *The Genteel Tradition*, ed. D. L. Wilson (Cambridge: Harvard University Press, 1967), 54–58. This was originally presented as a lecture at the University of California, Berkeley. Santayana was, however, more impressed with James's so-called radical empiricism than with the pragmatic philosophy of truth.

8. The "preluders" James mentions include Socrates, Aristotle, and Locke. But the historical matrix of pragmatism is the Enlightenment. Referring to "the new physical theory of knowledge, which owes its existence to Newton and Locke," Ernst Cassirer writes: "Every principle owes its truth and inner reliability solely to the use to which we can put it, and this use consists only in the aid we receive from the principle in comprehending the manifold of given phenomena and arranging them according to certain points of view" (Ernst Cassirer, *The Philosophy of the Enlightenment* [Princeton: Princeton University Press, 1959], 55).

9. Emerson, "Experience," in *Essays and Lectures,* 474–75. Frank Lentricchia suggests that "the Emerson/James connection may constitute the most influential enhancement of intellectual force in American literary history." See "The Ideology of Poetic Modernism, 1890–1913: The Example of William James," in *Restructuring American Literary History,* ed. Sacvan Bercovitch (Cambridge: Harvard University Press, 1986), 230. Cornel West underscores Emerson's importance for American philosophy from Peirce to the present; see Cornel West, *The American Evasion of Philosophy: A Genealogy of Pragmatism* (Madison: University of Wisconsin Press, 1989).

10. James, *P,* 24, 139–43; James, *M,* 124–25; A. R. Ammons, "Dunes," in *The Selected Poems 1951–1977* (New York: Norton, 1977). In psychology, James held that "the effort which [a man] is able to put forth to hold himself erect and keep his heart unshaken is the direct measure of his worth and function in the game of human life. He can *stand* this Universe. He can meet it and keep up his faith in it in presence of those same features which lay his weaker brethren low" (*The Principles of Psychology* [1890] [New York: Dover, 1950], 2.578–79). On the prestige of psychology in American culture at the turn of the century, and the reduction of political differences to psychological differences, see T. J. Lears, *No Place of Grace: Antimodernism and the Transformation of American Culture 1880–1920* (New York: Pantheon, 1981), esp. 304. These trends had long been in preparation; see Perry Miller, *The Life of the Mind in America* (New York: Harcourt, Brace & World, 1965), 321.

11. Hans Blumenberg, *The Legitimacy of the Modern Age* (Cambridge: MIT Press, 1983), 449. Four representative texts on the traditional estimation of truth's value: "Of all things good, truth holds the first place among gods and men alike" (Plato, *Laws* 730). "Add truth to life, and you get happiness" (Augustine, *Sermons* 306.9). "The inquiry of truth, which is the love-making or wooing of it, the knowledge of truth, which is the presence of it, and the belief of truth, which is the enjoying of it, is the sovereign good of human nature" (Bacon, *Essays* I). Finally Locke, who effortlessly mixes all three: "I know there is truth opposite to falsehood, that it may be found if people will, and is worth the seeking, and is not only the most valuable, but the pleasantest thing in the world" (Letter to

Molyneux, 1698, cited in J. Dunn, *Locke* (Oxford: Oxford University Press, 1984), 87.

12. Plato, *Philebus* 59; Plato, *Republic* 490; Emerson, "Self-Reliance," 271.

13. Nietzsche, *On the Genealogy of Morals* (1887; New York: Vintage, 1967), 3.24, 27. James does not seem to have been much of a reader of Nietzsche, though he did know his work, to which I have found three references: In *The Variety of Religious Experience* (*W*, 336), he cites from the third essay of the *Genealogy* (a key text for the question of truth's value); secondly, in a book review he says of his author's attitude that it "seems to resemble that of Nietzsche's *amor fati*!" (*W*, 312); and finally, a letter (1905): "As for Nietzsche . . . I recall . . . a posthumous article in one of the French reviews a few months back. In his high and mighty way he was laying down the law about all the European countries" (*The Letters of William James* [Boston: Atlantic Monthly Press, 1920], 2.233).

14. Cp. Nietzsche: "'Truth'? Who has forced this word on me? But I repudiate it; but I disdain this proud word: no, we do not even need this; we shall conquer and come to power even without truth. The spell that fights on our behalf, the eye of Venus that charms and blinds even our opponents, is *the magic of the extreme*, the seduction that everything extreme exercises: we immoralists—we are the most extreme" (*The Will to Power*, ed. W. Kaufmann [New York: Vintage, 1967], sec. 749).

15. Sacvan Bercovitch, *The Puritan Origins of the American Self* (New Haven: Yale University Press, 1975), 174–75.

16. Emerson, "Self-Reliance," 274, 259–60; "Experience," in *Essays and Lectures*, 481; Nietzsche, *Thus Spoke Zarathustra* (1883), in *The Portable Nietzsche*, ed. W. Kaufmann (New York: Viking, 1954), 251.

17. Bercovitch, *The Puritan Origins of the American Self*, 175–76.

18. Emerson, *Nature*, III; *Essays and Lectures*, 19.

19. Harold Bloom, *A Map of Misreading* (Oxford: University Press, 1975), 176.

20. William James, *The Will to Believe and Other Essays in Popular Philosophy* (1897), (New York: Dover, 1956), 191.

21. See Foucault, *Discipline and Punish* (New York: Vintage, 1979); *The History of Sexuality* (New York: Vintage, 1980); and *Power/Knowledge*, ed. C. Gorden (New York: Pantheon, 1980); and my *Truth in Philosophy* (Cambridge: Harvard University Press, 1993), chap. 8.

KATHLEEN FLANAGAN

6

The Orient as Pretext for Aesthetic and Cultural Revolution in Modern American Poetry

In *Orientalism* (1979) Edward Said describes the West's portrayal of the Middle East, or Orient, as a lesser entity and submits that for those who practiced it at the turn of the century "the essence of Orientalism [was] the ineradicable distinction between Western superiority and Oriental inferiority."[1] Another sort of "orientalism" developed in England and America at the turn of this century, however, which, while also portraying the Orient as an "other," created an ideal, or superior, category for the civilizations of the Far East, specifically China and Japan. Drawing on the positive accounts of such scholars as Ernest Fenollosa, Herbert Giles, and Lafcadio Hearn, many American poets, including Ezra Pound, Amy Lowell, and John Gould Fletcher, came to see Chinese and Japanese poetry of particular types and eras as models for dissent from traditional English poetics.

These modernist poets turned to the Far East to dissent not

only from prevailing aesthetic choices in poetry but even more so from Western culture. A prevailing high valuation of Far Eastern culture and civilization led these poets to view Japanese and Chinese art and literature as the means of achieving an artistic "revolution." And those involved in the new poetic movement considered it very much a revolution: Harriet Monroe, editor of *Poetry,* wrote in 1935 that she considered the changes in poetry at the beginning of the twentieth century "revolutions" and commented that she had been involved in two or three of them.[2] This was a revolution in many senses, for while poets revolted against the cultural and aesthetic requisites of nineteenth-century Western poetry, they also returned in a cyclical fashion to the poetics of English Romantic verse. Such an act poses questions about the nature of change and dissent in modern American poetry similar to those raised by Sacvan Bercovitch about classic American literature in *The American Jeremiad.* There Bercovitch observes, "To be American for our classic writers was by definition to be radical—to turn against the past, to defy the status quo and become an agent of change."[3] Michel Foucault in his account of the changes in the Western penal system, *Discipline and Punish,* asserts that what we generally view as the humane shift from public punishment and torture to correction and incarceration beginning in the eighteenth century was, in fact, a mark of a desire not to "punish less, but . . . to insert the power to punish more deeply into the social body."[4] One finds an analogy between the situation Foucault analyzes and modernists' appropriation of the Orient as a means of change, in that both show how dissent can simultaneously involve deep consent to political and cultural bodies.

American modernists legitimized their dissent from prevailing poetic practices with Far Eastern civilization, a civilization they found venerable because of its age and its attention to the arts. Modernists proclaimed a revolution in order to usher in a "new" poetics that was neither new nor intrinsically connected to the Far East. Bercovitch in *Ideology and Classic American Literature* has noted that utopian visions in American literature are often "adopted by repressed or ascendent groups to challenge the status quo."[5] I believe that a similar process occurred when American writers in the new poetic movement perceived the Orient as a utopian "other" in order to "challenge the status quo" of English poetics.

Not only poets were fascinated with the Orient. D. W. Griffith's 1916 film *Broken Blossoms* juxtaposed a gentle Chinese hero with a brutal London villain, showing that the appeal of China and

Japan at the turn of the century was not simply an aesthetic one but also constituted a reaction against Western industrial civilization. This is cultural primitivism as A. O. Lovejoy defined it, or "the discontent of the civilized with civilization, or some conspicuous and characteristic feature of it."[6] Bercovitch has pointed out the persistence of American myths of primitivism and pastoralism, "of individuals reintegrated with nature and society, and thereby empowered with the confidence to make their own world," and has argued their importance to the process of dissent (*Ideology,* 431). Twentieth-century American poets turned in just such a manner to what they saw as the primitive and pastoral qualities of the Far East in their reactions against science and realism to achieve their poetic dissent. Modernist poets believed that the way in which Chinese and Japanese art and literature portrayed human civilization and nature coincided with their own aesthetic principles. The Chinese and Japanese were seen, and rightly so, as people whose art eschewed direct imitation and actual representation of objects, presenting instead the essence, or "spirit," of objects through a conscious style. Speaking of Japanese paintings, W. B. Yeats wrote in a 1916 letter to his father,

> Everywhere there is delight in form, repeated yet varied, in curious patterns of lines, but these lines are all an ordering of natural objects though they are certainly not imitation. In every case the artist one feels has had to *consciously* and deliberately arrange his subject.[7]

In contrast, Yeats denied the validity of the similar Western aesthetics of the impressionists, believing they "were wrong in substituting abstract scientific thought for conscious feeling."

With these ideas of the Far East as a culture that valued literature over science, that reconciled people and nature, that justified imagination over realism as an aesthetic creed, poets of the time championed new poetic principles. Despite the dissent implied by their involvement with Oriental aesthetics, Pound, Lowell, and Fletcher ultimately reaffirmed an aesthetic derived from occidental sources, an aesthetic that remained unaffected by its articulation in oriental terms. If the poetry of Pound and others involved in the new poetry movement embodied their perception of a culture on the other side of the globe, then modern poetry, although preoccupied with form and aesthetics, did not stand in an aesthetic or cultural vacuum. The choices made in aesthetics were part and parcel of similar attitudes and choices in philosophy, religion, and art where they believed the Orient surpassed the Occident and therefore served as a model.

As I previously suggested, the "orientalism" of modernist poets at the beginning of this century was as much an extension of nineteenth-century English Romanticism as it was a revolution. Modernism was a revolution not only in the sense that it sought to revolt against existing poetics and propounded changes, but also in the sense that it marked a turn, or rotation, in the cycle of English poetics. With some twentieth-century variations, modernist poets returned to the poetics of the English Romantic writers, perceiving them as acceptable Oriental aesthetics, a bona fide revolt against Western poetic tradition. Bercovitch has noted the pervasive nature of such processes in American literature: "Every ideology, that is, breeds its own opposition, every culture its own counterculture. The same ideals that at one point nourish the system may later become the basis of a new revolutionary consensus, one that invokes those ideals on behalf of an entirely different way of life" (*Ideology*, 431). That is to say, in a sense, twentieth-century poets practiced the same sort of orientalism, as well as the same poetics, as did the English Romantics. As E. J. Hobsbawm has noted in *The Age of Revolution 1798–1848*, the English Romantics sought a means of replacing the "lost harmony of man in the world" with, among other things, the "ancient and profound mysteries and sources of irrational wisdom in the Orient: the romantic, but also the conservative, realms of Kublai Khan or the Brahmins."[8]

The new poetic movement at the beginning of the twentieth century advocated a freer choice of subjects, subjects not considered "poetic" by the late Victorians. T. E. Hulme, British philosopher and founder of the Poets' Club, to which Pound belonged, believed the subject of a poem could be "a lady's shoe or the starry heavens" as long as it had "any real zest in it."[9] Hulme predicted the end of the Romantic movement and prophesied a return to classicism, complaining that most romantic poets "cannot see that accurate description is a legitimate object of verse. Verse to them is always a means of bringing in of some of the emotions that are grouped round the word infinite" ("Romanticism and Classicism," 127). Hulme in the twentieth century predated the Imagists and other poets who insisted on accurate description of minute particulars, rather than abstract sentiment, as the basis of poetry. As Alun Jones argues, Hulme's poetics were formulated by 1908 when he founded the Poets' Club.[10] Hulme rejected nineteenth-century

English Romantic poets as models for the new poetic movement without noting that these poets themselves argued for many of the same poetic agenda as early twentieth-century poets. Although he briefly praised Keats for writing "verse strictly confined to the earthly and the definite," he categorically stated, "I object even to the best of the romantics" ("Romanticism and Classicism," 126–27). In this rejection Hulme ignored William Wordsworth's claim that in *Lyrical Ballads* he "at all times endeavoured to look steadily at my subject; consequently, there is I hope in these Poems little falsehood of description."[11] When Wordsworth wrote that "the remotest discoveries of the Chemist, the Botanist, or Minerologist, will be as proper objects of the Poet's art as any upon which it can be employed," he argued for the same freedom of subject matter as did Hulme.[12] Hulme overlooked the similarity between the poetics of the English Romantics and those he himself advocated for twentieth-century poetry in what readers have identified as an attack on late-nineteenth and early-twentieth-century practitioners of the Romantic tradition.[13] Thus Hulme came to reject, almost in its entirety, the English poetic movement of the nineteenth century. F. S. Flint noted in 1915,

> I think what brought the real nucleus of this group [Hulme's Poets' Club] together was a dissatisfaction with English poetry as it was then (and still is alas!) being written. We proposed at various times to replace by pure *vers libre;* by the Japanese *tanka* and *haikai.* In all this Hulme was the ringleader.[14]

Flint's statement shows that while Hulme and the Poets' Club ignored precedents in English poetry for the new poetic movement, they adopted Japanese verse as a suitable model. Since Hulme had decided on his poetic agenda before the formation of the club, one might assert that he first formulated a new poetics, then believed he found a model for it in Japanese verse *from a classical period.* In doing so, Hulme stood at the beginning of an "orientalist" trend that was to continue for at least two decades. Arthur Christy in 1929 argued that

> the reactions of English and American poets from the profuseness of the Victorian vogue to the concision of modern imagistic and vers libre movements was developing simultaneously with Occidental interest in the Pacific-Asian religions and literatures.[15]

The two interests did not develop simultaneously, however. Instead, poets at the beginning of the twentieth century first reacted against Victorian poetics. Then, because the Orient for them constituted an already-ideal land of the imagination, the utopian vision of the Orient became, in Bercovitch's terms, "an invitation to resistance and revolt" (*Ideology*, 431).

Hulme, and subsequently Ezra Pound, Amy Lowell, and John Gould Fletcher, saw in the subject matter of Chinese and Japanese poetry a method of expressing emotion in the "dry hardness" of the classics. In the Japanese tanka and haiku and in Chinese Tang and Sung dynasty poetry, these poets found a justification for conveying the emotion of lyric poetry through describing natural phenomena. They rightly believed that classical Chinese and Japanese poets had identified a means of expressing feeling without allowing abstractions. Fletcher, in the preface to his 1918 *Japanese Prints*, poems in imitation of Japanese verse, remarked that Basho would have agreed with William Blake that to write poetry was "to see a World in a grain of sand," with one exception:

> The only difference between the Western and the Eastern mystic is that where one sees the world in a grain of sand and tells you all about it, the other sees and lets his silence imply that he knows all its meanings.[16]

Although poets connected their revolution in poetry with the Far East, the ideology of dissent connected with Far East utopias was more important than actual Chinese and Japanese verse forms. In Chinese and Japanese poetry that has exceedingly complex rhyme and syllable schemes, poets saw a "primitive" simplicity they sought for their own poetry. Chang Hsin-Hai in a 1922 article, "The Vogue of Chinese Poetry," argued that translators, including Ezra Pound, used Chinese poets to vindicate their positions in English poetry.[17] Chang asked why poets of the free-verse movement in English found in Chinese and Japanese poetry the embodiment of their ideals (any poetic movement might do the same, he noted) and concluded that their admiration for things Chinese, including poetry, was "impressionistic" rather than a genuine understanding (100–102). One concludes, then, that poets in the new poetic movement were attracted to the forms of Chinese and Japanese poetry at least partially because they were a revolutionary tool, an exotic means of dissenting from prevailing poetic techniques in English. The Orient had already been portrayed for them as an ideal, a cultural "other." These writers went through the same process with regard to American poetry that Bercovitch has observed of the typical writer in the American Renaissance: "His identification with America as it ought to be impels the writer to withdraw from what is in America" (*American Jeremiad,* 182).

American poets Ezra Pound, Amy Lowell, and John Gould Fletcher all followed this pattern of first formulating their ideology of dissent by adopting similar models from what they saw as the utopias of China and Japan. They agitated for reform of English poetics (much as American Puritans moved toward social and religious reform), participated in the Imagist movement, and were instrumental in forming a twentieth-century English canon of Chinese and Japanese verse in translation. Bercovitch's remarks about the nature of protest and dissent in *The American Jeremiad* apply to these poets: "American writers have tended to see themselves as outcasts and isolates, prophets crying in the wilderness. So they have been, as a rule: *American* Jeremiahs, simultaneously lamenting a declension and celebrating a national dream" (180). When one examines these poets' work previous to their discovery of Far Eastern verse, one sees that they were predisposed by this ideology of dissent to find in Chinese and Japanese poetry the principles of versification for which they had earlier expressed a preference. Thus, while I would not argue that Chinese and Japanese verse changed the form of modern English poetry, I submit that these poets' ideas of Far Eastern verse encouraged them to develop and implement what they believed to be "revolutionary" standards in their dissent against nineteenth-century poetics. They abandoned what they considered rote forms of English rhyme and meter, and instead believed themselves to follow Chinese and Japanese verse forms, even though the forms of the Chinese Tang and Sung dynasty verse and Japanese haiku and tanka they invoked were as strictly regulated as any English verse.

In 1912 Ezra Pound wrote to Harriet Monroe, editor of *Poetry* magazine, explaining that his poem "The Epilogue," published in a 1913 issue of *Poetry,*

> refers to . . . the experiments and paradigms of form and metre—quantities, alliteration, polyphonic rimes in *Canzoni* [1911] and *Ripostes* [1912]. . . . It has been my hope that this

> work will help to break the surface of convention and that the raw matter, and analysis of primitive systems may be of use in building the new art of metrics and of words.[18]

In these collections of poems that precede the 1915 *Cathay* translations of Chinese poetry, one sees Pound's interest in achieving a revolution in English verse forms. In Pound's earlier books of poetry, *A Lume Spento* (1908), *Personae* (1909), and *Exultations* (1909), one finds examples of verse not rhymed in conventional English forms. With *Lustra* (1917), a collection of poems written between 1913 and 1916, Pound achieved the more complete poetic revolution: His verse is almost all "free," his diction is modern, and his choice and treatment of subjects is straightforward and objective. In the interval between *Ripostes* (1912) and *Lustra,* Pound published *Cathay,* translations of Chinese poetry from the Fenollosa manuscripts he received in 1913 from Mary Fenollosa. In the poems Pound wrote after perusing Fenollosa's works, one perceives a more confident use of the cadenced verse and modern diction we now associate with poetry of the modern period.

Lustra as a whole revolts against the form of traditional English poetry. The opening poem, "Tenzone," questions, "Will people accept them? / (i.e. these songs)."[19] Five poems later, Pound's tone is less hesitant—"Go, little naked and impudent songs, / Go with a light foot! (Or with two light feet, if it please you!)" (p. 18). Pound explored alternatives to traditional rhymes and meters in English verse before he made his free-verse *Cathay* translations, which indicates that Pound's poetic ideology, as well as the versification of Chinese poetry, influenced the form of the *Cathay* translations. His *Cathay* renditions, however, seemed to strengthen his revolt against forms of traditional English poetry. In a June 1913 letter to his father, Pound remarked as an aside that "'Ortus' means 'birth' or 'springing out'—same root in 'orient'" (*Letters,* 58). This idea of "springing out" perhaps led Pound to his great interest in the Oriental poetry in Fenollosa's manuscripts. Pound had these manuscripts by December 1913, for he wrote to William Carlos Williams, "I am very placid and happy and busy. Dorothy [Pound's wife] is learning Chinese. I've all old Fenollosa's treasures in mss." (*Letters,* 65).

One might compare a translation from *Cathay* to an earlier Provençal translation to see the difference in poetic form. In "Alba Innominata," a poem from the Provencal in *Exultations,* the "envoi," or refrain, praises a lady in pseudo-Middle English phrasing:

> Fair is this damsel and right courteous,
> And many watch her beauty's gracious way.
> Her heart toward love is no wise traitorous.
> Ah God! Ah God! That dawn should come so soon![20]

In contrast, when Pound rendered the Chinese poem "A Ballad of the Mulberry Road" from Fenollosa's manuscript, the English he used was very much what he had been advocating for English poetry—modern, concrete, and down-to-earth:

> Her earrings are made of pearl,
> Her underskirt is of green pattern-silk,
> Her overskirt is the same silk dyed in purple,
> And when men going by look on Rafu
> They set down their burdens,
> They stand and twirl their mustaches. (*Lustra,* 92)

Pound used the same diction and free verse throughout *Cathay.* The difference between the English Pound used for his Provencal translations and the English he used for his Chinese translations indicates that Pound in Provençal poetry dealt with a Western literature that had its analogue in English literature both in time and in content. That is, English poetry was written in a certain way in the Middle Ages, a way comparable to Provençal poetry. In contrast, Chinese poetry, especially that from the classical period of the Tang and Sung dynasties, was much more of an unknown and had no specific association with English poetry of the same era. Using the terms of Bercovitch's analysis of classic American writers, classical Chinese poetry represented the utopian past, even more ideal since it stemmed from a Far Eastern culture that was an "other" for Pound. Chinese poetry therefore became for Pound a malleable vessel for his own preferred poetic diction. Once he had established it as such, it became for him an example on which to model all English poetry.

Pound and his interest in Chinese verse influenced Amy Lowell's concept of the proper form for English poetry. Lowell did not use free verse in her poetry until her second volume of poetry, *Sword Blades and Poppy Seeds* (1914). This volume came out after Lowell's trip to England in 1912, on which she met Pound and became involved in the new poetic movement. In the preface to *Sword Blades and Poppy Seeds,* she claimed that "the Anglo-Saxon of our day has a tendency to think that a fine idea excuses slovenly workmanship," while "in France, to-day, poetry is so living and vigorous a thing, that so many experiments come from there."[21] One sees that Lowell was prone to find foreign models for a new vein of English poetry, for Lowell came to associate *vers libre* not only with French poetry, but with Chinese and Japanese verse as well. The association of free verse with Far Eastern verse came about not because Chinese or Japanese verse was, like French verse, actually written in free verse, but because Lowell, like Ezra Pound, had used it to translate Chinese and Japanese poetry.

One sees evidence of the association of free verse with Chinese and Japanese poetry in Lowell's long poem of 1918, "Guns as Keys: And the Great Gate Swings." In this poem Lowell described the gunboat diplomacy of Admiral Perry that opened Japan. All of the poems in the volume in which this poem appears, *Can Grande's Castle* (1921), are written in "polyphonic prose," verse resembling prose paragraphs, with the exception of the parts of "Guns as Keys" representing Japan. She attempted to "place in juxtaposition the delicacy and artistic clarity of Japan and the artistic ignorance and gallant self-confidence of America"[22] by writing those portions of the poem that represent the Western perspective in polyphonic prose and those portions that represent the Eastern perspective in free, or cadenced, verse. This free verse is written in briefer, simpler lines, especially when compared to the polyphonic prose. Most of the translations of Chinese poetry in *Fir-Flower Tablets,* on which she began work in 1917, were rendered in cadenced verse, and it is clear from her use of free verse in the "Japanese" portions of "Guns as Keys" that she associated the two.

At the beginning of "Guns as Keys," Lowell depicts Commodore Perry's sailing on the U.S.S. Mississippi for Japan:

> The wharves of Norfolk are falling behind, becoming smaller, confused with the warehouses and the trees. On the impetus of the strong South Breeze, the paddle-wheel steam frigate, *Mississippi,* of the United States Navy, sails down the flashing bay. Sails away, and steams away, for her furnaces are burning, and her paddle-wheels turning, and all her sails are set and full. (*Can Grande's Castle,* 50)

Lowell followed this passage by describing the presumably simultaneous activities of the Japanese:

> At Mishima in the Province of Kai,
> Three men are trying to measure a pine tree
> By the length of their outstretched arms.
> Trying to span the bole of a huge pine tree
> By the spread of their lifted arms. (*Can Grande's Castle,* 51)

This passage of free verse in short, simple lines depicts the more natural, almost primitive, activity of measuring a tree, juxtaposing it with the mechanical and forceful departure of the ship from the West in polyphonic prose. In between these passages, Lowell inserted a sailor's song, a song with a crude rhyme scheme that might represent the art of the "uncultured" West: "A Yankee ship sails down the river, / Blow, boys, blow; / Her masts and spars they shine like silver, / Blow, my bully boys, blow" (*Can Grande's Castle,* 50). Throughout "Guns as Keys," Lowell followed this practice of juxtaposing in both content and form the actions of West and East.

In *Pictures of the Floating World* (1919), Lowell again separated the East and West in both form and content, for she divided the volume into two parts, the first, the Japanese- and Chinese-inspired "Lacquer Prints" and "Chinoiseries," and the second, "Planes of Personality." Lowell in her preface wrote that the poems in the first part of the book were not translations, but were "written in a quasi-Oriental idiom."[23] She noted that she followed the Japanese haiku pattern more closely than the Chinese forms, but even with the Japanese poetry, she did not try to keep to the syllabic rules of Japanese poetry. Instead, she wrote, "I have endeavoured only to keep the brevity and suggestion of the *hokku,* and to preserve it within its natural sphere."[24] One sees in this statement that, again, Lowell valued the idea of Oriental verse, the "quasi-Oriental idiom," over exact duplications of these verse forms in English. Leonard Swartz observed in a 1928 article on Lowell that only seven out of the fifty-nine Japanese imitations "are cast in the tripartite arrangement that is characteristic of the *hokku.*"[25] While Lowell may have attempted, and failed, to preserve the exact arrangement of the haiku, she was actually interested in imitating in English poetry the suggestion, objectivity, and brevity of the haiku. In form she duplicated the free verse she used in the "Japanese" sections of "Guns as Keys." This repeated use of free verse to represent the poetry of the Orient indicates that, for Lowell, verse forms had associations with cultural, as well as aesthetic, stereotypes and demonstrates that her dissent was based on principles of English, not Far Eastern, poetry.

John Gould Fletcher, who knew both Lowell and Pound, also demonstrated an interest in Japanese and Chinese verse at the same time as he was attempting to reform English poetry. His comments often resembled the American jeremiad that Bercovitch ascribes to Emerson: "His jeremiads were couched in terms that reaffirmed the basic tenets of the culture" (*American Jeremiad,* 184). That is, Fletcher strongly dissented against prevailing poetic practices in English, only to reaffirm the earlier poetics of the English Romantics. In 1915 Fletcher wrote epigrams, published in 1918 as *Japanese Prints,* inspired by Japanese *ukiyoe* prints he saw at the Boston Museum. In his autobiography Fletcher explained his purpose in writing *Japanese Prints,* and it is clear that he intended the poems to be a lesson in form for English poetry:

> What I intended by *Japanese Prints* was a brief commentary on life and manners, a kind of "Spoon River" *à la Japonaise,* more compressed indeed, and more decorative, but not less valid and direct. . . . Poetry of this sort should be concentrated, suggestive, brief, much as the Japanese poetry itself had been. There was no need of all this proliferation of sprawling and prosaic detail. . . . If any imagist wished to comment on life, this was the way, I felt, the comment should be made.[26]

The use of the past tense "had been" in Fletcher's reference to Japanese poetry groups him with those poets who preferred the "Orient" of the past, or the imagination, to the modern Far East, and with those whose ideology allowed them to recognize only those types of Japanese poetry that dissented from prevailing poetics. Fletcher connected Japanese poetry with the form of "comment on life" appropriate for modern English poetry. Yet even before he wrote the poems in *Japanese Prints,* Fletcher stated preferences for the type of poetry that he justified there. In the preface to the earlier *Irradiations: Sand and Spray* (1915), Fletcher argued that English poetry of the time was "in a greatly backward state"[27] and blamed this decadence on the insistence on conventional rhyme and meter. Fletcher insisted that this traditional view of poetry was "barbarous; it derives from the stamping of feet, clapping of hands, pounding of drums, or like devices of savage peoples to mark rhythms in their dances and songs" (*Irradiations,* xiii). Fletcher, moreover, associated the beginning of this convention with "the breakup of the Latin civilization, and the approach of what historians know as the Dark Ages," or, in other words, with the decline of civilization. Fletcher connected the Orient with his discussion of the poetic line when he argued that a line of poetry "represents a single breath, and therefore a single perception," and remarked that this correspondence "is a commonplace of Oriental philosophy" (*Irradiations,* xii).

Fletcher's comments on the superiority of the form of Japanese poetry to English poetry in the preface to *Japanese Prints* are a restatement of the poetics he had declared in these earlier works. Here Fletcher described the syllabic rules of Japanese poetry (which call for seventeen syllables in haiku and thirty-one in tanka) and concluded,

> Other rules there were none. Rhyme, quantity, accent, stress were disregarded. . . . This method of writing poetry may seem to the reader to suffer from serious disadvantages. In reality this was not the case. Contrast it for a moment with the undignified welter of undigested and ex parte theories which academic prosodists have tried for three hundred years to foist upon English verse, and it will be seen that the simple Japanese rule has the merit of dignity. (17)

In describing the syllabic rules of Japanese poetry, Fletcher was blocked by his ideology of Japan as utopia from seeing that the syllabic restriction imposed on Japanese haiku and tanka is perhaps as limiting and mechanical as the very rules of rhyme and meter he chafed against in English poetry. This ideologically based perception of Japanese poetry prompted Fletcher to adopt that poetry as a utopian literature, rather than explore it as an actuality. Indeed, Fletcher wrote in this preface that one cannot write haiku in English; rather, "the thing we have to follow is not a form, but a spirit" (16). In describing the Japanese imitations contained in *Japanese Prints,* Fletcher wrote, "they are in some cases not Japanese at all, but all illustrate something of the charm I have found in Japanese poetry and art" (17). *Charm* is the operative word in his account. It is no coincidence that Fletcher described his poems in almost the same words Amy Lowell used to introduce her Japanese and Chinese imitations in *Pictures of the Floating World* (1919).

Modernist poets in England and America perhaps practiced an orientalism of a more "progressive" type than that which Said discusses, in that they idealized, rather than denigrated, the Far East. Yet these poets' ideology of dissent led them to perceive only idealized Far Eastern aesthetics that in turn allowed them to "imitate" the poetic practices they preferred and dissent from the poetic practices of the West. In the preface to his 1915 volume of poetry *Irradiations: Sand and Spray,* Fletcher wrote, "It is time to create something new. It is time to strip poetry of meaningless tatters of form, and to clothe her in new suitable garments" (xv). A Maxwell Bodenheim poem, "To Li T'ai Po," which appeared in a 1919 issue of *The Dial* along with Amy Lowell's poem, "Li T'ai Po," shows that some writers were aware of the uses to which modernist poets were putting Chinese verse. In a sense, Bodenheim also appropriates the Chinese poet Li Po by making him the subject of a poem; however, Bodenheim makes Li Po a person when he addresses him in the title "*To* Li T'ai Po" (my emphasis), while Amy Lowell conflates the Chinese poet with her poem in the title, "Li T'ai Po." Bodenheim apostrophizes the Chinese poet, saying,

> They are writing poems to you:
> White devils who have not
> Smeared the distant yellow of your life
> Upon their skins. . . .
> These faces bend over paper
> And steal from you a little silver and red
> So that their lives may seem to bleed
> Under the prick of a flashing need.[28]

What modernist poets, Bodenheim's "white devils," "stole" from Li T'ai Po was the justification for dissent from prevailing verse forms and treatment of subjects in English poetry. The Asian influence is superficial, however, consisting of sprinkling "a little silver and red" on English poetry that remained principally Western.

Many modernist American poets, while primarily compelled by formalist agenda, were affected by their perceptions of Western culture's deficiencies and of Eastern solutions to these problems. These poets' invocation of the Orient as a model for aesthetic dissent demonstrates that they believed they participated in a philosophical and cultural rebellion. As Bercovitch points out, many readers find "this sort of radical stance . . . is indeed 'representative,' *American:* It is the aesthetic flowering of an ideology adopted from the start precisely for its capacity to transmute radicalism of all forms, from religious protest to revolutionary war, into forms of cultural consensus" (*Ideology,* 436). Although modernist poets saw their desire for change in English poetics as revolutionary, this dissent was, in fact, a return to earlier English poetics and as such became consent. Michel Foucault remarks that "one can perfectly well conceive of revolutions which essentially left untouched the power relations which form the basis for the functioning of the state."[29] One can just as easily see that the modernists' revolution in language and form left untouched the foundation of English poetics as it had been since the English Romantic period.

NOTES

1. Edward Said, *Orientalism* (New York: Vintage, 1979), 42.

2. Harriet Monroe, *Chosen Poems* (New York: Macmillan, 1935), viii.

3. Sacvan Bercovitch, *The American Jeremiad* (Madison: University of Wisconsin Press, 1978), 203.

4. Michel Foucault, *Discipline and Punish,* trans. Alan Sheridan (New York: Vintage, 1979), 82.

5. Sacvan Bercovitch, *Ideology and Classic American Literature,* ed. Sacvan Bercovitch and Myra Jehlen (New York: Cambridge University Press, 1986), 431.

6. A. O. Lovejoy, Gilbert Chinard, George Boas, and Ronald S. Crane, *A Documentary History of Primitivism and Related Ideas* (Baltimore: Johns Hopkins Press, 1935), 7.

7. W. B. Yeats, *The Letters of W. B. Yeats,* ed. Allan Wade (London: Rupert Hart-Davis, 1954), 608.

8. E. J. Hobsbawm, *The Age of Revolution 1789–1848* (New York: New American Library, 1962), 312–13.

9. T. E. Hulme, "Romanticism and Classicism," in *Speculations* (New York: Harcourt Brace, 1924), 137.

10. Alun R. Jones, *The Life and Opinions of T. E. Hulme* (Boston: Beacon Press, 1960), 30.

11. William Wordsworth, *Preface, Second Edition of Lyrical Ballads,* in *English Romantic Writers,* ed. David Perkins (New York: Harcourt Brace Jovanovich, 1967), 323.

12. Wordsworth, *Preface,* 326.

13. Jones, 42.

14. F. S. Flint, "The History of Imagism," *The Egoist* 2 (5 January 1915): 71.

15. Arthur Christy, "Chinoiserie and Vers Libre," *Open Court* 43 (April 1929): 209.

16. John Gould Fletcher, *Japanese Prints* (Boston: Seven Seas Company, 1918), 14.

17. Chang Hsin-Hai, "The Vogue of Chinese Poetry," *Edinburgh Review* 236 (July 1922): 102.

18. Ezra Pound, *The Letters of Ezra Pound,* ed. D. D. Paige (London: Faber & Faber, 1951), 45–46.

19. Ezra Pound, *Lustra of Ezra Pound, with Earlier Poems* (New York: Knopf, 1917), 13.

20. Ezra Pound, *Collected Early Poems of Ezra Pound* (New York: New Directions, 1982), 125.

21. Amy Lowell, *Sword Blades and Poppy Seeds* (1914; reprint, New York: Macmillan, 1916), ix.

22. Amy Lowell, *Can Grande's Castle* (New York: Houghton Mifflin, 1921), xvi.

23. Amy Lowell, *Pictures of the Floating World* (New York: Macmillan, 1919), vii.

24. Lowell, *Pictures,* viii.

25. Leonard Swartz, "Amy Lowell's Far Eastern Verse," *Modern Language Notes* 43, no. 3 (March 1928): 148.

26. John Gould Fletcher, *Life is My Song* (New York: Farrar Rinehart, 1937), 200–201.

27. John Gould Fletcher, *Irradiations: Sand and Spray* (New York: Houghton Mifflin, 1915), ix.

28. Maxwell Bodenheim, "To Li T'ai Po," *The Dial* 67 (1919): 428.

29. Michel Foucault, *The Foucault Reader,* ed. Paul Rabinow (New York: Pantheon, 1984), 64.

Part III

Cohesion, Dissent, and Contemporary Cultural Boundaries

PRISCILLA WALD

7

"Chaos Goes Uncourted": John Yau's Dis(-)Orienting Poetics

In a 1990 interview in *Talisman,* John Yau describes the dilemma of alterity in the United States:

> What would someone who is Chinese or Afro-American or Latino return to in this country, its history? What would they be nostalgic for? In my case, my parents left China. They could never go back to live there, so the notion of return seems to me both an impossibility and a repressive illusion.[1]

A present intensified by the inaccessibility of the past calls for a poetics that moves forward, fashioned, to cite one of Yau's favorite images, from "an ever-changing tale." The genesis of such a poetics centrally concerns him. With neither history nor country to which he can return, Yau finds himself struggling with the terms that constitute subjectivity in the United States, profoundly distrustful of "a language that comes from an 'I.'" By contrast, he strives to write "from . . . that 'I' who doesn't know who the 'I' is" (*T,* 46).

His poetry evinces what Elaine Kim recognizes as a common desire among Asian-American writers: "the desire to remain as 'others' by defining our own 'otherness,' not as foreigners but as American 'others.' "[2] As the interview makes clear, Yau's poetry evolves from his discomfort with the correspondence between conventional forms and expressions of subjectivity in the United States. Instead, he expresses his Chinese-American identity in his poetic engagement with what he sees as the terms of that subjectivity.

Kim ranks Yau among those Asian-American writers who refuse to "be confined by 'Asian American' themes or by narrow definitions of 'Asian American' identity. Their writings are all the more 'Asian American' because they contribute to the broadening of what that term means."[3] That broadening is critical to Yau, not only to his struggle to survive "out there" (*T*, 46), but to the critique occasioned by his poetry. Yau's model is less a particular poetic form than a geo-conceptual space—like Chinatown, which remains perpetually in uneasy dialogue with an ambivalent culture. Through that dialogue, and the hyphen that manifests it, Yau attends to competing claims that complicate, and therefore make him conscious of, his subjectivity. His hyphen is not the "plus sign" that Michael Walzer describes; he is very clearly not, like Walzer's "ethnic American[,] . . . someone who can, in principle, live his spiritual life as he chooses, *on either side of the hyphen.*"[4] Nor does he, however, with Amy Ling, reject the hyphen because it "keeps elements apart.[5] Ling's term *Chinamerican,* "coined . . . because of [her] own dissatisfaction with the conventionalized hyphenated form," expresses her "wish to assert that we're not a wobbly balancing act but something together, a wholeness" (77). But for Yau, the unrelenting desire, the nostalgia for nowhere that a hyphenated identity can suggest, calls attention to certain inherent contradictions in all subjectivity. Yau's project differs from both in stressing the verb rather than the noun: The hyphen refashions a site into a process, representing the dialogue—often as a clash—between two cultures, as one attempts simultaneously to absorb and to exclude the other.[6] "By concentrating on the interplay of areas," Yau says of painter Ross Neher, "the artist has evolved a space that is far more ambiguous than before."[7]

The aesthetic as well as critical potential offered by this space fascinates Yau. His study of subjectivity takes shape as an experimentation that encourages the reader to contemplate rather than submit to or resist cultural identity. In a review of Michael Kessler's drawings from which I have taken my title phrase *Chaos*

Goes Uncourted, Yau praises the artist for his control: "Although the drawings originate in the artist's bodily gestures, the lines never become frenzied. Chaos goes uncourted. Control rather than freedom is the issue. Aggressiveness is transformed into a dance."[8] This transformation of a possible anarchy into a graceful expression of possibility represents, for Yau, the highest artistic achievement. His own work demonstrates not only a critical dimension of aesthetic experimentation, but also an aesthetics of critique.

CROSSING BORDERS

In "The Music of America," an autobiographical introduction to a collection of essays, United States culture critic Sacvan Bercovitch describes his own cultural dislocation—his "border-crossings"—as the genesis of his "cross-cultural criticism" (*MA,* 5).[9] Striking resonances between Yau's poetry and Bercovitch's criticism underscore the poet's theoretical concerns. Both Yau and Bercovitch depict Americanization as ambiguous, involving a potential violation, and where Bercovitch talks of "the threat of assimilation" (*MA,* 2), Yau admits that he "respond[s] more readily to artists whose work resists assimilation into the accepted discourses" (*T,* 37). Both, moreover, respond to the dramatically appropriative capacities of United States rhetoric with what Bercovitch calls a "hermeneutics of non-transcendence" (*MA,* 5), a strategy that substitutes an interpretation for a (futile) resistance of the processes of Americanization. This critical paradigm helps to explain why Yau fashions an aesthetic in dialectical engagement with its own impossibility.

Bercovitch argues that the hermeneutics of nontranscendence entails the recognition of "universals as culture-specific barriers [that], so specified, may become (within limits) avenues of discovery" (*MA,* 5). Yau's "avenue of discovery" is figured in Canal Street, a boundary of New York's Chinatown that constitutes the landscape of his first volume of poetry, *Crossing Canal Street* (1976). His refusal to specify the direction of that crossing stresses the activity of *crossing* rather than of *having crossed* Canal Street. Yau moves between the droll cosmopolitanism of the New York School (including his future teacher, John Ashbery) and the"accident of birth" by which, he remarks, "you're imprinted in all sorts of ways" (*T,* 48). He inscribes his self-discovery within a cultural transformation, a sense that being Chinese

American means actively looking—rather than appearing—in a certain way. Yau makes the reader aware of how a Chinese American looks at and transforms New York's Chinatown, how he shapes his world. The urbane New York poets' consciousness of being watched as they are watching becomes Yau's consciousness of a certain complicity with the symbolizing process of Americanization.

In "Suggested by a Waitress in YEE's," for example, the poet's similes transform the waitress into an emblem both of her function as a waitress and of his orientalizing fantasies:[10]

> Holding the pencil like one lonely chopstick
> & grasping the pad like an empty plate
> waiting to be filled:
> words such as shrimp almonds pork rice
> thoughts of brocade pearl silk rain verbs

The second and final stanza foregrounds the observer's role in creating the subject:

> Nothing decorous but *our own clinging minds*
> & the piling of her smooth black hair
> (emphasis added)

The poem, which concludes the volume, turns on the discordant word *verbs,* which interrupts the list of nouns to call attention to the poet's activity—encasing and "creating" the waitress within the catalogue. The opening clause has no referent, because "she" has disappeared into the poet's vision. The poetic subject's resurrection in the poet's language suggests the cultural subject's similar creation by a cultural discourse.

The inevitability of such creations interests Yau, who is concerned with investigating rather than condemning them. Subjects divested of cultural identity haunt the poetry as much as subjects reified by its processes. A macabre image in a later poem, "Postcards from Nebraska" (*The Sleepless Night of Eugene Delacroix,* 1980), for example, embodies the horrifying consequences of divestiture. The poet-narrator reports having

> learned how to avoid sending your parents to an old age home. . . . What happens is that the children take their senile parents on a vacation. This usually means somewhere far

> from home. Along the way they eliminate all forms of identification; labels and tags from dresses suits and gloves etc. Then they stop for lunch at a Howard Johnson's. When the parent or parents go off to the bathroom, the children drive off. It's quite difficult to trace where these people came from. And often they themselves don't know.[11]

The children literally deprive their parents, already without memory, of all remaining means of cultural identification, from home, family, and name to the labels that define a particular consumer status. Extreme expressions of Yau's own dilemma, these parents have no history and nowhere they can return to: They cannot locate a home. Here is unaccommodated man/woman, uncannily embodying the fate of any cultural subject disconnected from the culture's symbolic system and potentially undefinable: the only real possibility for (and the consequences of) transcendence. In fact, the site of the senile parents' abandonment, the Howard Johnson, stands as a monument to the "home" as a generic concept. Designed to offer the mobile American traveler predictability, a Howard Johnson restaurant underscores the traveler's temporary homelessness as a consequence of mobility. Howard Johnson patrons retreat into the comforting indistinctions of a familiar symbolic system that hints at the possibility of a generic and mass-produced self. The patrons disappear—and transcend—as effectively as their mirror images, the senile parents. The analogy reconceives the abandoned parents as culturally liminal figures, like the often ghastly corpses drifting through Yau's works, strangely familiar, haunting precisely in their mirroring the cultural subjectivity that they can no longer experience.

The children's complicity in this middle-American fantasy certainly bespeaks the guilty conscience of a consumer society that commodifies youth—of a nation forever young. Yet Yau's primary concern is with the immigrant family; the process of Americanizing notoriously entails an erasure of the past. Yau reverses the roles in "Postcards from Nebraska" when, in the *Talisman* interview, he depicts the parents rather than the child as the agents of Americanization. Here immigrants willfully divesting themselves of home, family, and memory flesh out the senile parents' symbolic dimensions. Yau defines himself as a sort of Frankenstein's monster, whose parents "wanted [him] to be American, and then . . . were shocked by how American [he] became" (*T,* 40). Their efforts end in his dislocation. "[B]eing Chinese-American," he could "liv[e] in, but not belong to," what he perceives as a "homogenous community," but his family offers only an "intense feeling of disconnection from their past, present, and future" (*T,* 50). While the senile parents cannot go home because they have literally forgotten who they are, his parents have repressed who they are because they cannot go "home." He, in turn, is threatened with a symbolic *self*-annihilation.

Yau is particularly concerned with the disappearance of the subject as it is produced. Every identification entails a corresponding loss. In "Postcards from Nebraska," for example, while the senile parents emblematize cultural disenfranchisement, the writer of the postcards embodies (or disembodies) the subject as it disappears into the terms of its construction (what Yau calls "cultural subjection"). The sender is identified in the penultimate section of the poem in what first appears to be "a case of mistaken identity" (*RS,* 45), an invitation or summons from an unfamiliar hand. The recipient calls to inform the stranger that his invitation to a party has reached the wrong person: "I protested for about four minutes, in the drugstore phone booth, told him that since I didn't know him he couldn't know me, etc" (*RS,* 45). But the dropped subject ("told him") suggests more than postcard shorthand; it rhetorically announces her imminent reconstitution: "He then asked if I weren't the woman who spent spring semester running every morning in mauve gym shorts. I couldn't deny that now, could I?" (*RS,* 45). Here the narrator, expecting mutuality, is hierarchically re-cognized by a male gaze that she "couldn't deny." That gaze (re)constructs the narrator for the reader as a gendered subject. The previously disembodied voice, initially like the parodically "sweet voice, no body" of the man's answering service, is engendered into silence. The last postcard briefly reports, "I'm keeping my trip to Calgary for another time because it takes so long to treat the subject properly" (*RS,* 45). This subject, reduced to her mauve gym shorts, is hardly treated "properly."

The poet-narrator's engendering establishes her as a fictional voice—not Yau, who is, in turn, cast into an ambiguous position. As the poet, he is identified to some extent with his narrator; as her creator, however, he plays a role analogous to that of the voyeur, the man who constructs her undeniable subjectivity. This double identification at once implicates and victimizes him. Unable to transcend his own subjectivity, he complies—both analogously and instrumentally—with the creation of cultural subjects. Yet the double role of perceiver and perceived at least conceptually enables him to envision his nontranscendence. Thus aware of his complicity, he can imaginatively transform Canal Street into an "avenue of discovery."

This transformation reverses the Americanizing strategy of the mother's stories in "Two Kinds of Story-Telling" (*Corpse and Mirror,* 1983), which turn the activity of crossing into an archetypal crossing.[12] Her "stories are symbolic narratives incorporating the idea of change. The inspiration behind them is the passage of the *Mayflower* to the New World." Having no recognizable past, but only a "childhood . . . composed of fairy tales," she is especially susceptible to a cultural narrative that prescribes her identity. The poet changes tenses—from past to present to future—to underscore the narrative's *erasure* of history:

> Her stories begin fitting into this genre after she has lived in America for a few years. At different points in her life she attempts to write them down. They will be about the moment her life changed.

She cannot write because she is herself emplotted within an immutable narrative. Her own crossing of the border, in other words, is obscured by a border-crossing mythically inscribed in a national identity. She assimilates by substituting one "past" for another, rather than experiencing a dissonance that could lead to confrontation. Her stories are inattentive not only to the facts of her immigration, but even to an official historical narrative: "she remembered almost nothing of American history." That amnesia allows her to disappear into a history to which she cannot *in fact* return. She is simultaneously dis-oriented by a history that significantly excludes her and disoriented by a cultural representation that erases history: "In her mind the names—*Mayflower, Pilgrim,* and *Plymouth Rock*—were associated with businesses; one on a moving van, the other two in insurance ads." Images meant to be evocative instead mark her cultural displacement, as history itself becomes a referent in the business of culture.

The figure of the mother dramatizes what Bercovitch theorizes: "a principle of socialization" wherein "the discovery of 'America' is converted into a process of self-discovery."[13] The result, in Yau's poem, is the disappearance of that self, a disappearance that the poet uses to interrogate the concept of selfhood. Bercovitch similarly notes that his own "shock of discovery proved a continuing barrier to Americanization" (*MA,* 1), where "continuing" insists on the sense of an ongoing activity, what Yau calls "the reading of an ever-changing tale." For both Yau and Bercovitch, the clash of cultures arising from confronted barriers potentially inheres in the identity hyphen, a confrontation that occasions other hyphens—dis-orientation and re-cognition, for example. The space between a first and second look clarifies, as it reasserts, the nontranscendence of both.

THE EVER-CHANGING TALE

That confrontation becomes a dialectic in Yau's central metaphor of the ever-changing tale. The title of his second volume of poems, *The Reading of an Ever-changing Tale,* offers a gerund, "the *reading,*" verb turned noun, which can suggest an activity turned static. In this case, *reading* becomes *the reading,* either an activity or a fixed *interpretation.* The difference is crucial, as it is for Bercovitch, who claims that "the reciprocity between the personal and the professional has hinged on [his] ability to channel [his] resistance to the culture into a way of interpreting it" (*MA,* 1). The verb *interpreting* is always potentially undermined hereby, because restricted by "a way." The ongoing activity of interpreting, for both, threatens to become a more fixed interpretation, and Bercovitch remarks that "interpretation is a strategy for evading or repressing the actual worlds around us which expresses itself through yearnings for a world elsewhere" (*MA,* 4). An ever-changing tale entails an ongoing interpreting that also implies the subject's engagement with, rather than circumscription by, the culture's prescribed narratives of identity, such as the mother's "border-crossing" evinces.

Yau's poetry manifests an enduring interest in the relationship between fixed interpretations and circumscribed subjectivity. Poetic efforts to preserve the activity of interpreting simultaneously foreground cultural strategies to produce subjects. These efforts come together in the elusive title poem of Yau's second volume, a poem that appears subsequently in *Sometimes* (1979), *Corpse and Mirror* (1983), and *Radiant Silhouette* (1989). "The Reading of an Ever-changing Tale" presents interpreting as a dialectic between naming and perceiving:[14]

> Certain colors got lodged under
> the fingernails before their names

> came to grace our speech. But
> what of the phenomena whose
> colors can only be imagined?

Colors precede names, but names in turn shape perception. The poem asks the reader to consider how we organize perception, how we color our world, as the passive voice ("can only be imagined") calls attention to the perceiver's susceptibility to names. The possibility of a racial pretext offered by the colors under the fingernails extends the inquiry into the shaping of (cultural) identity. Yet that is only one among many ever-changing tales.

The poem offers hints of a story line, but turns those hints into "restraints" that simultaneously constrain and refocus the tale. The poem proceeds through increments that become associations:

> What did you do with the pills?
> And why were you without any gasoline?
> Today, these questions are a restraint
> on your memory as the color
> 'blue' is a box opened up
> like a sky under which
> no grass grows.

Compiled metaphors suggest a kind of repressed associating, as of the pressing of memory itself. The impossibility of experiencing an unmediated world emerges in the mediated experience of "the color 'blue.'" The poem ends with an image of such mediation:

> . . . But the traces remain.
> The war you only just heard about
> inextricably mixed with a face
> you will probably never see again.

But mediation, which involves two terms, can unfold into a dialectic: The inextricable mixture of the war and the face discloses the way in which each colored encounter in turn recolors the experience of the world. The omission of any form of *to be* makes the last phrase, the three final lines, the poem's only nonsentence, stressing the image, perhaps a breakthrough in which an ongoing dialectic makes the tale "ever changing." "Traces remain," in the memory, as in the poetry.

An ever-changing tale challenges the symbolic process that stabilizes experience; the world becomes less knowable, less predictable. In this sense, it appeals to Yau, who comes to poetry effectively homeless, as an immigrant, but in search of an alternative way of conceiving of his experiences, himself, and, in general, "home" rather than in search of another country. In the story he tells about himself, his interest in "the wonderful possibility" of poetry emerges from his "feeling kind of out of it and nonconnected or disconnected from the world [he] lived in" (*T,* 50). There is a subtle difference between "*non*connected" and "*dis*connected," in which "*dis*connected" implies a previous connection. For Yau, however, the disconnection, which, with nostalgia, he inherits from his parents, points to a fundamental threat of *non*connection that social rituals at once cover up and implicitly suggest. This is the threat as well of the "ever-changing tale." Yau recalls "trying to write about what my experience was that I felt unable to discuss with anyone else. And learning from the writing that you are incredibly distant from your own experience, that it remains incoherent and so do you" (*T,* 50). The move from first to second person rhetorically articulates an alienation, a self-as-other, that his poetry works to foreground. Accordingly, he writes especially to interrogate the rituals that foster social cohesion and position subjects within a culture.

In "Toy Trucks and Fried Rice" (*Sleepless Night,* 1981), Yau begins to fashion an ever-changing tale out of "The Chinese Benevolent Association's Annual Christmas Party"; each of these parties "reenact[s] the previous one down to the smallest detail" (*RS,* 68).The tale emerges from disjunctions in the ritual, through which an evident clash of cultures is embodied, for example, by the "Santa Claus . . . [who] was never Chinese . . . [but] was chosen from among the middle-aged men and women who studied Chinese in a Saturday class held in the church basement" and dramatized by these "sincere students['] put[ting] on a skit, and [singing] Christmas Carols in Chinese" (*RS,* 68). The students sing songs presumably translated from their own language, conveying the distance between the two cultures that the event is trying to bridge. When "Father Kwo . . . [makes] the blessing in both Chinese and American" (*RS,* 71), Yau turns a culture, American, into a language. This analogy, which implies that grammar and rules, arbitrary structural principles, define a culture, envisions cultural identity as acquired behavior. The boy attending the party "had been told ever since he could remember that he was Chinese" (*RS,*

68). In "Toy Trucks and Fried Rice," cultural collisions unravel his parents' accounts of his identity, which shape his memory and name him into his "Chinese" identity.

Each parent tells a story of Chinese identity that expresses a prescribed American narrative. The mother uses such a narrative to distinguish herself from the other Chinese at the party:

> His mother was from Shanghai and spoke the dialect common to that area. The people at the party (he assumed this was true of the students as well) spoke another dialect, Cantonese, and were, according to his mother, only farmers anyway. The analogy his mother made had to do with how people spoke in Louisiana as compared to those in Boston, except that in China they didn't understand each other at all. (*RS,* 69)

Significantly, she casts her analogy in American terms, those with which her "Chinese" son is apparently most familiar. And her comparison evokes, as it parallels, the historical and political vocabulary through which New England, extending into the Northeast, has traditionally laid claim to a privileged (and representative) American status. Her distinctions extend more nebulously to her proud reminder "that his grandfather was taller than anyone in this room, as were most people from Shanghai" (*RS,* 69). She, herself "only a shade above five feet tall, and . . . thus indistinguishable from the rest of the women in the room" (*RS,* 69), expresses distinction through stature, a term that, echoing an American stereotype of Asians, could also indicate an Americanization of her own Chinese identity. She seems in effect to see herself in the unflattering mirror of W. E. B. DuBois's "double-consciousness."[15] Having grown up "in a 27 room house on *Great Western Way,*" the daughter of "the Ambassador to Belgium in Sun-Yat Sen's doomed republic" (*RS,* 69, emphasis added), she is doubly dislocated when "thrown irretrievably into the past, as at this party" (*RS,* 69). The language suggests a cultural act of violence inherent in the party, a violence to which she responds with the analogy through which she "trie[s] to convey to her son the belief that isolation, whether social or spiritual, was the inevitable result of being better than what was around you" (*RS,* 70).

The father offers no satisfactory alternative to the mother's isolation, having himself been "abandoned" by his own Chinese father to "his . . . father's mother, an English Catholic, [who] had had him baptized, curled his long hair, and dressed him in girl-like clothes until he was nearly six" (*RS,* 69). As the father is abandoned by his father to his mother's feminization of him, so the boy feels similarly abandoned to his mother's Americanized construction of a confused Chinese identity. He never asks "his father if he felt *like* he was Chinese" (*RS,* 69, emphasis added), where Chinese identification rhetorically becomes a simile, a figure that implies the mutability of cultural identity.

His father constructs his identity indirectly through displacement onto a reconstituted American history:

> The one thing his father talked to him about, besides World War II, was American history. Every week his father went to the public library and brought home old diaries, documents and studies about the Indians, especially the Sioux, Apaches and Seminoles. They were the fighters his father told him about. His father also told him the Indians were the only true Americans and everyone else was a fake. (*RS,* 69).

The father's legacy Americanizes the son as effectively as, if more subtly than, the mother's; his apparently oppositional values, as his son recognizes, are readily appropriated into affirmation of the dominant culture. His visits to the library become rituals of socialization that contextualize the historical documents and stories through which he communicates with his son. The father unwittingly resorts to a familiar cultural iconography when he transforms the heroic Indian fighters into representatives of the culture they opposed. As early as the mid-nineteenth century, "Indians" were appropriated to emblematize an indigenous United States culture; Abraham Lincoln, for example, belonged to a group of young Whigs who signaled their Americanness by calling themselves the "Young Indians."

The father's implied identification with the conquered fighters, the "true Americans," uncannily returns to the earliest efforts of the United States to legislate the subjectivity of Chinese residents. In 1854, the California Supreme Court decided on the inadmissibility of the testimony of a Chinese witness against a white defendant in a court of law. Citing precedents in acts disqualifying, variously, the testimony of "Indian or Negro" witnesses and of any "Black, or Mulatto Person, or Indian" against white defendants, the court sought to determine "the legal significance of the words, 'Black, Mulatto, Indian and White person.' "[16] The argument asserts the interchangeability of Columbus's mistake and geographical speculation to define the tribal nation's descent from "the great Mongolian race" as a "meaning" subsequently "fixed by law" (*PH*, 432). In the eyes of the law, the "Indians" and the Chinese become racially indistinguishable.

The significance of this indistinction emerges in the national uneasiness that the case articulates. *People v. Hall* evinces an almost hysterical indecision concerning the real threat of admitting the testimony of a Chinese witness. On the one hand, the court warns that "[t]he same rule which would admit them to testify, would admit them to all the equal rights of citizenship, and we might soon see them at the polls, in the jury box, upon the bench, and in our legislative halls" (*PH*, 434). On the other hand, the court juxtapositionally evokes "[t]he anomalous spectacle of a distinct people, living in our community, recognizing no laws of this State, except through necessity, bringing with them their prejudices and national feuds, in which they indulge in open violation of law" (*PH*, 435). The chief justice, who appears to have forgotten that a white American citizen has been accused (and convicted) of murdering a Chinese resident, seems also unable to decide whether the Chinese residents' desire to assimilate or their refusal to assimilate poses the greater threat. *People v. Hall* strives to cover up its anxious ambiguity in a vow to "protect . . . life and property" from "the corrupting influences of degraded castes" (*PH*, 433). Throughout his poetry, Yau makes use of the anxiety generated by his own ambiguous position to foreground the ever-changing tale of a constructed subjectivity.

In "Cenotaph of Snow" (1984), the son becomes a poet by retelling the father's story as an ever-changing tale in which identity is always in question. The father tells the son a bedtime story about men—Indians in an earlier version—lying in wait beneath a "treacherous blanket" of snow for settlers to leave a church. The poem rehearses the story line until the middle of the poem, when the past tense and a description of the narrative's mechanisms and the boy's reaction begins to pull them apart:

> V
>
> The bells united the villagers kneeling inside the church with the men waiting beneath the snow. They located precisely where in the narrative everyone could be found.
>
> VI
>
> After his father reads him the story, he begins
> each night by pulling

> the blanket over his head and listening. Will he
> be able to stay awake
> long enough to hear the bells? Has he finally learned
> how to shape his dreams?
> Afraid of the answer, he retells the story once more.

Each retelling postpones the story's—and the father's—conclusion. Initially, the boy retells the story out of fear: to avoid confronting the subjectivity (or commitment to a subjectivity) evident in his ability to shape his dreams. At the same time, he longs to organize the events that confuse him: In a moment "of calm frenzy[,] . . . he wishe[s] he could become like the bells, and float above the consuming flames" (*RS*, 155). Increasingly, as he moves toward sleep, his own identity becomes more explicitly the point of confusion; he finds it ever "harder . . . to discover if he [is] kneeling inside the church or hiding beneath the snow" (*RS*, 155). Here he reflects the disorientation of his father's narrative in which the term *Americans* collapses the opposition between "Indians" and white settlers. The boy cannot locate himself in his father's narrative. "In order to keep circling," the poem continues, "he had to tell himself the story once more" (*RS*, 155). Yau uses the same expression—"I kept circling it" (*T*, 45)—in the *Talisman* interview to describe the experiences of trying to write about a childhood memory. In both cases, the retelling defers commitment and coherence; the father's straightforward narrative—his interpretation—becomes the boy's ongoing interpreting. But the boy's more suggestively imagistic account of the father's story also brings out psychological and cultural aspects of that story of which the father is unaware. The reader is drawn into the ongoing interpreting through which the boy-turned-poet links his poetry to a deferred narrative of identity.

The shaped dreams risk becoming an interpretation and manifesting an "I" that, for Yau, "accept[s] an academicized, historical legacy— . . . fulfill[s] the terms of the oppressor" (*T*, 49); the "I," in other words, embodies the hallucinated coherence through which an oppressively prescriptive rhetoric fixes the mother's crossing as a culturally primal and ceaselessly determinative moment, or the father's struggle in a mythologized (and appropriated) heroism. Yau instead presents subjectivity in the poetry as a complicated dialogue between ways of perceiving and of being perceived. Suggestive parallels between agents and objects of perception confound "the" subject's fixed position in a poetry committed to rewriting narrative coherence as an ever-changing tale.

REVISIONARY POETICS

In the exotic landscape of a sequence of poems entitled "Corpse and Mirror," the poet imagines a fantastical alterity that increasingly reflects the gaze turned upon it. The first poem of this sequence, which begins "When one of our citizens dies, his corpse is placed in his chariot" (*RS*, 126), constructs the speaking subject as a kind of anthropological informant. Prescriptions and prohibitions surrounding the treatment of the dead depict a highly ritualized mythical culture, an impression amplified by the structural repetitions of the poem. The sequence suggests a parodic transposition of the poet's self-consciousness as a "Chinese American" poet, a curiosity attracting sociological rather than aesthetic interest.

When "Corpse and Mirror III" brings the corpse and a mirror into a movie theater, the poet turns the anthropological gaze on the implied anthropologist's—or the audience's—culture. Resonance among sentence structures continues to link the landscapes:

> When the movie ends and the lights come on, the audience is puzzled by the sight of a corpse reclining on a velvet couch in clothes of human hair. . . . When the movie ends, the lights come on. The audience is puzzled by the sight of a large oval mirror leaning awkwardly against a column, which wasn't there at the beginning of the evening's entertainment.'(*RS*, 133)

The echo that structurally replaces the corpse with the mirror suggestively analogizes the audience's reflection to a dead body. But the poem replaces this expected reflection with a spectral illusion: "A reflection pierces the mirror, though the stage is empty. The men see a woman brushing her hair, while the women see a man trimming his beard" (*RS*, 134). The anomaly of a reflection that *pierces* replaces complacent mirroring with the possibility of investigating. Here the reflections register cross-gender fantasies or identifications as men and women see each other in the mirror, engaged in the gendered rituals of hair brushing and beard trimming. The reflections mark the construction of the subject as an ambiguous engendering. Allusions to human hair, which thread the sequence, open out from that ambiguity. The hair takes the reader back through the corpse's clothes and to the "conversation made of human hair" that passes "back and forth between" the movie and the corpse (*RS*, 133) in the poem's first section, and to an "old woman, who embroiders tablecloths with human hair" (*RS,* 130) in "Corpse and Mirror II." Hair is significant in race discourse as well as in a culture's gendered rituals, but it also marks an eery border world, being one of the two parts of the human body that continue to grow after death. In this liminal space, the corpse and the mirror suggest two ways of being a person who is not quite a person.

Such figures fascinate Yau as embodiments of the "I," the cultural subject. The poet uses the sacrificial victims in "Halfway to China" (1984), for example, or the exhibited dead in "Two Meditations on Guanajuato" (1984) to envision—or re-vision—his own complicated subjectivity. "Halfway to China" begins with the displaced personae of a third-person subject:

> While lying on a beach, he remembers the photographs he once saw in a magazine. On a strip of white sand, nestled between the movie lot palm trees and sculpted turquoise waves. Beneath the brownish-red mask that clamps tightly over his face when he closed his eyes.
>
> The children—their eyes are open and their faces immobile. (*RS,* 156)

After the double displacement of memory and photography in the first sentence, two ways of "fixing" a subject temporally, the subject disappears in the second sentence, which ambiguously could refer to either the beach or the scene in the photographs. Subjectivity itself seems suspended or deferred, perhaps to suggest connection in the contiguity of the "brownish-red mask" and the open-eyed children. Here are versions of cultural subjects, although the children, sacrificial victims of an Incan ritual, resurface only allusively until the eighth stanza. Liminal times and places recall the photographs of the children—as the poet is falling asleep or crossing a bridge—and they are fitting emblems of his own liminality:

> Incas guided groups of children up the mountain, and left them as offerings to their gods. They have been waiting for centuries when they are discovered by accident. Frozen and intact. Replicas of themselves. Ice, not wax. Brightly woven blankets their crustacean shells. (*RS,* 157)

"Replicas of themselves," the children are, literally, ossified subjects, sacrificial offerings of a cultural ritual; they are equally subjected to, as they are contextualized by, a photograph that turns them into curiosities, victims of "savage" rites. The photograph, which freezes the subjects in time, oddly mirrors the ritual. The children's meaning in the photograph corresponds both to their sacrifice within the Incas' ritual and to the "mask's" analogous cultural subjection.

The title evokes a metaphysical rather than geographic landscape. China courses through the poem as an implication until the last stanza, when

> [b]eneath the mask he remembers his friend telling him a story about what it was like to grow up in China. After being led into the room, she was ordered to go over to the canopied bed, draw the curtain back, and kiss her dead grandmother farewell. (*RS*, 159)

His evident experience of her apparent reluctance, like his memory of her memory, suggests his (and probably her) distance from China. But the "brownish-red mask" expresses an alienation from America as well. In the geographically and temporally unidentified landscape, he is ambivalently Americanized, "Halfway to China," homeless, and a haunting emblem particularly of the (sacrificial) rituals of identification of the United States, *his* native culture.

"Two Meditations on Guanajuato" considers the source of those rituals in an (auto)biographical impulse, an urge for "self"-representation. Cultural selves are gruesomely mirrored in a postcard of Guanajuato's main attraction, in which the disinterred of an overcrowded graveyard, mummified from the dry climate, are "stood up in a hallway of some kind of graveyard museum" (*RS*, 140). The living experience the dead through grim crises that reflect their own existence:

> The man on the left is clutching his chest with both hands in obvious hysteria. His mouth is agape, his face contorted. Has he just realized he has lost his wallet and cannot pay the bill? Has he only just this minute consulted his watch and seen what time it is? (*RS*, 141)

The poet understands his interest in the Guanajuato museum as a complicitous desire for culturally reified selves: "Isn't my urge to go to Guanajuato similar to the one I have when I go to the bookstore and buy an autobiography or biography?" (*RS*, 143). As a tourist and a reader, he participates in the analogous processes of displayed mummification and cultural subjectivity, a "self" framed and made comprehensible by a conventional narrative form.

In the second meditation, Guanajuato has become an explicitly private space in which an uncharacteristic explicitly autobiographical voice revisions his own poetic project—notably "Toy Trucks and Fried Rice":

> So why do I read autobiographies if I am unwilling to write one? It grows more complicated. For the postcard has become increasingly entangled with the idea of Christmas, my memories of it. And if the connection has remained constant yet vague—which it has—comical yet dull and unspecified, like a restless ache, then I must make it clear, at least to myself, if I am to get on with my daily activities. (*RS*, 143)

Poetry is, like Guanajuato, a private space, in which, however, the poet hopes to re-present the process by which the "contorted faces" have become haunting representations—haunting because they are so obviously representations. The poet risks the ossification of conventional autobiography because it is only in that risk, in the confession of his complicity with cultural representation, that he can make his limitations visible. Writing, in other words, can only imagine a transgressive struggle with (rather than conform to) cultural representation when the tourist becomes the museum's curator:

> if I am going to dig up the recent past and place it in a museum, if I am going to endow its banality with meaning, as anyone who writes about *themselves* does, I want it done quickly and efficiently, like the men who push their spades into the warm soil of Guanajuato. For it will be a museum I have no desire to visit. Arranging it will be enough. (*RS*, 144, emphasis added)

This process is revisionary rather than oppositional, relying on slippage and indirection. The speaking subject flickers at several points even in this passage: The plural "themselves" attests to a writer's multiple, rather than coherent, experiences of the "self." *Arranging,* which insists on remaining a verb (an activity) and refuses, conversely, to become a gerund (or noun), and possibly subject of the sentence (the arranging), implies the absent subject in the structuring activity: Someone is doing the arranging. Understood as such an activity, autobiography becomes an example of how a person's experience is written into coherent subjectivity. It tells the story of cultural representation. Writing thus re-presents, as it mimics, cultural representation; limitations that may not be transcended may at least be imaginatively perceived.[17]

Yau expresses his concern with the dilemma of representation—how to keep mimicry from becoming recapitulation—in his treatment of the difficulty of such imaginative perceptions. They are not, for example, readily available to the moviegoers in "Corpse and Mirror III," who "will [not] be able to agree on what they saw" (*RS*, 134). Memories "twist around" each other, leaving only "the ache of trying to recall a moment, whose slanting roof of sunlight has long since fallen in" (*RS*, 134), like Yau's "restless ache" in "Guanajuato." The moment itself is almost imperceptible, like Emily Dickinson's "certain slant of light," possibly fantasized into a meaningful event and just beyond recall. But it also evokes the moment between frames when perceptual illusion itself comes very nearly into focus; here it is the cultural subject as corpse, barely perceived, quickly repressed, and yet returning in the legacy of a former continuity left no longer intact: "By then the mirror will have vanished and the movie will have started. This time *in pieces*" (*RS*, 134, emphasis added).

Cinema serves at once as metaphor and medium for the processes of cultural representation that enlist the agency of the subject, or viewer. The audience is drawn into the spectacle, which determines what the viewers perceive. But that process is disrupted when the movie resumes "in pieces." The poem ends with the implication that the poet can "pierce" the mirror to foreground the viewers' culturally produced perceptions, an implication that Yau develops in a later poem that also uses a movie set, "No One Ever Tried to Kiss Anna May Wong" (*Dragon's Blood*, 1985–88). Wong, another orientalized and gendered subject, is less complacent than her earlier counterparts. Moreover, the poet's relationship with Wong diverges significantly from the relationship with characters in the earlier poetry. In "Anna May Wong," he pierces the "celluloid scrim" to enter the film and the poem simultaneously:

> No longer lashed to this oily chatter
> I enter her compartment
>   She is languishing
> On a ledge, annoyed at all the times
> she's been told to be scratched, kicked,
> slapped, bitten, stabbed, poisoned, and shot.

> Lightning flickers between the frames.
> On the seat beside me I find a circle
> smaller than one left by a wet apple. (*RS*, 187)

Desire finds its own voice in the poem, in which the speaker shares his uninterpreted discovery of a wet spot with the reader. He will not repeat culture's speaking for the subject, but instead presents the sign of her desire, hitherto erased.

As in the "Corpse and Mirror" poems, the poet is uncertainly located between the film and the audience, perceiving *as* he is perceived. A fantasized Wong inhabits the poem as much as the fantasized waitress in "Suggested by a Waitress in YEE's," but here she is joined by an equally fantasized (and fantasizing) poet. The drama of cultural subjectivity is ritually staged in the flicker between frames, where the eye retains the image to give the illusion of movement to contiguous representations, where the spectator, that is, participates in the spectacle. Like many modern experimental writers, notably Gertrude Stein, Yau acknowledges being "influenced by movies, that kind of *speed* of seeing, the seamless jumps, the echoes, and the way something dissolves something else" (*T*, 48). His project is to stop the camera, to capture "the time inside the camera before light casts its shadows on the wall" ("Cenotaph," *RS*, 151), before the image has definitively formed and "where seeing might actually take place" (*T*, 48). The "colors lodged under the fingernails *before their names.*"

Yau's art criticism of the late 1980s registers an increasingly articulated relationship between visual representation and cultural subjectivity. The concerns ever present in the poetry emerge as an insistent inquiry into the "visionary impulse." Writing of artist Paul Laffoley, Yau urges that "the term 'visionary' . . . be reserved for the handful of solitary sojourners who have been both blessed and cursed with believing in the sanctity of the world."[18] "Revisionary" more accurately describes Yau's sensibility. His revisionary impulse challenges the "sanctity of the world," foregrounding the cultural construction of a putatively universal selfhood, but the revisionary retains the visionary's faith in representation. The representation of nontranscendence is, after all, a representation of cultural dynamics. Yau's description of "Bluff," a painting by Anna Bialobroda, describes this revisionary aesthetic:

> Given that the title of the painting is *Bluff,* the viewer asks, Does this painting depict a false sense of display or does

> it challenge my power to define and therefore limit? The empty auditorium functions as another mediated zone between the viewer and the painting. Self-conscious of what is being looked at, the viewer begins to look through his or her own act of looking. It is this zone the painting focuses on, the place where the defining, circumscribing look begins to be felt, and the Hidden Self and the Subjected Self begin looking at each other.[19]

Yau is intrigued by Bialobroda's investigation of "the confines of [the] subjected condition" evident in "culture's way of looking at women."[20] Self-expression emerges as the Hidden Self confronts the Subjected Self, and their mirroring promotes a dialectic between faith in a visionary expression and awareness of circumscription; this is the dialectic of the revisionary moment, an ever-changing tale that keeps subjectivity *in process.*

These concerns virtually explode into a recent poetic meditation on the visionary artist, inspired by "Bluff":

> Today it is no more than an empty theater where small boys search the floorboards for corroded coins. A bareheaded man is standing at one end of the stage. After consulting the list of rumors he inherited from his father, he begins painting orgies on the sides of caskets. Some believes these are forgeries of a world that never existed, while others remember the morning the river set out towards the ocean never to return.[21]

There is a certain nostalgia in the image of a space that was once "more than an empty theater." Great dramas, perhaps, were staged here. But the artist has only a diminished legacy, the "list of rumors" inherited from the father, unsubstantiated stories that are ways of making sense in and of the world. Out of that legacy, he stages a new drama, envisioning an alternative creation myth as a way of representing creating. The viewers' subjectivities emerge in their differing responses to make the reader self-conscious about his or her role in the poem.

In the audience's response, Yau depicts what I earlier called "an aesthetic in dialectical engagement with its own impossibility." The "orgies on the sides of caskets" evidently prompt speculating and interpreting among the viewers but then apparently incorporate their consequent efforts to refashion the work into the creating of the work itself. The audience tries to make sense of the work by reading it through their own stories. The first group sees "forgeries," hopefully calling the painter's authenticity into question, as though his imagination has retreated into a prefabricated vision, perhaps even a cultural prescription. A forgery (as opposed to a forging) undercuts the apparently threatening newness of the vision. But "forgeries" also sonorously picks up on "orgies," hinting that the viewers respond in accordance with an imperceptible suggestion from the work itself; the language of their response may be supplied by their own unwitting reactions to the subject matter. In the underscored coincidence of "forge"/make and "forge"/copy, everything made seems in some sense copied, a dialectical engagement that represents a nontranscendence. This group's response expresses what its members do not know that they have seen, or re(-)cognized.

Alternatively, the second group "remembers" what seems to be a legendary event; this group, although also distanced from the artist's vision by memory, nevertheless evinces a more visionary spirit. The first group articulates what Yau calls "a kind of demand, a kind of repressive fact, that" stems from our "want[ing] our artists to be normal, to fit into our definition of history, to do what we think is the right thing to do" (*T*, 34–35). The second group, evidently more receptive to "conditional instances, . . . impurities" (*T*, 35), more readily accepts the artist's "rewriting" in which "[t]he past is as fluid as the present" (*T*, 36). That fluidity allows the painter to enter, and create, the audience's memories, crossing the boundaries of cultural subjectivity to envision its genesis in mutual constraints. Here again is no transcendence, but a vision of nontranscendence, thus a *re*visionary moment.

The relationship between Yau's description of Bialobroda's painting and his poetic image unfolds into a seemingly endless series of double mirrorings. Yau *is* "the viewer . . . look[ing] through his . . . own act of looking," looking at a painting and describing his own poetic project, knowing that his looking is simultaneously transforming and transformed and incorporated by the painting of reflexivity. The poem is about a self-reflexiveness, "being looking," that it demands.

As a poet, Yau resiliently and defiantly resists categories. He is only marginally and often uncomfortably affiliated with the experimental poetics of the so-called LANGUAGE poets or the New York School, and, as Elaine Kim implies, he is not necessarily immediately associated with Asian-American writers. As an art critic, he champions similarly unaffiliated artists, asking the audience to consider the threat the artist evidently poses precisely by resisting affiliation. There will always be cultural subjects, but cultural subjects, Yau suggests, can be dialectically engaged with the processes of their creation and location—and with the epic task of founding a "home." In his poetry, as he writes of Michael Kessler's drawings," "[o]ur perceptions shift between an observed world and a world made visible."[22] In the contrast, we see our observation turn into the possibility of an imagined alternative. It is as a Chinese American who is a poet that Yau embarks upon his revisionary project, but it is as a poet who is Chinese American that he presents it.

NOTES

I wish to thank Joseph Alkana, Christopher Beach, Sacvan Bercovitch, Cordelia Candelaria, Patricia Chu, Carol Colatrella, Joseph Donahue, David Palumbo-Liu, Michael Tratner, and John Yau for reading and commenting on versions of this essay. I am also grateful for a summer research grant from the Council for Research in the Humanities of Columbia University and a Mellon Fellowship from Stanford University, both of which gave me time to write the essay.

1. Edward Foster, "An Interview with John Yau," *Talisman: A Journal of Contemporary Poetry and Poetics* no. 5 (Fall 1990): 31–50; hereafter cited as *T.*

2. Elaine Kim, "Defining Asian American Realities through Literature," *Cultural Critique* 6 (Spring 1987): 111.

3. Elaine Kim, "Asian American Literature," in *Columbia Literary History of the United States,* ed. Emory Elliot (New York: Columbia University Press, 1987), 821.

4. Michael Walzer, "What Does It Mean to Be an 'American'?" *Social Research* 57, no. 3 (Fall 1990): 611.

5. Amy Ling, "A Perspective on Chinamerican Literature," *MELUS: The Journal of the Society for the Study of Multi-Ethnic Literature of the United States* 8, no. 2 (Summer 1981): 7.

I do not mean to suggest contrariety between Yau's concerns and Ling's assertion that "[a]cceptance of both the Chinese part of oneself and the American part, exploring and forging both to create a whole that may be something other than either but nonetheless strong in itself—that, it seems to me, is our goal" ("Chinamerican Literature," 80). Rather, Yau's emphasis on a process rather than an end product represents a different strategy for a related but different project. Where Ling's interest is in conceptualizing a Chinese American identity—and, in "A Perspective on Chinamerican Literature," from which I am quoting, in classifying a new literary category—Yau's concern is to use the tensions of his own Chinese-American identity to inquire into the obscure(d) dynamics of American cultural subjectivity.

Yau, Ling, and Kim are all concerned with the dynamic described by Lisa Lowe in "Heterogeneity, Hybridity, Multiplicity: Marking Asian American Differences" *Diaspora* 1, no. 1 [Spring 1991]: 24–44): "To the extent that Asian American discourse articulates an identity in reaction to the dominant culture's stereotype, even to refute it, . . . the discourse may remain bound to, and overdetermined by, the logic of the dominant culture" (30).

6. In his stunning "Other: From Noun to Verb," a currently unpublished essay delivered as a talk at Intersection for the Arts in San Francisco, California, on 10 June 1991, Nathaniel Mackey draws on Amiri Baraka's description in *Blues People* of white appropriation of black music. Mackey distinguishes between "otherness" and "othering, black linguistic and musical practices which accent variance, variability—what reggae musicians call 'versioning'" (3) to demonstrate how "othering practices implicitly react against and reflect critically upon the different sort of othering to which their practitioners, denied agency in a society by which they're designated other, have been subjected" (4). Mackey, in other words, shows how a number of black artists in the United States reversed the appropriation that Baraka figures in the transformation of verbs such as *jazz* and *swing* into nouns. Following Baraka, Mackey sees this transformation as both an erasure and a circumscription or containment, and he suggests that the reversal—insistence on the *verb*—marks an aesthetic and cultural resisting. I have benefited significantly from Mackey's essay. See also Baraka/Leroi Jones, *Blues People: Negro Music in White America* (New York: William Morrow, 1963).

7. John Yau, "Light and Dark—the Art of Ross Neher," *Sulfur 18* (Winter 1987): 184–85.

8. John Yau, "Michael Kessler's Drawings: Gesture as Image," *Sulfur 14* (Winter 1985).

9. Sacvan Bercovitch, "The Music of America," Introduction to *The Rites of Assent: Transformations in the Symbolic Construction of America* (New York: Routledge, 1993), 1–28. Hereafter cited as *MA*. A version of this essay is reprinted in this volume as "Discovering America: A Cross-Cultural Perspective."

10. John Yau, *Crossing Canal Street* (Binghamton, N.Y.: Bellevue Press, 1976). This is the last poem in the volume. There are no page numbers. The complete poem is cited herein.

11. John Yau, "Postcards from Nebraska," in *Radiant Silhouette: New and Selected Work 1974–1988* (Santa Rosa, Calif.: Black Sparrow Press, 1989), 41–45.

12. John Yau, *Corpse and Mirror* (New York: Holt, Rinehart & Winston, 1983), 72.

13. A central task of Bercovitch's project has been to elucidate the rhetorical strategies of American "ritual[s] of socialization" through which opposition is appropriated into affirmation. (See Sacvan Bercovitch, *The American Jeremiad* [Madison: University of Wisconsin Press, 1978], 172). In *The Puritan Origins of the American Self* (New Haven: Yale University Press, 1975), Bercovitch explicates the introducing of an American "self" into the ritual through "auto-American-biography: the celebration of the representative self as American, and of the American self as the embodiment of a prophetic universal design" (136). Bercovitch's "border-crossings," like Yau's, set ongoing marginalizing in dialogue with the teleological model of progress that incorporates reform into a national design.

14. John Yau, *The Reading of an Ever-Changing Tale* (Clinton, N.Y.: Nobodaddy Press, 1977); *Sometimes* (New York: Sheep Meadow Press, 1979), 17; *Corpse and Mirror*, 51; *Radiant Silhouette*, 20.

15. In his well-known formulation of "double-consciousness," W. E. B. Du Bois describes the "sense of always looking at one's self through the eyes of others, of measuring one's soul by the tape of a world that looks on in amused contempt and pity" (*The Souls of Black Folk*); he depicts a distorted act of mirroring, in other words, an internalized self-devaluation. See *W. E. B. Du Bois: Writings* (New York: Library of America, 1986).

16. *People v. Hall*, in *California Reports*, vol. 4, 429. Hereafter cited as *PH*.

17. For my understanding of this concept, I am indebted to two discussions of "mimicry." In *This Sex Which Is Not One* (trans. Catherine Porter with Carolyn Burke [Ithaca, N.Y.: Cornell University Press, 1985]), Luce Irigaray describes the two alternatives available to women as the deliberate assumption of the feminine role: a "mimicry," or the "direct female challenge," which entails speaking as a male subject and therefore "maintain[ing] sexual indifference." Mimicry makes visible "the cover-up of a possible operation of the feminine in language" (76). The woman engaged in mimicking her "historically assigned" role is presumed to "*remain elsewhere*"; the act of mimicking, in other words, implies distance from the mimicked discourse (76).

Homi Bhabha extends this concept into a theorizing of mimicry and colonial discourse in "Of Mimicry and Man: The Ambivalence of Colonial Discourse" (*October* 28 [Spring 1984]: 125–33). For Bhabha, the "slippage" of mimicry—"to be Anglicized, is *emphatically* not to be English" (128)—simultaneously constructs the colonized subject as incomplete and arrests the discourse in the act of this construction. Bhabha is interested in the "process by which the look of surveillance returns as the displacing gaze of the disciplined, where the observer becomes the observed and 'partial' representation rearticulates the whole notion of *identity* and alienates it from essence" (129).

Whereas for Bhabha, "[m]imicry *repeats* rather than *re-presents*," whereas, that is, for Bhabha, as for Irigaray, mimicry implicitly rather than explicitly challenges a colonizing discourse, for Yau the activity inheres in the hyphen of a re-presenting. Yau makes "slippage" apparent, as his poetics *articulates* both the grammar of cultural subjectivity and grammar *as* part of the process of cultural subjecting.

18. John Yau, "In the Visionary Tradition: The Art of Paul Laffoley," *Sulfur 17* 6, no. 2 (Fall 1986): 88.

19. John Yau, "Anna Bialobroda: Self-Portraiture as Self-Representation," *Sulfur 24: A Literary Tri-Quarterly of the Whole Art* 9, no. 1 (Spring 1989): 164.

20. John Yau, "Michael Kessler's Drawings: Gesture as Image," *Sulfur 14* 5, no. 2 (Winter 1985): 88.

21. This is the first stanza of "Sixth Ode to My Desk," *o blek: A Journal of Language Arts* (Spring 1991): 69.

22. Yau, "Michael Kessler's Drawings," 88.

JOSÉ DAVID SALDÍVAR

8

The Hybridity of Culture in Arturo Islas's *The Rain God*

What is hybridization? It is a mixture of two social languages within the limits of a single utterance, an encounter, within the consciousness, separated from one another by an epoch, by social differentiation or by some other factor. . . . We may even say that language and languages change historically primarily by means of hybridization, by means of a mixing of various "languages" co-existing within the boundaries of a single dialect, a single national language, a single branch, a single group of different branches or different groups of such branches, in the historical as well as paleontological past of languages—but the crucible for this mixing always remains the utterance.

Mikhail Bakhtin, *The Dialogic Imagination.*

In recent years critical interest in the theorizing of ethnic, Third World, and "minor" literature has increased.[1] For the most part, however, this new writing has not emphasized what Charles Newman in *The Post-Modern Aura* calls "the new agencies of production, transmission, and administration of knowledge as dominant cultural institutions,"[2] processes that pose distinctions between minor and major work. For example, William Boelhower's

Through a Glass Darkly: Ethnic Semiosis in American Literature, whose first chapter, "A Modest Ethnic Proposal," valuably traces, with the help of Henry James, the identity crisis of Americans, concludes that "everybody in America is willy-nilly an ethnic subject."[3] Throughout his study, however, Boelhower defers analysis of the ideological function of the canon, and blurs the binary opposition that continually haunts his work, namely, the collapsing of a radically minor literature into one that seeks a major function. Likewise, Werner Sollors declares in *The Invention of Ethnicity* that ethnicity is "an invention, a cultural construction." To be sure, Sollors's analysis of U.S. mainstream and minority discourses has a structuralist slant, for he claims that even if Puritan and minority discourse differ in their application, they are the same in their grammar. Puritan and what he calls "non-*WASP*" discourses all find redemption in representing themselves as outside radical dissent, for, as Sacvan Bercovitch's work describes, the minority becomes incorporated in inoculated form as part of the mainstream.

To produce an adequate understanding of ethnic, minor, or Third World writing, it is necessary to understand the criteria that determine the constitution of a canon at every juncture, and to grasp those criteria in relation to the general ideological forms that legitimate domination at any given historical moment. Arnold Krupat's *The Voice in the Margin: Native American Literature and the Canon* goes a long way toward engaging this issue. What Krupat effectively demonstrates is how Anglo-American New Critics consciously chose to privilege texts "that could accommodate the wider context of international—or at least of Western—literature."[4] In other words, Anglo-American New Critics, for Krupat, defined international literature as independent of all sociotemporal determinants—"as if one actually could read globally (and timelessly), passing directly to the highest levels of generalization (linguistic, philosophical), bypassing the mean and ordinary local—as if rhetoric were a matter of figures and of no occasions" (*V,* 183).

Indeed, rhetoric and, let me add, American literary history tells us how writers' works of art are packaged, distributed, sold, or censored in the postmodern marketplace. This essay contests Boelhower's and Sollors' generalizations about ethnic and minor literatures by discussing the editorial deliberations of some mainstream editors and reviewers (male and female) who read Arturo Islas's *The Rain God* within an Anglocentric monocultural matrix, thereby refusing to see his magical narrative as a hybrid novel with a difference. Because the reviewers were incapable of crossing cultural boundaries, they could not recognize Islas's narrative as going beyond their vision of what Bercovitch describes as "the myth" or "the symbol" of America.[5]

Put in Krupat's terms, *The Rain God* reveals the local and ordinary but accommodates its own critical "cosmopolitan" context. A study of the editors' and reviewers' reading practices will reveal the complex ideological calculations and negotiations of a particular fraction of the Anglo-American middle class as it attempts to define itself within the already established taste hierarchy.[6] By tracing some of the editorial deliberations of the editors who read Islas's novel in manuscript, we can learn something about the taste and underlying ideological and ethnic assumptions of those key individuals who are, in Janice Radway's and Richard Ohmann's words, "controlling the gate, deciding not only what cultural creations will be formally produced but also which among those will be distributed"[7] "in an urgent or attractive way."[8]

New York publishers who read *The Rain God* in manuscript largely directed their attention to Islas's Chicano background and the ethnic cultural gaze in his work. This narrow view failed to reveal the complex literary and cross-cultural influences from both North America and Latin America that shape his writing. Put differently, white middle-class editors refused to consider his narrative as part of the hemisphere's pan-American traditions.

In a letter of 30 December 1975 to John Meyers, Islas's agent, Frances McCullough, senior editor at Harper and Row, made this comment about Islas's novel: "I think what's wrong with the characters is tha[t] they are so busy conveying a cultural message that they have no time to be real people. This is true also of the plot; whatever happens has a heavy cultural message but you don't feel its weight in terms of the people's lives."[9] This characteristic reading of Islas's fiction precisely addresses the very problem that Chicanos and Chicanas are confronted with in New York: the ethnic "cultural message" label imposed on them by mainstream editors draws simplistic attention to their "otherness," while their place in U.S. society and the relation of their work to global literature tends to be undervalued.

The temptation to examine Islas's work only for its "insider" Chicano cultural message has been considerable. Two examples are enough to show their shortcomings. A reviewer, Raymond

Mungo, suggested that the Chicano essence of *The Rain God* is the author's "striving for the key to some Castanedan, soulful mystery in the lives of these [Chicano] people."[10] Likewise, Carol Fowler operated with similar racial criteria in her 1985 review. She claimed that Islas's Chicano characters "seem" to have "a sense of clannishness stronger than Anglo families."[11] The suggestion that Islas's work is reflective of some aboriginal "soulful mystery," or some "clannishness," betrays an insufficient understanding of the background to his writings. Such critical stances lead to an unbalanced and restricted view of his importance as an American writer with a difference and give rise to pernicious stereotypes.

Henry Louis Gates, Jr., has convincingly argued that the trope of "race" is an important concern of many U.S. writers and thus demands our critical attention.[12] And since Chicano and Chicana cultural identities are shaped in the tension between cultures—U.S. and Mexican—they embrace double-voiced elements and patterns from different backgrounds. In other words, Islas does not work in an artistic vacuum. He is free to incorporate elements from literature and art outside his immediate "Latino" cultural sphere.

The value of Arturo Islas's *The Rain God* lies not in the author's depiction of traditions alien to American readers but in the specific way he bridges the gap between North American and Latin American cultures and unites literary and transnational traditions. The label *ethnic* used by New York editors therefore distracts from these qualities.

Islas's personal background and his academic interest in American literatures—he was until his death in February 1991 professor of English at Stanford University and had served as a visiting professor of creative writing at the University of Texas, El Paso—explain why his work is marked by cross-cultural hybridization. Yvor Winters and Wallace Stegner, two of his Stanford mentors, and such writers as William Faulkner, Wallace Stevens, Maxine Hong Kingston, Juan Rulfo, and Gabriel García Márquez have left their mark on his double-voiced writing. Similar to Bercovitch, who developed a critical perspective out of his experience of moving to America,[13] Islas used his own experiences of migration to create an idea of himself out of his Mexican and American background, his knowledge of New World Amerindian cultures, his experiences in a postmodern American society, and his study of classic American literatures. All of these factors must be considered in an assessment of Islas's fiction.

Another reason editors were incapable of acknowledging the true character of his novel was their fear that *The Rain God* would be bought only by a limited number of Chicano readers. Henry William Griffin, a senior editor at Macmillan, put it this way in a 5 April 1976 letter to Bob Cornfield, Islas's agent at the time: "Interesting, very interesting indeed, but I'm afraid our sales force would be very hard put to sell a thousand copies" (*IP*, 1). Seven years after its publication by Alexandrian Press, *The Rain God* has sold approximately eleven thousand copies.[14] One can only imagine how many copies of Islas's novel might have been sold if the book had been published, distributed, and marketed with understanding by the mainstream presses in New York.

Comments such as Mr. Griffin's led Islas to remark, "The constant observation from New York was that publishers felt there was no audience for this work—no market. And market is really the word because it means money."[15] Although Islas did not deny that his novel describes Chicanos and Chicanas who live in a southwestern border town, he repeatedly noted that "it was not intended solely for a Chicano audience" (*W*, 1) But after eight years of struggle with unresponsive New York publishing houses (he submitted his novel to more than twenty), he gave up trying to convince the editors and publishers that his story about the Angel family would have what he called "universal" appeal. "I finally decided," he tells us, "to stop banging my head against the wall" (*W*, 1).

To his credit, Islas claims that his comments aren't evidence of "sour grapes." But he does point out that people he went to school with at Stanford, who are now editors in New York, have consistently ignored Chicano and Chicana writers: "I know that world. I went to Stanford with a lot of the [people] who are editors, and it's a very circumspect and provincial world; they publish their own" (*W*, 1).

To show how the novel can be read as a direct refutation of the New York publishing world's view of ethnic literature, as well as of a narrow U.S. sense of literary and historical "tradition," the following sections draw upon Islas's letters and interviews to trace the classic American and Latin American literary backgrounds of *The Rain God*. In other words, Islas dissents in *The Rain God* from what Bercovitch has called the "consensus ideology" of classic American literature that projects onto that vast and diversified body of literature a totalizing cultural homogeneity.[16] Seen in this light, Bercovitch's depiction of American ideological consensus takes on rather different nuances when we explore the ways that

U.S. writers such as Islas use racial and sexual differences to question and rewrite American literary and social history.

Two statements by Arturo Islas in a letter to his agent are particularly pertinent to an initial understanding of *The Rain God.* He suggests that his novel is in the U.S. southern tradition of Faulkner's classic *Absalom, Absalom!* (1936): "I am chronicling," he writes, "the life of a historical creature who happened to live at a time when he was taught to hate what he perceived himself to be" (*IP,* 1). In the same letter Islas elaborates: "[Miguel Chico is] my Quentin Compson; he would say in exactly the same tone Quentin uses at the end of *Absalom!*: 'I don't hate Mexicans! I don't hate Anglos! I don't hate gays!'" (*IP,* 1).

In *The Mind of the South,* W. J. Cash notes of U.S. southern writers—and Islas, like García Márquez and Carlos Fuentes, stresses an affinity with them: "[they are] romantics of the appalling," who only hate the South, "with the exasperated hate of a lover who cannot persuade the object of his affections to his desire," much as "Narcissus, growing at length analytical, might have suddenly begun to hate his image in a pool."[17] Presumably, what Islas wants us to see is that his central consciousness, Miguel Chico, like Faulkner's Quentin Compson, comes under Cash's definition. There is every reason to see, at least on a first reading, Islas's *The Rain God* as a compressed exploration of Miguel Chico's narcissistic hatred and resentment. Put differently, Miguel Chico exemplifies what Nietzsche saw in intellectuals as a form of profound *ressentiment.*[18] He suffers in a "psychological" sense from the destructive envy of the have-nots for the haves.

Thus envisaged, Islas would have readers center the novel's interest in Miguel Chico. Those who do so, he believes, at least will see the primary importance he places on the contemplative mind and its exploratory, interpretive acts. Hence, early in *The Rain God,* he describes the protagonist as central consciousness:

> He, Miguel Chico was the family analyst, interested in the past for psychological, not historical reasons. Like Mama Chona, he preferred to ignore factors in favor of motives, which were always and endlessly open to question and interpretation. Yet unlike his grandmother and Maria, Miguel

> Chico wanted to look at motives and at people from an earthly, rather than otherworldly, point of view.[19]

Clearly, the hero's consciousness is the fixed point of view from which readers overhear the various generations of the Angel family. It follows that instead of attempting to give readers an "ethnic cultural message," as many editors in New York narrowly claimed, Islas's Chicano narrative is in the long tradition of psychologically complex novels, for *The Rain God* constantly draws attention to its ideas and labyrinthine methods. The central task of Miguel Chico as "family analyst" therefore is clear: to penetrate and attempt to see below the surface of things, and so arrive at psychological judgments. Like a bookish Henry James character, Miguel Chico is "affected with a certain high lucidity."[20] For Islas, his character becomes not simply exceptionally intelligent and sensitive with a "value intrinsic," but, as in James's best work, "a compositional resource" of the highest order. From the aspect of narrative structure, Islas places Miguel Chico's point of view, the play of his impressions and reactions, at the book's center to produce a unity and intensity of focus that could not easily be easily achieved by other means. But his interest in such a character clearly extends beyond his structural use, for, like James before him, he sees the "large lucid reflector" as no less than "the most polished of possible mirrors of the subject" (*N*, 122).

As a consequence of this method, the novelist seems to withdraw from the action, allowing his intense perceiver to discover the subject for himself and in the process to reveal it to the reader. Miguel Chico's function is to create the story out of its particulars by gradually perceiving the full significance of events in which he is involved. A word of qualification about Miguel Chico is in order here, for like John Marcher in James's classic tale, "The Beast in the Jungle," in which Marcher spends most of his time staring his fate (in the person of May Bartram) in the face and failing to get the point precisely because it so apparent, Miguel Chico often tends to (mis)read experience. Miguel Chico, Islas writes, "was still seeing people, including himself, as books. He wanted to edit them, correct them, make them behave differently. And so he continued to read them as if they were invented by someone else, and he failed to take into account their separate realities, their differences from himself. When people told him of their lives, or when he thought about his own in the way that is not thinking but a kind of reverie outside time, a part of him listened with care. Another part fidgeted, thought about something else or went blank, and wondered why once again he was being offered such secrets to examine" (*RG*, 26). In *The Rain God,* as in James's fiction, failure to get the point that directly confronts one is often a matter of life and death.

Another source of difficulty for early mainstream reviewers and readers is Islas's use of chronological dislocation: the free wandering flow of mind, back and forth in time, over names and events at least known to the narrator but not to us on a first reading. Early reviewers, like the editors of major publishing houses, were baffled by these techniques in Islas's art. "The first 78 pages," one reviewer wrote, "seemed to me nothing more than a long introduction to the scores of characters in the novel, in which each is described but not given enough depth or color to be believable. The net effect is one of wholesale confusion as the reader tries to memorize dozens of names and figure out their relationships in this fictional middle-class Mexican-American family" (*M*, 5). Capable of such remarks, the reviewer seems never to have read a Faulkner or García Márquez novel!

Additionally, Wallace Stevens's influence on *The Rain God* has not been noted by either Islas's mainstream or his brown "inside" reviewers and critics. Briefly, Stevens's entire poetic enterprise, as Daniel Hoffman pointed out, can be seen as a heroic and brilliant attack against the emptiness of "heaven," where "the death of one god is the death of all."[21] For Stevens, the withering away of traditional religion leaves the poet-artist of the twentieth-century with only the impoverished earth and what Stevens termed "the gaiety of language." Spirituality and its waning are also central to *The Rain God.*

Specifically, Stevens's classic poem "Sunday Morning" informs much of Islas's thinking about traditional religion, for the poem, as Stevens said in one of his letters, "was simply an expression of paganism" (Hoffman, "Poetry after Modernism," 442). Like Stevens's "Sunday Morning," Islas's *The Rain God* mounts a counterrhetoric against the words of idealism (*holy, divinity, lord, Jesus, soul*) by bringing those words into his Chicano narrative and bringing them to the southwest borderlands: freedom is rain, soul is sexual passion, the lord is the Amerindian Tlaloc (the rain god), and angels are well-built young men.

Stevens's "Sunday Morning," moreover, argues in a provocatively erotic language, what Frank Lentricchia calls a "gutsy, wet, blooming passion,"[22] that the Christian myth has outlived its usefulness, for just as Jove stayed inhuman in the clouds only until he could move among us, so a later God-myth went unrealized until "our blood" mingled with Christ's at Bethlehem and the "very hinds" or shepherds discerned it in a star. Stevens contends, the myth of Christ is as obsolete as the myth of Jove. Like Stevens, Islas argues in *The Rain God* that we are unable to look beyond the human for our gods. Thus, he suggests, even the gods need human flesh.

In short, Islas, like Stevens, gives his idealistic readers a lesson: we must avoid abstraction, fixed principles, and closed systems. Throughout *The Rain God,* he challenges the legitimacy of universals, repeatedly offsetting images of hollow spiritual categories with a wet, blooming imagery of a vibrant sexual world. To be sure, Islas, like Stevens, replaces the desolate Christian mythology with one of his own: he inverts the procedure of Christianity in which people reach toward paradise in humble supplication. Naked in the desert, gay Uncle Felix, the rain dancer, in a male utopian vision, chants not to but from paradise, not in supplication but in triumph, projecting himself from the center of the world, not from its margins.

If Islas belongs among those U.S. writers whose works have been defined by region, his double-voiced novel also has direct lines of kinship to the Latin American new writing by Juan Rulfo, Gabriel García Márquez, and Isabel Allende. Throughout Islas's desert tale, there are New World-Amerindian qualities that clearly identify the book with the Latin American and, more specifically, with the Mexican-Amerindian obsession with death. Islas digs deeply into the reality of his Chicano border culture by showing how the Angel family fits together in a postcontemporary borderlands cultural pattern.

Foremost in this Amerindian-New World context is the author's assumption that the moment of death does nothing to inhibit communication. This characteristic, thematized in Rulfo's classic Mexican novel, *Pedro Paramo,* García Márquez's *One Hundred Years of Solitude,* and Allende's *The House of Spirits,* stems from the New World idea of *almas en pena* (souls in torment) that wander the earth even after death.

At the novel's end, for example, Islas writes of Mama Chona's familiarity with *almas en pena:* "In the daytime, usually before the late afternoon meal, she would ask, 'Where is your father?' The first time she asked, Mema, surprised, told her straight-forwardly that he was dead. Without blinking, Chona retorted, 'Yes, but why doesn't he come to see me? Where is he?'" (*RG,* 172). On another occasion, Mama Chona, like Ursula Buendía in *One Hundred Years of Solitude,* matter-of-factly reveals to Mema that she has visited with her dead husband, Carlos: "I saw your father today. He was with that woman Josefina. They came to see me together, can you imagine? I knew he was seeing a great deal of her, but it was shameless of him to bring her here when there are children in the house. I will not forgive him for that" (*RG,* 172).

Mama Chona, to be sure, is not the novel's only character who is conversant with the Amerindian spiritual world. Nina, Miguel Chico's godmother, also is intimate with the supernatural: "The otherworldly side of her," Islas writes, "came to the surface before her son's death, and she explored it with the care and precision she used to prepare the annual income tax accounts of various business firms in town" (*RG,* 33). Like the best magic realist writers, Islas often turns his back on conventional realism. But it is important to note how, like García Márquez, he extends a magic realist situation to the edge of comedy and parody:

> It was not until she discovered the spirit world that Nina began to recognize that death might not exist as she imagined it in her terror. At the bi-weekly seances in the basement of her friends' Mexican food restaurant, her nose itched from the Aqua Velva they sprinkled into the air to induce serenity, Nina gradually became aware of two women waving at her from a strange and unknown region. They were about the same age and Nina saw with joy that one of the women was her sister, Antonia, who had died in her late twenties. The other woman was her mother, who at twenty-nine had died giving birth to Nina. (*RG,* 34)

The comical "signifyin[g]" distortion of reality at the seance—induced by the sprinkling of the aftershave in the air—conveys an absurd and humorous effect in Islas's *The Rain God*. Indeed, this humorous critique of the magic realist tradition informs much of Islas's comic-tragic novel. For example, when Juanita, Nina's sister, begins attending Nina's "classes in mind control," Islas "signifies" on García Márquez's fantastic world in *One Hundred Years of Solitude,* where one character literally ascends to heaven: "As a gesture of good will toward Nina's interest, Juanita had begun attending classes in mind control. It was her way of seeing to it that Nina did not ascend into heaven without her" (*RG*, 40). Like García Márquez's writing, then, Islas's prose style is usually plain, exact, and easily leaps into the comical and the exuberant. Although Nina's seance is accurately described, and with a wonderful, inventive touch, his desert tale in the end is always brought back to ordinary, local experiences.

Almost a year after Islas published *Migrant Souls*, a novel continuing the saga of the Angels, he died in February 1991 of complications from AIDS at his home on the Stanford campus. Though he did not identify himself as an openly gay Chicano writer, he did not shy away from presenting what we might call "the spectacle of the closet" as one of the truths of the Chicano homosexual on the bridge of sexuality. I want to end by discussing this as one of the most difficult problems of reading Islas: Is it possible to read *The Rain God* as the author's attempt to represent a male-gay thematics as precisely a liminal presence? Throughout the novel these gay thematics are absences. At the novel's beginning, the first, and perhaps the only, thing we learn about Miguel Chico is that he and his family have secret "sins," things unknown that he reveals in the writing of the book that we are reading. "Because he was still not married and seldom visited them in the desert," Islas writes, "they suspected that he, too, belonged on the list of sinners" (*RG*, 4). I would suggest that to the extent that Miguel Chico's "sin" has a form, that form is homosexuality. Certainly the Angel family suspect what the content of Miguel Chico's sin is, but, like Mama Chona, their looks and words "gave him that lost, uneasy feeling he had whenever any of his younger cousins asked him why he had not married. Self-consciously, he would say, 'Well, I had this operation,' stop there, and let them guess the rest" (*RG*, 5).

But why does Islas keep Miguel Chico closeted in the novel? Is the reader's "guessing" of the hero's sexuality merely a stylish narrative and Jamesian intertextual device? Male same-sex genitality, Eve Kosofsky Sedgwick suggests, has been historically "unspeakable, unmentionable, *nefandam libidinem*, that sin which should be neither named nor committed."[23] Silence is thus rendered throughout *The Rain God* as pointed and performative as speech in social spaces around the closet.

There are other lexical pointers as well throughout the novel to a gay meaning: "Maria made [Miguel Chico] a skirt and they watched him dance to the jitterbug music on the radio. . . . Miguel Grande had caught them at that once and made a terrible scene. . . . His father said nothing to him but looked at Juanita and accused her of turning their son into a *joto*" (*RG,* 16). Later, Islas writes that Miguel Chico "always felt that his father disliked him for being too delicate, too effeminate" (*RG,* 94). At the novel's end, Islas associates the hero's sin with the monster that "wake[d] him during the night": "The monster held Miguel Chico closely from behind. . . . Miguel Chico wanted to escape but could not. The monster's breath smelled of fresh blood and feces. . . . Although it moved away from him, Miguel Chico continued to feel its form pressed tightly against him, and the odor of its breath lingered, forcing him to gasp and struggle for air" (*RG,* 159–60). Why can't Miguel Chico face the gaze of the monster? Why does the author have him turn his back? As with James's move to have Marcher turn his back on the beast, for Miguel Chico to face the gaze of the monster is—as Sedgwick might put it—to erase the closet.

For critics intent on reading *The Rain God* as a depiction of a particular culture, "the epistemology of the closet" represented in Islas's narrative cannot easily be reconciled with elements of Latin-Amerindian spirituality or the allusions to canonical works of American literature. That Islas's multiply voiced fiction was stereotyped and ignored by mainstream presses demonstrates the Bercovitchean principle that innovative narratives often engender hostile criticism. My revisionist criticism recuperates Islas's work as a multiple syncretism of narrative practices of several pan-American traditions (Western European, Latin-Amerindian, southern, Chicano, gay) in recognizing that a postcolonial novel derives its power from its "discrepant" hybridity.[24]

Originally titled *Día de los Muertos* (Day of the Dead), Islas's novel challenges classic American literature's very concept of a straight, white male "tradition" as it has been traditionally taught in the academy, and deconstructs the one-dimensional (linear) view of history on which it is often predicated. Freed from strictly national U.S. genealogical imperatives, tradition in the author's sense of the Américas can be perceived as a system of affinities that are made independent of racial, ethnic, national, sexual, or linguistic criteria. Islas thus combines historical with literary revision by demonstrating the impact of what Mikhail Bakhtin called "hybridization" on literary production, specifically on questions of American literary canonization. Translating cultural interaction into an exchange of literary forms, Islas invalidates distinctions and proposes his own distinctive U.S.-Amerindian mythology of writing.

NOTES

A version of this essay appeared in *Dispositio* 16/41 (1991): 109–19. I would like to thank Carol Colatrella for her helpful reading of this work.

1. See, for example, Werner Sollors, ed., *The Invention of Ethnicity* (New York: Oxford University Press, 1989); Fredric Jameson, "Third World Literature in the Era of Multinational Capitalism," *Social Text* 15 (1986): 65–88; David Lloyd, *Nationalism and Minor Literature: James Clarence Mangan and the Emergence of Irish Cultural Nationalism* (Berkeley: University of California Press, 1987); and Arnold Krupat, *The Voice in the Margin: Native American Literature and the Canon* (Berkeley: University of California Press, 1989).

2. Charles Newman, *The Post-Modern Aura: The Act of Fiction in an Age of Inflation* (Evanston, Ill.: Northwestern University Press, 1985), 185.

3. William Boelhower, *Through a Glass Darkly: Ethnic Semiosis in American Literature* (New York: Oxford University Press, 1987), 33.

4. Krupat, *Voice in the Margin,* 183; hereafter abbreviated *V.*

5. See Sacvan Bercovitch, *The American Jeremiad* (Madison: University of Wisconsin Press, 1978).

6. Of course, editors at major publishing houses are agents of the professional-managerial class and are by no means neutral cultural workers. See Pierre Bordieu, *Distinction: A Social Critique of the Judgment of Taste,* trans. Richard Nice (Cambridge, Mass.: Harvard University Press, 1984).

7. Janice Radway, "The Book of the Month Club and the General Reader: On the Uses of 'Serious' Fiction," *Critical Inquiry* 14 (Spring 1988): 521.

8. Richard Ohmann, "The Shaping of a Canon: U.S. Fiction, 1860–1975," *Critical Inquiry* (September 1983): 202.

9. Arturo Islas, Arturo Islas Papers, Folder 1—Correspondence, Special Collections, Green Library, Stanford University; hereafter abbreviated *IP.*

10. Raymund Mungo, "Strange Murder in the Desert," review of *The Rain God* by Arturo Islas, *San Francisco Chronicle,* 4 November 1985, 5; hereafter abbreviated *M.*

11. Carol Fowler, "Death and Family Dominate Novel," review of *The Rain God* by Arturo Islas, *Contra Costa Times,* 26 January 1985, 1.

12. See Henry Louis Gates, Jr., "Introduction: Writing 'Race' and the Different It Makes," in *"Race," Writing, and Difference,* ed. Henry Louis Gates, Jr., (Chicago: University of Chicago Press, 1986), 1–20.

13. See Sacvan Bercovitch, "Discovering America: A Cross-Cultural Perspective" this volume.

14. Computer Curriculum Corporation of Palo Alto, California, was one of the first northern California Silicon Valley businesses to lend support to literature. Alexandrian Press was established as a division of Computer Curriculum to publish a few novels each year.

15. Eileen Walsh, "The Book Report," *Campus Report,* Stanford University, 16 January 1985, 1; hereafter abbreviated *W.*

16. For an historical analysis of the consensus ideology in classic American literature, see Sacvan Bercovitch, "The Rites of Assent: Rhetoric, Ritual, and Ideology of American Consensus," in *The American Self: Myth, Ideology, and Popular Culture,* ed. Sam B. Girgus (Albuquerque: University of New Mexico Press, 1981), 5–42.

17. W. J. Cash, *The Mind of the South* (New York: Knopf, 1941), 386–87.

18. Friedrich Nietzsche, *The Genealogy of Morals,* trans. Walter Kaufmann and R. J. Hollingdale (New York: Vintage, 1969). I am indebted to Rosaura Sánchez's graceful reading of resentment in Islas's novel. See her "Ideological Discourses in Islas' *The Rain God,*" in *Criticism in the Borderlands: Studies in Chicano Literature, Culture, and Ideology,* ed. Héctor Calderón and José David Saldívar (Durham, N.C.: Duke University Press, 1991), 114–26.

19. Arturo Islas, *The Rain God: A Desert Tale* (Palo Alto: Alexandrian Press, 1985), 28; hereafter abbreviated *RG.*

20. Stephen Donadio, *Nietzsche, Henry James, and the Artistic Will* (New York: Oxford University Press, 1984), 122; hereafter abbreviated as *N.*

21. Daniel Hoffman, "Poetry after Modernism," in *Harvard Guide to Contemporary American Writing* (Cambridge, Mass.: Harvard University Press, 1984), 442.

22. Frank Lentricchia, *Ariel and the Police: Michel Foucault, William James, Wallace Stevens* (Madison: University of Wisconsin Press, 1988), 156.

23. Eve Kosofsky Sedgwick, *Epistemology of the Closet* (Berkeley: University of California Press, 1990), 202.

24. For a sharp critique of the loose and ahistorical uses and abuses of the terms *postcolonial, hybridity,* and so on, see Ella Shohat's "Notes on the Post-Colonial," *Social Text* 31/32 (1992): 99–113. The term *discrepant* hybridities is James Clifford's. See his "Borders and Diasporas," unpublished manuscript, University of California, Santa Cruz.

KATHY SMITH

9

Norman Mailer and the Radical Text

Historical narration without analysis is trivial,
historical analysis without narration is incomplete.
Peter Gay, *Style in History*

CROSSING FRONTIERS

In order to oppose the state's power over the control and production of words, PEN, the international writers' organization, established a charter that expressed the need to protect writers from potential political oppression resulting from what they wrote. "Literature," reads the charter, "national though it be in origin, knows no frontiers, and should remain common currency between nations in spite of political or international upheavals."[1] To many PEN members, it must indeed have seemed like crossing new frontiers into enemy territory when their 1986 president, Norman Mailer, invited U.S. Secretary of State George Schultz to deliver the keynote address at the forty-eighth PEN conference in New York.

As Ronald Reagan's State Department chief, Schultz could not very well have been regarded as a facilitator of liberal thought. It was Schultz's public relations charge to rationalize spending cuts in arts and education programs while increasing the military budget. His rhetorical weapon was an un-self-consciously ironic one—

government noninterference in the private sector. Moreover, the administration's desire for control of words and information for ideological purposes was manifested, for example, in tacit support of attempts to have certain works of literature banned from public schools. Perhaps the most direct affront to the spirit of PEN's charter was the administration's decision to revive and enforce the McCarran-Walter Act, which denies individuals, including writers who are considered politically dangerous, entrance into the country. Mailer thus risked embarrassment, scorn, and political confrontation by asking Schultz to speak to a group that was alienated from that state's political acts and expressions.

Mailer, it seemed, was forcing the literary community to accept the state's chief administrator in order to dramatize the PEN topic of the day, "The Imagination of the Writer and the Imagination of the State." By so doing, he introduced and promoted a carnival quality in the literary-cum-political event; by inviting this confrontation he thereby made an appropriately incongruent spectacle. I say "appropriately" incongruent for two reasons. First, because Mailer's choice of speakers seemed calculated to create a disturbance, and that impulse is in keeping with Mailer's controversial public persona as a troublemaker. Second, because Schultz's being there raised two interesting speculations in relation to the imaginative connection between writing and the state: How would Schultz's voice, narrated in a traditional space of literature, call into question the "facticity" of state truth or institutionalized media truth? And what cultural effects proceed from the expansion of literary space to include the state as an author?

It seems likely, given the self-consciously political context of so much of his works and activities, that Mailer staged the event in a deliberate effort to politicize the literary and, conversely, to narrate the state's story in a literary setting. This act is clearly consistent with his criticism of the "cult of professionalism," which standardizes and opposes "fields" of cultural practice. He seems to share Edward Said's conviction that

> culture works very effectively to make invisible and even 'impossible' the actual affiliations that exist between the world of ideas and scholarship, on the one hand, and the world of brute politics, corporate and state power, and military force, on the other.[2]

By this grossly unpopular gesture, Mailer meant to make the invisible visible, the impossible, possible. Mailer also capitalized on a certain rhetorical freedom gained by another, nonaffiliative position in respect to PEN in order to test the literary forms that the group was willing to embrace. His connection with the press corps (PEN's purview extends to poets, playwrights, essayists, editors, and novelists) kept him "strange." Mailer the novelist converged with Mailer the journalist when he invited a media show at a conference that had meant to limit its politics to a *literary* discussion of the state's imagination. This freedom jeopardized his position as president of the organization, who, it was assumed, would speak for PEN with a certain measured, liberal authority. But it also allowed him to take up a position from which speculation on the notion of the writing "frontier" could take place.

Mailer's and Schultz's positions as "outsiders" and irritants at the conference did little to disguise their differences, which were glaringly obvious when they spoke. Schultz expressed predictable loyalty to, if not total agreement with, the rhetoric of the Right when he declared himself aligned with a government that upheld the autonomy of the private sphere:

> and that is why I am proud to represent an Administration that more than any in this century is committed in philosophy and in fact to reducing the intrusion of government into the lives, minds and livelihoods of the individual.[3]

Such claims serve a cultural history that continues to affirm, either through romance or parody, its ineluctable ties to the notion of rugged individualism as well as such prevailing dualities as head/heart, state/individual, public/private, and totalitarian/free. In his essay on ideology and American literature, Sacvan Bercovitch makes the important observation that the American experiment—its errand into the wilderness—has itself been a symbol of such affirmation.[4] According to its paradoxical logic, free choice and dissent appear to be the natural handmaidens of democracy. Individual difference, freedom, and opportunity are rhetorically championed, despite, and of course because of, our insistence on consensus. Bercovitch suggests that a peculiar feature of our cultural history is that the need for consensus is played out in a vital interchange between politics and culture:

> What could be a clearer demonstration of ideas in the service of power than the system of beliefs which the early colonists imposed on the so-called New World? What clearer demon-

> stration of the shaping power of ideology than the procession of declarations through which the republic was consecrated as New Israel, Nature's Nation in the Land of Futurity? 'America' is a laboratory for examining the shifting connections between politics . . . and cultural expression.[5]

Bercovitch's discussion of ideology and literature has a particular relevance here, since Schultz failed to satisfy Mailer's desire for border crossing in one important regard: He refused to recognize the rhetoric of consensus—"We the People"—or privileged exclusion—"The New Israel"—as part of a mythology that could break down when its fundamental assumptions were tested. Schultz would have Mailer believe that our "city on the hill" is protected by a truth that simply emerges from common sense and nature. The functional state metaphors could not be perceived as anything other than a natural outgrowth of Truth, Justice, and the American Way. The real, then, in the context of state imagination, is never allowed to be an unaccommodating or unwilling subject; rather, it is legitimized in the oxymoronic structure of the "true story."

Schultz's rhetoric rests on the oppositional structure that can, by consensus, replace one abstraction with another (individual vs. state) without admitting any overlap. These values operate within a system that produces a dichotomy between art and politics in order to, as Bercovitch suggests, "enforce the separation of 'spheres of influence.'"[6] While Schultz would keep those spheres discrete and uncontaminated, Mailer would like to run the "laboratory" where their shifts and collisions are produced. Schultz's division of individual and state into two neat and separate categories opposed Mailer's sense of movement between them. While in his speech to PEN Schultz expresses his conviction that the state must not be personified and that it has no imagination, Mailer's response on this occasion is to remark that this very imagination of the state and its intrusion into, and production of, our historical consciousness is what necessitates keeping records:

> I might go so far as to suggest that if the State does not possess imagination, then we are left with no need to write history . . . When states begin to perceive themselves as protagonists, that is to say, as embodiments of a creative vision, we may be entitled to speak not only of the imagination of the state, but to perceive of such states as actors in a scenario, or characters in a novel.[7]

In his assigning imagination to the state, Mailer seems to agree with Hegel's proposition that the state shapes the historical consciousness out of which form takes meaning:

> it is only the state which first presents subject-matter that is not only *adapted* to the prose of History, but involves the production of such history in the very progress of its own being.[8]

While for Mailer the state acts as a dynamic organism, not only selecting and disseminating a particular history that will conform to its own needs but actually producing it, Schultz characterizes the state as a kind of passive engine of the collective peoples' wills. If for Mailer the state is a living, breathing body, for Schultz it is a kind of shadow. Schultz's conception of statehood does not work for Mailer, because, in his view, politics take place in shifting narrative scenes whose true stories change with the telling.

COHESION AND DISSENT IN *ARMIES OF THE NIGHT*

Bercovitch writes that in creating America, the Puritans adopted a style of rhetoric capable of establishing a social contract that held forth the promise of fulfillment through a process that would continually invest the secular with the sacred.[9] Bercovitch "reads" America as a symbol of that fusion, and what attracts him to the living mythology of the American dream is the notion that the country,

> despite its arbitrary territorial limits, could read its destiny in its landscape, and a population that, despite its bewildering mixture of race and creed, could believe in something called an American mission, and could invest that patent fiction with all the emotional, spiritual, and intellectual appeal of a religious quest.[10]

In his Pulitzer Prize-winning novel, *Armies of the Night,* Mailer prompts his readers to examine that fiction by forcing political interference in the literary and vice versa. By reconstituting the connections between events and narrative interpretations of history, he thereby seeks to challenge the rhetoric of the American social contract.

By challenging the conventional workings of both narrative

and cultural symbology, Mailer's aim is twofold: to produce change in the way we come to knowledge and to avoid being disarmed and commodified by the ideological machine of consensus. If, as Bercovitch claims, the paradoxical logic of the American dream reveals that "progress and conformity stand . . . as the twin pillars of the American temple of freedom," and that "process and essence merge in the symbols of the Revolution,"[11] it is all the more interesting that Mailer should choose a seemingly subversive historical moment, the 1967 civil disobedience at the Pentagon, to test how he and other culture makers reshape history.

Rhetoric thematizes the individual *will* to truth or the desire to make sense of history. In *Armies of the Night,* Mailer implies that the history of his subject, America, is increasingly difficult to recognize, not only because of the absurdity of events, but because the historian must place himself in an ambiguous position when he attempts to record them:

> Either the century was entrenching itself more deeply into the absurd, or the absurd was delivering evidence that it was possessed of some of the nutritive mysteries of a marrow which would yet feed the armies of the absurd. So if the event took place in one of the crazy mansions, or indeed the crazy house of history, it is fitting that any ambiguous comic hero of such history should be . . . very much to the side of the history . . . thrusting itself forward the better to study itself . . . at home in a house of mirrors.[12]

Mailer makes the perhaps obvious but compelling point that if history does indeed inhabit a crazy house, and if the historian himself resides in a house of mirrors, the better to reproduce the craziness, it will be difficult to determine just where the missing center of history can be placed.

In journalism, the play on "center" and "self" is doubly interesting, because the codes built up by the profession act as a deterrent to the forbidden play of ego in the text. Mailer's strategy throughout *Armies of the Night* is to question the authority of the newspaper text and to discover the limits of the reporter's narrative practices by counterposing a more imaginative recorder of events:

> an eyewitness who is a participant but not a vested partisan is required, further he must be not only involved, but ambiguous

> in his own proportions, . . . is he finally comic, a ludicrous figure with mock-heroic associations; or is he not unheroic, and therefore embedded somewhat tragically in the comic? Or is he both at once, and all at once? (*Armies of the Night,* 67–68)

Mailer's ruminations proceed from a constant shifting of subject positions throughout the text. One of the effects of this shifting is to offset the conceptual associations that accumulate around and cling to the notion of "center." Of course, in the two passages quoted above, it is easy to locate a structural bias in Mailer's construction of history. He positions himself, for example, off "to the side" of history. Spatial metaphors are grounded in a structural philosophy whereby meaning can be permanently fixed (in a center, to the side). Their use here indicates Mailer's need to ground his provisional remarks in the language of authority. But that authority is contradicted by the house-of-mirrors metaphor and the unstable self as it mutates in an effort to make order out of confusion.

Mailer implies elsewhere that it is bad fiction to historicize events by claiming to have determined their natural boundaries. His purpose is certainly not to defer all judgments. Indeed, it is clear that Mailer is finally against the war in Vietnam that the "armies" have come to protest. It is more to his purpose to uncover connections where none seem to exist and to find differences "within" logical formations that the state imagination and media practices obscure by insisting on objective writing as truth rather than as metaphor for truth.

In the fun-house mirror, the subject watches the transmogrifying self observing the self-observing subject. What Mailer has come to know as history is reflected in this metaphor of the distorted images created by the act of looking. The metaphor is a rich one, inviting distortion of meaning, inviting the preemption of the event by the self, whose difference from itself requires a reexamination of the true story. For Mailer, the viewing subject's eye is the only legitimate mediator between the word and the event, but this eye is no longer "sanctified."

The assumption of the eye's sanctity is, of course, a major feature in the paradigm of the American dream, in the ideology of objectivity, and therefore in the rhetoric of the state and the media. For truth in history, the most credible and sought-after form of evidence has always been the eyewitness account. In *Armies of the Night,* the self's preemption of the story, the self *as* story, is the only strategy that can precipitate a radical rethinking of how history provides cohesive explanations of ambiguous events. If Mailer succeeds in disrupting the logic behind the truth of history, then he has corrupted, too, the equation by which the secular and sacred can fuse.

Within the context of the antiwar movement, Mailer develops the reader's wariness by distorting his own political views, calling himself a "Left Conservative." It is with this label in mind that Mailer wants us to receive his impressions about why we are in Vietnam. They are presented in such a way as to complicate apparently polarized positions: you are either for the war or against it. By way of condemning the war in Vietnam, he suggests that he will think "in the style of Marx in order to attain certain values suggested by Edmund Burke" (*Armies of the Night,* 208). He sets up several criteria by which a good war can be differentiated from a bad. As a Left *conservative,* Mailer finds that there are "roots" worth fighting for even at the cost of full-scale war: the preservation of a world in which justice, patriotism, and equality, for example, are valued in practice over genocide, colonization, class oppression, and exploitation. As a *Left* conservative, he also understands that these concepts do not operate in a vacuum. Supporters of the war in Vietnam use this rhetoric of worthy causes to support the very things they purport to fight against. A hidden agenda of the pro-Vietnam War rhetoric of making the world safe for democracy was spreading what Mailer calls the "cancer" of corporation land, a symptom of the colonizing adventure.

Mailer is not merely reciting whimsical, equal-but-opposite opinions that cancel each other out; those same opinions are marked by change and movement between contradictory positions. The bad war in Vietnam, ironically enough, is also a source of energy for him. Because it is a physical manifestation of the American sickness that he has been talking about for so long, he experiences the fulfillment of his prophetic ideas. According to Mailer, the war is also energizing for the country, because it allows what Bercovitch has argued is at the very heart of the American experiment—a convergence of state acts and cultural expression.

In Mailer's contextualizing of the war, objectivity is not reduced either to pure relativism or to absolute truth. He works the border between. And like the fun-house image of himself, the border is an impersonation, a mythical form that he wants to rewrite continually. Even when he pronounces upon specific social phenomena, the conclusions are apt to partake of a symptomatic inconclusiveness. It is not that he gives no clear message, but rather the message is itself clearly contradictory:

> He had come to decide that the center of America might be insane. The country had been living with a controlled, even fiercely controlled, schizophrenia which had been deepening with the years . . . Any man or woman who was devoutly Christian and worked for the American Corporation had been caught in an unseen vise whose pressure could split their mind from their soul. For the center of Christianity was a mystery, a son of God, and the center of the corporation was a detestation of mystery, a worship of technology. (*Armies of the Night,* 212).

The deep-seated affliction of the schizophrenia indicates that the effects of both the war and the demonstration on the national psyche will be difficult to assess. On the one hand, "the good Christian Americans needed the war or they would lose their Christ," assuming that Christianity is predicated on sacrifice and purification. By a strange convoluted logic, the Christian supporters of the war wanted it so that they could get their payback on the middle class, whose identification with "technology land" and the corporation targeted it as the oppressor. The war presented for the working class the possibility for a potential destruction of technology in an all-out war that would signal a new beginning, a return to the roots. Being hopelessly victimized by his own schizophrenia, however, the average American did not resist the war in Vietnam, for precisely the opposite reason: to join the protest was to fight "the cold majesty of the corporation," which had come to be regarded as another promise of peace:

> The Corporation was what brought him his television and his security, the Corporation was what brought him the unspoken promise that on Judgment Day he would not be judged, for Judgment Day—so went the unspoken promise—was no worse than the empty spaces of the Tonight Show when you could not sleep (*Armies of the Night,* 212–13).

The absurdity of the march thematized in *Armies of the Night* makes sense to an historian who understands how the events of history serve as media fetishes, that is, how events are made to act as symbols of events or spectacles of themselves. One aspect of the absurdity of the protest march on the Pentagon, for example, is that it was negotiated in advance, on the one hand so that it could remain controlled, predictable, and safe, and on the other so that it would receive the kind of media coverage that would reflect its radical departure from the everyday. The march is a wonderful example of Bercovitch's claim that cultural symbols do the work of ideology by pushing continually for consensus. The potential subversive quality of the march was undercut before it began by everyone involved in its orchestration. The one chance for what Yippie leaders called "revolution by theatre and without a script" (*Armies of the Night,* 249) was summarily squashed, not only by armed National Guardsmen but by the protest organizers themselves.

One can only give lip service to the forms of dissent already destined to be absorbed into the consensual language of American politics. The march's revolutionary aesthetic, as David Eason suggests, turns on the protest organizers' "absorption in the techniques of media production that threatens to transform protesters into actors."[13] The house-of-mirrors metaphor calls attention to this imminent transformation and suggests that a critical self-reflexivity could act as a corrective to what Eason calls the "disjunction between the symbolic and the real that pervades modern culture."[14] It is the historical "lie" that results from the perceived *conjunction* between real and symbolic that Mailer's book is about.

In the process of writing, Mailer feeds into the narrative something like a confession of the author's entrapment from within; characters and witnesses are unable to break from the "tower" of their egos, and that creates a vague awareness that choice is mere illusion. Mailer senses, too, that the massive institutions of America have an independent life of their own that he cannot check or change regardless of what he writes. Moreover, he is frightened by the ambiguous episodes of history that force him to question his fractured memory: at these moments he can never be sure of the clarity of his own record. Society, represented as a thing with its own dynamics, quite beyond human control, keeps expanding to accept more towers, and as the towers proliferate, they all begin to look alike.

The metaphor of the tower is one that appears often in our literary culture. It is manifested as prison, asylum, and privileged vantage point. As in the Rapunzel myth, the tower imprisons the subject and keeps it from the broad possibilities of experience. It keeps us safe from our own "bad" desires, creating the illusion of a natural fate and an appropriate end. It is both safety and confinement. It also commands a superior view of the forest and the liberating hero, the one fate that may make escape from the tower possible. However, despite one's having made eye contact with a world that appears separate and outside the tower, the suspicion remains that it is the tower itself that creates the special illusion of pattern. The meaning we assign reality and from which we gain control and assurance, the meaning that conditions choices, is a function of the tower, and escape may thus be impossible.

Is the tower all? This question remains strategically posed between the text's two books, "History as a Novel" and "The Novel as History." The first book, which reads like a novel, is the only accurate "firsthand" version of the march that Mailer can produce. It is a more "reliable" account because it does not make claims to truth but instead shows a grim determination to record his own participation in the event even at the risk of appearing unreliable. The second book, which reads like a journalistic account, is really a "condensation of a collective novel" in which every bit of information is gathered from other sources and then remodeled (*Armies of the Night,* 284)

The word "as" in the titles of Books 1 and 2, respectively, "History as a Novel" and "the Novel as History," operates by displacement. That is, "as" denotes a metaphorical relationship between history and fiction, implying not only that history is *like* fiction, and vice versa, but that one always contains the other even when the writing does not happen to be overtly metaphorical or self-conscious. Mailer uses "as" to complicate the terms, allowing them to merge into one another. The disturbing relativity that threatens public truth when it is made up of only individual truths is held off by the parameters of the historical event and the self-conscious positioning of the author in a specific place in respect to that event.

So, rather than produce a stabilized version of history through what looks like a balanced presentation of the event in two separate books, Mailer disrupts his own scheme by constantly reinterpreting his observations. His provisional contexts have the effect of uniting the writing act and the event, but the union is always fraught with tensions—between text and context, and between his direct experience of the event and its subsequent reproduction as text. For example, in book 1, Mailer describes his arrest after deliberately crossing a military police line at the demonstration in the Pentagon parking lot. He is taken by a U.S. marshal to await his incarceration and notes that while he is being escorted away, the marshal's hand, which now encircles his arm, is trembling. For Mailer the incident is worth noting in the context of the march and subsequent arrest precisely because, added up, such details describe and limit the way in which the event can be interpreted. However, the significance of this detail cannot clearly be determined from Mailer's account. It must be held in suspense, and consequently it colors the event, which vibrates with possibilities:

> Mailer's arm was being held in the trembling grip of a U.S. Marshal . . . Whether this was due to a sudden onrush—quote Freud from a letter to Fliess—of "unruly latent homosexuality" or whether from a terror before God that they judged other men sufficiently to make arrest, or whether simply they were cowards, or if to the contrary they trembled from the effort it cost them to keep from assaulting the prisoner, whatever, Mailer could not quite decide—he had sometimes even wondered if it had to do with the incongruities of his own person. (*Armies of the Night,* 156)

Mailer directs us to a story that is *as* true as author is *as* self, both story and self are compositers of an indistinct meaning constructed with unreliable tools. More important, however, is Mailer's message that once one comes to recognize the true story as a replica of or metaphor for truth, then history becomes a more reliable record, capable of being distinguished from ideological practice.

The problem for Mailer's readers, in trying to access history through an historian who "is not one," corresponds with the conflicts Mailer encounters when he explores the nature of communication itself. He finds that those official media channels one relies on for recognizable representations of reality are the less reliable the more they are seen as institutionalized information centers that claim to tell the facts but do not add, as Carlin Romano convincingly demonstrates in his essay, "The Grisly Truth about Bare Facts," that these facts are really statements "based on inferences from traces of the events."[15]

Mailer's advertisement is always for a self that is different from what it says it is, and these personae eventually clash with the historian who wants to recreate the world in its own image. Traditionally, the historian tries to silence these other voices so that his masterpiece might be purified of any romantic taint of subjectivity. Mailer, of course, encourages those personae to speak. For example, in the penultimate chapter of book 1, "The Communication of Christ," Mailer ministers to the waiting crowd after just having been released from a night in jail:

> '. . . You see, dear fellow Americans, it is Sunday, and we are burning the body and blood of Christ in Vietnam. Yes, we are burning him there, and as we do, we destroy the foundation of this Republic, which is its love and trust in Christ.' He was silent. Wow. (*Armies of the Night,* 239)

One of the things that Mailer should *not* say here is that he is a Jew. His positioning of himself as a member of a group whose foundation was not the love of Christ would have nullified his speech and made him appear not himself, an impostor, insincere and ridiculous. And it is precisely in this "existential" moment that Mailer wants to appear most sincere, most docile, most responsible. In fact, though, Mailer starts the speech by mentioning that he is not a Christian. He hopes to give the impression, perhaps, that his Jewish self is subsumed or assimilated in his American one. He emphasizes his participation in the demonstration in order to ground his evocation of mystery and faith in Christ (whom he refers to as a "revolutionary") in concrete political acts that could identify hopeful change. Because he senses that his audience needs some sense of closure after the events of the march, he calls up the most reassuring associations of love, forgiveness, and regeneration. Moreover, he cleverly connects Christ with America, again multiplying associations between state and cultural practice, associations he reinforces throughout the text, for example, when he compares Christ and Jerry Rubin as revolutionaries.

The speech testifies to Mailer's capacity to understand what Bercovitch calls the centrality of the Puritan errand of revolution in the wilderness to American culture. At the same time, he is very much aware of the incongruent spectacle he makes when he envelopes the last words of perhaps his finest hour of the weekend in a romantic rhetoric at odds with an earlier harsh and obscene speaking stint at the Ambassador Theatre. Rather than ignore the contradiction between his previous public speech act as the "beast" and this "modest" Judeo-Christian version, he interrupts his speech twice precisely to call attention to his masquerade. His speech, therefore, is another "act" of speech. Twice referring to himself in the third person, he establishes an effective literary distance between his writing and speaking self, a strategy he uses throughout the text. He is only able to *say* the difference that would negate the Christian self—"I am Jewish"—by creating separate personalities that coexist, and, at the same time, have in common the trait that they are aware of themselves as incomplete and unreliable.

Mailer ends book 1 with a report from the *Washington Post* based on this same Sunday speech on America and Christianity. Mailer's words are effectively undercut in the context of the report, which ends as follows:

> Mailer said he believed that the war in Vietnam 'will destroy the foundation of this republic, which is its love and trust in Christ.' Mailer is a Jew. (*Armies of the Night,* 240)

Clearly the *Post* cannot be faulted for deliberately "misrepresenting" the facts. What the newspaper story has kept silent, however, is that those facts have been arranged in such a way as to produce a calculated response. Because the newspaper business operates on the assumption that provisional truth is no better than a lie, "salience" must substitute for complexity as a measure of understanding history. Of course, it is this very desire for salience that often causes an important context of historical events to go unrecorded. Also, the expectation of salience is a convenient screen for editorializing even when the "facts" seem to speak for themselves. By beginning the *Post* story with the lead, "Novelist Norman Mailer using a makeshift courtroom to deliver a Sunday sermon on the evils of the Vietnam war . . . ," the writer sets up for a satirical treatment of the subject. Readers might bring a more serious consideration to the subject had the report begun, for example, with "Arrested demonstrator, novelist Norman Mailer . . ." Beginning with "Novelist Norman Mailer" and ending with "is a Jew" gives the report a neat balance: We are invited to take Mailer's modest comments about Vietnam and Christianity with a grain of salt because he is, first of all, a novelist prone to fictionalizing, as he himself has taken pains to show, and, second of all, a Jew, who, perhaps, lacks the authority or conviction to proselytize for Christianity. The newspaper account, then, *also* calls attention to Mailer's speech as a speech *act.* But it is a one-dimensional account that offers no counter to the sarcastic tone with which Mailer is treated.

Clearly, *Armies of the Night* includes other journalistic reports in it so that readers can compare texts and intertexts and make their own judgments about reliability. Indeed, Mailer's invitation to Schultz tested the PEN event's capacity to bear such intertextuality. It is to be expected, perhaps, that in a style-conscious city like New York, in the midst of politically conscious writers like Grace Paley, it was difficult even for Schultz to take his role as author seriously. He opened his speech with a glib remark about his lack of artistic credentials: "I can only regard Norman Mailer's invitation to me as another shining example of that charitable spirit for which New York literary circles have long been famous."[16] Indeed, his presence there makes little sense if we continue to regard the domain of narrative as a strictly novelistic one. But the power of story and narrative to "assist" truth is not an exclusively novelistic practice. The fear of the state's misuse of the power of language to construct cultural truths occasioned the establishment of PEN in the first place.

Since Mailer is so self-consciously directing our own reading event, it is perhaps fitting to end with a final note on his own style of dissent. As he is being arrested, Mailer reveals that he has made a deal with the BBC to photograph his every move during the demonstration. How, we are invited to ask, has the BBC's role in filming Mailer "meddled" in the playing out of history and increased, if that is possible, Mailer's already "disproportionate" egotism and self-consciousness? Mailer's confession emphasizes once more how he comes to terms with doubt and uncertainty about the real. By agreeing to have himself filmed, he once more complicates the fun-house-mirror metaphor and forces us to question the image (in this instance the one that depicts Mailer as moral hero) he desires to be true and natural.

For politicians and journalists, narrative's capacity to challenge the notion of the real as a bare fact presents a theoretical crisis of monumental proportions, if only because the codes for guaranteeing accuracy and protection against the invasion of fiction are so firmly entrenched in cultural practice. The crisis remains an issue for the state and the media because ideology breaks down under the skeptical scrutiny of central symbols like "the City on the Hill." The city cannot be replaced by a faulty tower.

Mailer's nonfiction novel introduces a critique of the value system based on an ahistorical, Aristotelian notion of immutable forms, and commensurability between the logos and the real. Read as literature, texts conventionally received as nonliterature can be reassessed in light of a metaphorical play. By reinvesting nonfictional discourse with literary possibilities, Mailer disturbs carefully drawn categories, and the consequent convergence of historical, novelistic, and ideological practices undermines consensual logic.

NOTES

1. Richard Stern, "Penned In," *Critical Inquiry* 13 (Autumn 1986).

2. Edward Said, "Opponents, Audiences, Constituencies, and Community," in *The Anti-Aesthetic: Essays on Postmodern Culture,* ed. Hal Foster (Port Townsend, Wash.: Bay Press, 1983), 145.

3. George Schultz, "The Writer and Freedom," Current Policy No. 782, (Washington D.C.: Department of State, Bureau of Public Affairs), 2.

4. Sacvan Bercovitch, "The Problem of Ideology in American Literary History," *Critical Inquiry* 12 (Summer 1986): 641.

5. Ibid., 635.

6. Ibid., 636.

7. Norman Mailer, "The Writer's Imagination and the Imagination of the State," *New York Review of Books,* 13 February 1986, 23.

8. G. W. F. Hegel, *Lectures on the Philosophy of History,* trans. J. Sibree (New York: Dover, 1956), 63.

9. Sacvan Bercovitch, *The American Jeremiad* (Madison: University of Wisconsin Press, 1978), 9.

10. Ibid., 11.

11. Ibid., 149.

12. Norman Mailer, *Armies of the Night: History as a Novel, the Novel as History* (New York: Signet, 1968), 68.

13. David Eason, "The New Journalism and the Image-World: Two Modes of Organizing Experience," *Critical Studies in Mass Communication* 1 (March 1984): 62.

14. Ibid., 60.

15. Carlin Romano, "The Grisly Truth about Bare Facts," in *Reading the News,* ed. Michael Schudson and Robert K. Manoff (New York: Pantheon Books, 1986), 77. In his discussion of truth as historically conditioned concepts, Romano is referring specifically to Richard Rorty's *Philosophy and the Mirror of Nature* and to the work of Hans-Georg Gadamer and Michel Foucault.

16. Schulz, "The Writer and Freedom," 1.

Part IV

Problems of Marginality in America

HELEN BURKE

10

Problematizing American Dissent: The Subject of Phillis Wheatley

In his *History of Sexuality,* Michel Foucault argues that our conceptual model of power has not changed very much since the Middle Ages. "At bottom, despite the differences in epoch and objectives," Foucault writes, "the representation of power has remained under the spell of monarchy. In political thought and analysis, we still have not cut off the head of the king."[1] This critique may not at first seem relevant to America, a political entity that originated in a struggle against kings and that defined itself in the apparently very antimonarchical discourse of pluralism, a rhetoric that asserts the "unalienable rights" of all "men." However, if we follow Foucault in identifying monarchy with a particular formulation of power—its conceptualization in juridical terms—the significance of this critique and its implications for political dissent become apparent. Despite the shift to a pluralist model of government, America, it could be argued, continues to conceive of power in a traditional way, shaping its political debate in terms characteristic of juridical monarchy by focusing on problems "of right and violence, law and illegality, freedom and will, and especially the state and sovereignty (even if the latter is questioned insofar as it is personified in a collective being and no longer a sovereign individual)."[2] Disenfranchised social groups, "the many," thus continue to pit themselves against "the one," though now the "one" is the existing consensus and not the king. Sacvan Bercovitch identifies the particular American variant of this ancient struggle in his description of how this country deals with dissent:

> The American way is to turn potential conflict into a quarrel about fusion or fragmentation. It is a fixed match, a debate with a foregone conclusion: you must have your fusion and feed on fragmentation too. And the formula for doing so has become virtually a cultural reflex: you just alternate between harmony-in-diversity and diversity-in-harmony. It amounts to a hermeneutics of laissez-faire: all problems are obviated by the continual flow of the one into the many, and the many into the one.[3]

What is omitted in this juridical conceptualization of power, whether in its monarchist or pluralist formulation, is the operation of those factors that are not reducible to the representation of law. Relations of power, as Foucault points out, "are not in a position of exteriority with respect to other types of relationships (economic processes, knowledge relationships, sexual relations), but are immanent in the latter, and conversely they are the internal conditions of these differentiations."[4] This connection with other types of relations is, however, obscured in the monarchical and in the pluralist models that locate power in a superstructural position and that frame the questions of power in terms of rights and prohibitions. As Ellen Rooney points out, in order to work, pluralism must create the fiction of a community in which the participating subjects all have equal rights and are equally vulnerable to persuasion, but it can create this fiction only by ignoring the historical, unavoidable givens that make for the inequality between subjects in power relations; it has to exclude the differences that Wayne Booth, in defending pluralism, calls "irrational forces (your id, your class, your upbringing, your inherited language)."[5] The rhetoric of pluralism in Bercovitch's words, can thus itself become "an ideological trap,"[6] a means of avoiding the questions raised by dissent that often originates in the felt disjunction between rhetoric and reality. The problem of the differential relation to power created by material differences—a lived experience for many who are, for example, born poor or black or female—cannot be articulated, much less addressed, in a legalistic model of power that constructs each person, no matter of what class, ethnicity, or gender, as an equal subject in discourse.

To make this point more concretely, I will turn here to the subject of Phillis Wheatley, an African-American writer who wrote poetry in this country in the late eighteenth century. I am focusing on Wheatley because as a black woman and a slave, Wheatley is representative of those traditionally excluded from American political discourse on the basis of ethnicity, sex, and class. Her struggle to constitute herself as a political subject is illustrative of the struggle of many such marginalized subjects to gain political recognition in America. As the first black writer to publish a book in the United States, Wheatley, Henry Louis Gates, Jr., points out, has also stood for many years in a synechdochal relation to "black art,"[7] so that her struggle is also emblematic of the struggle of nontraditional literary subjects to gain inclusion in the hegemonic literary culture. I will argue that in both these domains, the political and the artistic, we can see the same complex operation of an ideology that establishes the subject in discourse as a fiction that makes it difficult to see the position of the historical subject, the workings of an ideology that, as Bercovitch argues, "denies limitation rhetorically, in order to facilitate the continuity of certain rhetorical forms."[8] In Wheatley, I will suggest, we can see both the potential and the limitation of a particular rhetoric of "equal rights," the success and failure of the concept of America.

What has first to be acknowledged is the Phillis Wheatley American success story, the remarkable degree to which Phillis Wheatley achieved her goal in establishing herself as a subject in American political and cultural discourse. Arriving in this country as a slave, "a poor, naked child" who had "no other covering than a quantity of dirty carpet about her like a fillibeg,"[9] Wheatley began her career in a state of deprivation that was symbolic as well as material. The captors who had deprived her of her freedom had also deprived her of her family, her community, her name, and her language, so that Wheatley had to reconstruct her identity on every level. Although the conditions under which she labored were very different, her story of identity making, in these respects, is not dissimilar to that of many other emigrants who came to this country. Like these other politically and culturally displaced persons, she set about making an alien culture her own, adopting a strategy of symbolic appropriation in the best tradition of the melting pot.

Wheatley appropriates, first of all, the literary conventions of her time. She uses the heroic couplet popularized by Pope, Dryden, and Johnson as her verse form; the New England funeral elegy as her predominant genre; and the poetics of the mid-eighteenth-century sublime as her aesthetic.[10] More important then her use of traditional forms for her success, however, is her understanding of how the process of poetic legitimation works in the Western European literary tradition. Wheatley accepts, as does, for example, her predecessor Alexander Pope, that the individual writer has significance strictly in relation to this tradition. To establish a literary identity, to earn the title *poet,* one had to insert oneself into this tradition, recognizing the tradition, even while asserting one's own right to speak. When, in the first poem of her 1773 volume of poetry, Wheatley discusses her own poetic talents in the context of Homer and Virgil, she implicitly makes this assertion. The fact that she derides her talents in relation to these great classical writers—"But here I sit, and mourn a grov'ling mind / That fain would mount and ride upon the wind"[11]—should not obscure the fact that she is claiming the Muse. The young African-American writer's self-deprecation here is as conventional as the young Pope's in his "Essay on Criticism," where he similarly defines himself as an unworthy inheritor of the classical tradition, the Muse who "no more attempts to *rise* / But in low Numbers short Excursions tries."[12] Wheatley's negative comparison of her own talents to that of "the happier *Terence,*" who, as she explains in a note, "was an *African* by birth," is similarly merely conventional but is even more significant to her process of poetic self-definition. This insertion of a black literary predecessor into the Western tradition is a demand for recognition by the tradition of her own black voice, a right she reemphasizes constantly by identifying her writing persona with her ethnic background; as "an *Ethiop*" ("To the University of Cambridge . . .") (16); "Your vent'rous *Afric*" ("On Recollection") (62); "*Afric's* muse" ("An Hymn to Humanity") (97).

Wheatley exploits, then, the potential for the emergence of the new inherent in the traditional concept of the poetic tradition, a potential that T. S. Eliot best articulated. Eliot's essay "Tradition and the Individual Talent" is an excellent elaboration of the kind of literary pluralism that permits a new voice like Wheatley's to emerge. If, as Eliot argues, "the existing order is complete before the new work arrives," this order is nevertheless subject to constant modification. With the introduction of the new, "the whole existing order must be, if ever so slightly altered: and so the relations, proportions, values of each work of art towards the whole are readjusted; and this is conformity between the old and the new."[13] In literary terms, this process also entails "the continual flow of the one into the many, and the many into the one," a process that allows the "mind of Europe"[14] to remain constant, while permitting new voices to be heard. It is this literary pluralism that Wheatley engages when she defines herself as "*Afric's* muse" while at the same time conforming to the existing literary tradition. She makes a space for herself, gains admission, as it were, into the canon by engaging the tradition in its own terms, by making its language her own.

Wheatley's ability to comprehend and manipulate traditions and conventions is not, however, confined to the literary realm. She knows her new country's political as well as its poetical ideology, and she engages the former as much as the latter in the process of identity making. It could be said that in one of her earliest poems, "America," she acknowledges this function of political rhetoric in establishing her rights as a subject: "Thy Power, O Liberty, makes strong the weak / And (wond'rous instinct) Ethiopians speak" (134). It was indeed the power of "Liberty," the power of a rhetoric of "America," that gave her a voice, a rhetoric that she uses skillfully to claim her place in the political symbolic structure.

In a letter to the Rev. Samson Occom, the converted Mohegan Indian, a letter printed in the *Connecticut Gazette* in 1774 and then widely reprinted in other New England papers, Wheatley makes her strongest statement about liberty and the rights of African Americans. Her "Vindication" of the rights of "the Negroes" is based on her notion that religious and civil liberties are "so inseparably united, that there is little or no Enjoyment of one without the other" and also on the notion that the "Love of Freedom" is a divinely implanted "Principle" in all people. Biblical narrative is used to substantiate the claim that the struggle for freedom has a religious dimension. An implicit comparison is made between the bondage of the Israelites and the enslaved black people, so that the present supporters of slavery become "Modern Egyptians" (176–77). Wheatley's conflation here of secular history with divine is a defining characteristic of American political rhetoric. "Of all symbols of identity," Bercovitch writes in his discussion of American symbology, "only *America* has united nationality and universality, civic and spiritual selfhood, secular and redemptive history, the country's past and paradise to be, in a single synthetic ideal."[15] It is this kind of ideal that Wheatley holds up when she writes of the "Love of Freedom," and it is the failure on the part of slaveholders in relation to this ideal that she condemns, "the strange Absurdity of their Conduct whose Words and Actions are so diametrically opposite" (177). But it is not only the message but also the voice here that is embedded in the tradition. In the last line of her letter, Wheatley writes, in a tone that is uncharacteristically sharp: "How well the Cry for Liberty, and the reverse Disposition for the Exercise of oppressive Power over others agree—I humbly think it does not require the Penetration of a Philosopher to determine" (177). The professed humility here does not mask the note of condemnation, a condemnation that is reminiscent of what Bercovitch calls "the American jeremiad," the political sermon that both praises the American ideal and often scathingly criticizes the community for its failure to live out the dream.[16] It is again her unerring sense of the tradition that permits Wheatley to claim this rhetorical stance for her own advantage. Just as she cleverly invokes the literary tradition to establish her poetic authority, so here she invokes the ideological tradition to establish her political authority, an authority that allows her to speak forcefully on the issue of racial inequity.[17]

This strategy of engaging the rhetoric of "Liberty" and using it against itself is also apparent in a number of her poems, though usually applied less overtly than in her letter to Occom. Frequently (and to the dismay of those who look in her work for evidence of opposition to the dominant culture),[18] she, like the Puritan political preachers, praises America as a providentially chosen defender of freedom. This is "the land of freedom's heaven-defended race," she writes in a poem in praise of George Washington (146), while in her poem "Liberty and Peace" she sees the success of the Revolution as a divinely ordained victory for freedom: "LO! Freedom comes. Th'prescient Muse foretold, / All Eyes th'accomplish'd Prophecy behold" (154). But, as in the Occom letter, she often accompanies praise with a reminder of America's failure toward black people. In her poem "To the Right Honourable William, Earl of Dartmouth," in the most self-revelatory passage in her writing, she uses her own experience of oppression to make her point. After celebrating the newly won freedom of "America," which now will no longer suffer "the iron chain, / Which wanton *Tyranny* with lawless hand / Had made, and with it meant t'enslave the land" (74), she turns to her own case to explain her interest in and "love of *Freedom*":

> I, young in life, by seeming cruel fate
> Was snatch'd from *Afric's* fancy'd happy seat
> What pangs excruciating must molest,
> What sorrows labour in my parent's breast?
> Steel'd was that soul and by no misery mov'd
> That from a father seiz'd his babe belov'd:
> Such, such my case. And can I then but pray
> Others may never feel tyrannic sway? (74)

The criticism of slavery is again evident, though her desire here is clearly to reach the conscience of her readers by moving them rather than by pointing out logical inconsistencies. In an elegy on General David Wooster, a revolutionary leader, her condemnation is, however, more forcefully stated, the use of the dramatic persona (she places the following prayer in the dead general's mouth) allowing her more license to speak openly:

> "But how, presumptous shall we hope to find
> Divine acceptance with th'Almighty mind—
> While yet (O deed Ungenerous!) they disgrace
> And hold in bondage Afric's blameless race?
> Let Virtue reign—And thou accord our prayers
> Be victory our's, and generous freedom theirs." (149–50)

Again the tone of the preacher is heard in this denunciation, the rhetoric of the Old Testament prophet who denounces his society while at the same time acknowledging his people's special destiny.

Wheatley thus can be placed in a long line of American writers from John Winthrop to Martin Luther King, Jr., who used the rhetoric of the American dream with its central value of "Liberty" to win acceptance by the American people. Like these other interpreters of the American "errand," she plays a role that is both supportive and adversarial, the role of what Michael Walzer calls the "connected critic":

> He is not a detached observer, even when he looks at the society he inhabits with a fresh and skeptical eye. He is not an enemy, even when he is fiercely opposed to this or that prevailing

> practice or institutional arrangement. His criticism does not require detachment or enmity, because he finds a warrant for critical engagement in the idealism, even if it is a hypocritical idealism, of the actually existing moral world.[19]

It is this stance that Wheatley adopts. Her criticism works from within the culture's own controlling metaphors, exploiting the possibilities inherent in America's assumptions and beliefs to create a place for herself within its symbolic structures.

Given her aim to acquire a political and literary identity, it could be said that her strategy worked. Phillis Wheatley made, and is still making, a name for herself. In her own lifetime, her writing won her the notice of the governing elite of her day, both in this country and in Europe, and was no doubt instrumental in forging her own freedom as a political subject (she was manumitted shortly after the publication of her poems in London, probably because of the moral pressure on the Wheatleys from the reviewers of her work).[20] As a literary subject, her claim to an equal place within the tradition was also successful. Since her death, her small volume of poetry has been reprinted more than two dozen times, appearing most recently at the head of the Schomburg Library Series of Nineteenth-Century Black Women Writers, where she is given an honorable place as the founder of the black American literary tradition.[21] As more scholarly attention is paid to her work, her more general literary and historical contribution is also being acknowledged (her originality in the use of the elegy; her significance as a poet of the American Revolution).[22] As Wheatley was marginalized because of her ethnicity, gender, and class, her career could be read as a success story that is indicative of the potential for all nontraditional subjects to be heard, a tribute to America's liberal pluralism, with its ability to absorb constantly new subjects, to expand and redefine who "we the people" are, whether in art or politics.

But then there is the problem of Phillis Wheatley, historical subject, a problem that the success story of Phillis Wheatley, rhetorical subject, tends to obscure. The problem is that the real Phillis Wheatley and the black people whose voice she represented continued to experience social and economic deprivation, even while "*Afric's* Muse" was being privileged and celebrated—a continued material inequity that itself was outside the parameters of Phillis Wheatley's pluralist discourse. It is true, as we have just seen, that Wheatley's writing itself draws attention to the injustices of slavery and even, on one occasion, draws specific attention to the poet's own personal suffering. What her writing could not address, however, was the power structure that determined this writing's production or that occasionally permitted such a critique to take place. As Bruce Erlich points out, "ontological and epistemic-methodological pluralism are themselves abstractions into a specific philosophic vocabulary of preexisting contexts of choice and power—and so is 'communication.'" To overlook these contexts, "the power of the world in which texts and criticism reside," is to feed into the existing structure: to cede "even greater power to the forces that already exist and that remain untouched by gestures of 'dialogue.'"[23]

To survive, to be heard at all, Phillis Wheatley had to cede this power, though to say this is by no means to subtract from her great achievement in exploiting the system to its fullest potential. Wheatley's reaction to her predicament as an artist in white America may have been similar to James Baldwin's. Speaking of his initial relation to the white tradition, Baldwin recalls his recognition that he would have to use that culture: "I would have to appropriate those white centuries, I would have to make them mine—I would have to accept my special attitude, my special place in this scheme—otherwise I would have no place in *any* scheme."[24] Wheatley too had to accept the scheme, in both its literary and its social manifestations, because there was no other scheme, and, as we have seen, she worked this scheme to say as much as she could. But as we have also seen in the discussion of her writings, it is the similarities between herself and the larger culture (a similar literary understanding, a similar acceptance of the rhetoric of "Liberty") that she had to emphasize if she was to be accepted. What Phillis Wheatley could not address was the difference that her ethnic background, sex, and class made in her ability to express herself freely, a difference that, if elaborated, would have exposed the inequity of the power relations in which she operated.

It is these inequitable power relations, then, that we must readmit if we are to understand the constraints under which Wheatley operated, constraints that the ideology itself sought to exclude with its myth of "the extraordinary negro girl" who produced great art "by her own application, unassisted by others."[25] As is evidenced by the many prefatory letters that precede her 1773 volume of poems, Phillis Wheatley exists as a speaking subject only within the boundaries defined by the hegemonic culture. The title page that describes her as "Negro Servant to Mr. John Wheatley of Boston, New England" and John Wheatley's own letter to the publisher both indicate the degree to which she was not her own subject, while the letter of attestation, signed by eighteen of Boston's social and economic elite (including such notables as John Hancock and His Excellency, Thomas Hutchinson, governor of Massachusetts), indicates the broader social and political context that controlled her. Earlier attempts to solicit subscriptions to a proposed edition of Phillis Wheatley's work had failed because of doubts in the public mind that a black slave, described in the newspaper proposals for printing as one who had been "but a few Years since she came to this Town an uncultivated Barbarian from Africa" (188), could produce anything worthwhile. The letter of attestation by these eighteen notables, "the most respectable Characters in *Boston*" (7), however, served to secure a publisher and therefore a readership.

The making of a Phillis Wheatley, writer, far from being a radicalizing move, was achieved at the cost of reinscribing the very structure that oppressed her, and this structure continued to oppress her and other black people, even while legitimizing this one African American's right to speak. As William H. Robinson notes, most of the eighteen Boston notables and almost all the identifiable whites mentioned in Wheatley's writing owned one or more black servants or slaves. Even the Countess of Huntington, the English noblewoman who helped Wheatley first get published and to whom Wheatley, consequently, dedicated her volume of poetry, considered slave owning. Writing to those who were administering her estate in Georgia in 1771, the countess asks them to buy a black female slave for her: "I must request that a woman slave be purchased . . . and that she might be called Selina, after me."[26] The fact that the countess seems to have been talked out of this purchase by an abolitionist is beside the point. The cultural climate existed in which it was possible to enslave a "Selina" while at the same time privileging a "Phillis." The site of symbolic inclusion is the site of further real exclusion, and the power to mark the boundaries remains unchallenged.

The following anecdote, which has come down to us from a early biographer of the Wheatley family, further illustrates this anomaly, the anomaly by which the nontraditional subject can, apparently, be constituted both inside and outside the structures of power. Mrs. Wheatley, mindful, because of bad weather, of the health of her protégée, sent another black servant, Prince, to bring the young girl home in a chaise. The nineteenth-century biographer takes up the story:

> When the chaise returned, the good lady drew near the window, as it approached the house and exclaimed—"Do but look at the saucy varlet—if he hasn't the impudence to sit upon the same seat with my Phillis!" And poor Prince received a severe reprimand for forgetting the dignity thus kindly though perhaps to him unaccountably, attached to the sable person of "my Phillis."[27]

Prince, the other black servant, is not allowed to occupy the same position as a Phillis Wheatley, who is, significantly, not her own Phillis Wheatley, but "my Phillis," the creation of her white mistress. This fictional "Phillis" is used to deprive Prince of his place, such that the price of the integrated "one" becomes the creation of a further marginalized "other."

In Phillis Wheatley's own later life, this deprivation of the actual black subject in eighteenth-century America is more fully revealed when the fiction of Mrs. Wheatley's "Phillis" finally disappears. After Mrs. Wheatley died in 1774, Phillis Wheatley, who had been manumitted in late 1773, began her life as an independent black woman. Little is known about the short rest of her life,[28] but her extant letters from this time indicate that her life was not easy. Immediately after Mrs. Wheatley's death, she notes that some of those "who seem'd to respect me while under my mistresses patronage . . . have already put on a reserve" (183). In 1778, she writes to her friend Obour Tanner in a "hasty scrawl" that the events in her life in the past three years have "serv[d] to convince us of the uncertain duration of all things temporal" (185). We know she did not stop writing poetry during this period, but she had little success in getting her work published. For six weeks in 1779, she ran proposals in a Boston newspaper for a second volume of poetry but found no takers. In her last extant letter, dated from that year, she apologizes to Obour for being "silent," mentioning that "a variety of hindrances" had prevented her from writing (187). Without the aid of her powerful friends in the white establishment—Mr. and Mrs. Wheatley, the Countess of Huntington, and the eighteenth

Boston notables—Phillis Wheatley was indeed silent and silenced. In 1784, at the age of 31, she, and the last of her three children, died, by all accounts in obscurity and poverty.[29]

To conclude, then, we could say that, despite appearances to the contrary, the inclusion of Phillis Wheatley in the political and literary discourse of America did not substantially improve life for her. It did not empower her as a real subject or effectively improve her material conditions. Wheatley's relation to the dominant culture was one of connectedness but difference, and it was that difference based on a racial, sexual, and class specificity that finally prevented her from participating as an equal subject in American life. June Jordan, the contemporary black poet, commenting on the end of Wheatley's life, points to this difference as the source of the poet's final silence, suggesting that there was no place in America for an independent black woman's art.

> I believe that no one would have published the poetry of Black Phillis Wheatley, the grown woman who stayed with her chosen Black man. I believe that the death of Suzannah [sic] Wheatley, coincident with the African poet's twenty-first birthday, signalled, decisively, the end of her status as a child, as a dependent. From there we would hear from an independent Black woman poet in America.
>
> Can you imagine that, in 1775?
>
> Can you imagine that, today?[30]

As Jordan suggests here, the Wheatley tragedy is not over. If, as I have argued above, we take social and economic equality as a fundamental condition of political equality, then the Wheatley drama, as a drama of exclusion and deprivation, is still being played out today. While a differential relation exists between the social and the economic status of subjects in this society, there is no more chance of hearing from "independent" and equal voices in America in 1992 than in 1773. The gap between the ideology that claims that all subjects have an equal chance of participating in the dialogue of American poetry and/or politics, and the historic reality in which people are socially and economically disadvantaged, still exists. In the educational context, to take but one example, the rhetoric of equal opportunity for all is contradicted by statistical research that reveals a widening gap in the past decade between the proportion of white and black high school graduates who go on to college (a difference of 14 percentage points in 1987 as contrasted with a difference of 5 percentage points in the mid 1970s), a gap that can be attributed to the worsening social and economic situation of minorities during that period.[31] It is this same discrepancy that accounts for the odd fact that while Toni Morrison is now on the syllabus of many of our literature courses, black students are not, in any representative numbers, present in our classrooms. It is possible that future generations, looking back at this practice of integrating black literary subjects while perpetuating a social system that results in the exclusion of historical black subjects, will accuse us of being as blind as Mrs. Susanna Wheatley, will condemn us, as Phillis Wheatley once condemned her white contemporaries, for "the strange Absurdity of" a "Conduct whose Words and Actions are so diametrically opposite."

Finally, it is important to add that in making such a critique of pluralism, I am not undermining the importance of integrating nontraditional subjects into the political and cultural discourse of America, which means continuing to establish the rights of these subjects in law as well as in literary canons and academic curricula. But it is to emphasize that such a rhetorical integration is only part of what needs to be done. If, as Bercovitch argues, "ideology transmutes history into myth so as to enable people to act in history,"[32] what we must do to avoid being used by ideology is to reverse this transmutation, and that means continually opening up the space between myth and history, the rhetorical and the material—a space that ideology seeks to obscure. This praxis of ideological deconstruction is not, of course, an escape from ideology or power, but it offers what Foucault calls a "resistance" that is itself both engaged in and different from power. "Where there is power," Foucault says, "there is resistance, and yet, or rather consequently, this resistance is never in a position of exteriority in relation to power." Resistance is rather what he calls the "irreducible opposite" of power, functioning in a mobile and transitory way, "producing cleavages in a society that shift about, fracturing unities and effecting regroupings, furrowing across individuals themselves, cutting them up and remolding them, marking off irreducible regions in them, in their bodies and minds."[33] In marking the "irreducible regions" (differences of ethnicity, gender, and class) in subjects political and literary, we can offer such a resistance. As a result, we will indeed effect what Wayne Booth describes as a "critical killing," destroying the ideological unity, the imaginary harmony, of the pluralistic discourse.[34] But in so doing we may also finally kill the king and open the potential for revolutionary change.

NOTES

1. Michel Foucault, *The History of Sexuality*, trans. Robert Hurley (New York: Random House, 1980), 88–89.

2. Ibid., 89.

3. Sacvan Bercovitch, "The Problem of Ideology in American Literary History," *Critical Inquiry* 12 (Summer 1986): 649.

4. Foucault, *History of Sexuality*, 94.

5. Ellen Rooney, "Who's Left Out? A Rose by Any Other Name Is Still Red: Or the Politics of Pluralism," *Critical Inquiry* 12 (Spring 1986): 561–62. The Wayne Booth citation is from his *Critical Understanding: The Powers and Limits of Pluralism* (Chicago: University of Chicago Press, 1979), 259. For a particularly helpful discussion of the ideology of pluralism and its relation to power, see also Bruce Erlich, "Amphibolies: On the Critical Self-Contradictions of Pluralism," *Critical Inquiry* 12 (Spring 1986): 521–49. Laurie Finke's article, "The Rhetoric of Marginality: Why I Do Feminist Theory," *Tulsa Studies in Women's Literature* 5, no. 2 (1986): 251–72, provides a useful discussion of pluralism in the specific context of women's studies.

6. Bercovitch, "Problem of Ideology," 649.

7. Henry Louis Gates, Jr., "Phillis Wheatley and the Nature of the Negro," in *Critical Essays on Phillis Wheatley*, ed. William H. Robinson (Boston: G. K. Hall, 1982), 225.

8. Bercovitch, "Problem of Ideology," 636.

9. This quotation is drawn from Phillis Wheatley's first biography as cited by William H. Robinson, *Phillis Wheatley and Her Writings* (New York: Garland, 1984), 6. Robinson's book provides the best source for biographical information on Wheatley, information that has often been misrepresented (see Robinson's Introduction to his *Critical Essays*, 2–5, for a discussion of the dating inaccuracies in relation to Wheatley's life).

10. In Robinson's *Critical Essays*, see Albertha Sistrunk, "The Influence of Alexander Pope on the Writing Style of Phillis Wheatley," 175–88; Mukhtar Ali Isani, "Phillis Wheatley and the Elegiac Mode," 208–14; and John C. Shields, "Phillis Wheatley and the Sublime," 189–205.

11. Phillis Wheatley, "To Maecenas," in *The Collected Works of Phillis Wheatley*, ed. John C. Shields, Schomburg Library of Nineteenth-

Century Black Women Writers (New York: Oxford University Press, 1988), 11. All references to Wheatley's writing, whether poetry or prose, will be to this edition and will appear in parentheses in the text. This edition will be referred to in the notes as *Collected Works.*

12. Alexander Pope, *The Poems of Alexander Pope,* ed. John Butt (New Haven: Yale University Press, 1963), 168.

13. T. S. Eliot, "Tradition and the Individual Talent," in *Selected Essays* (New York: Harcourt, Brace, 1950), 5.

14. Ibid., 6.

15. Sacvan Bercovitch, *The American Jeremiad* (Madison: University of Wisconsin Press, 1978), 176.

16. See Bercovitch, *American Jeremiad,* esp. chaps. 1 and 6.

17. For a similar argument about Wheatley's appropriation of revolutionary rhetoric, see Betsy Erkkila's essay, "Revolutionary Women," *Tulsa Studies in Women's Literature* 6, no. 2 (1987): 189–223. Erkkila argues that Wheatley "turns the racial codes of the dominant culture back upon themselves, giving them an ironic inflection. What appears to be repetition is in fact a form of *mimesis* that mimics and mocks in the act of repeating" (206).

18. Wheatley has been vehemently attacked by some black critics for not being sufficiently critical of her oppressors. See Robinson, *Critical Essays,* 8–9, for an account of this criticism. A representative sample of this kind of criticism can be seen in Angelene Jamison's article, "Analysis of Selected Poetry of Phillis Wheatley," which appears in Robinson's volume (128–35). Jamison concludes that "it is a mistake to refer to her [Wheatley] as a Black poet" because "her mind was controlled by them [Whites], her actions were controlled by them, and consequently her pen" (134).

19. Michael Walzer, *Interpretation and Social Criticism* (Cambridge: Harvard University Press, 1987), 61. Walzer sees this kind of critic as the ideal critic, and he links his (or her) task to the work of priests, teachers, poets, all of whom do "the activity of cultural elaboration and affirmation" (40). He opposes this critic to the overly detached or the overly committed critic, neither of whom, he argues, is as effective (40).

20. See Robinson, *Critical Essays,* 1, for an account of Phillis Wheatley's contemporary fame. For speculation on the reasons why the Wheatleys granted Phillis her freedom, see Robinson, *Phillis Wheatley and Her Writings,* 39–40.

21. See Henry Louis Gates, Jr., "Foreword: In her Own Write," in Wheatley, *Collected Works.* Gates notes that Wheatley "launched two traditions at once—the black American literary tradition *and* the black woman's literary tradition" (x).

22. See Isani's "Phillis Wheatley and the Elegiac Mode," in Robinson's *Collected Essays,* 208–14, for a discussion of Wheatley's contribution to the elegiac form. For a discussion of Wheatley in the context of the American Revolution, see, in the same volume, Charles W. Akers, "'Our Modern Egyptians': Phillis Wheatley and the Whig Campaign against Slavery in Revolutionary Boston," 159–71, and Betsy Erkkila's essay, "Revolutionary Women." John Shield's article, "Phillis Wheatley's Struggle for Freedom in her Poetry and Prose" (Wheatley, *Collected Works,*" 232–40) also contains a good assessment of her political writing.

23. Erlich, "Amphibolies," 541.

24. Cited in J. Saunders Redding, "The Negro Writer in American Literature," in *Anger and Beyond,* ed. Herbert Hill (New York: Harper & Row, 1966), 2.

25. This description of the poet appeared in a headnote to an early Wheatley poem, "Farewell to America," which was published in the *London Chronicle,* 1–3 July 1773, as cited in Robinson, *Critical Essays,* 25. Robinson speculates that Phillis's "mistress," Mrs. Susanna Wheatley, wrote the headnote.

26. Robinson, *Phillis Wheatley and Her Writings,* 108–10. The Countess of Huntington, Robinson speculates, may have been shown the error of her ways by the American Quaker abolitionist Anthony Benezet, and it may have been as a compensation for her injustice that she became Wheatley's patron.

27. Cited in Robinson, *Phillis Wheatley and Her Writings,* 24.

28. For the uncertain history of Wheatley's life after Susanna Wheatley's death, see Robinson, *Phillis Wheatley and her Writings,* 47–69. The facts of her existence, as Robinson notes, are obscure, and her early biographers, descendants of the Wheatley family and more mindful of the Wheatley name than concerned for the truth, are not necessarily reliable.

29. Though there are reasons, as Robinson points out (*Phillis Wheatley and Her Writings,* 61) to doubt the accuracy of many of the details in the Wheatley family biographer's account of Phillis Wheatley's last years (the charges against John Peters, Phillis's husband, as a ne'er-do-well seem particularly the product of white bias against an enterprising and independent black man), the overall picture does seem to suggest that Wheatley's final years were bleak. Two other contemporary sources corroborate the account of Wheatley dying in indigence (see Robinson, *Phillis Wheatley and Her Writings,* 60).

30. June Jordan, *On Call* (Boston: South End Press, 1985), 96.

31. United States, Department of Education, *The Condition of Education 1990,* vol. 2, *Postsecondary Education* (Washington: GPO, 1990), 5,

16. This report shows that in 1987, 58 percent of white students went on to college in the October following graduation, as compared to 44 percent of black students, while in 1974, the difference between the groups was at its minimum, with 49 percent of white students and 44 percent of black students going on to college. As a *New York Times* editorial comments, the decline in federal financial aid and the failure of student benefits to keep up with inflation during the Reagan years are clearly important in explaining this recent difference in black and white participation in higher education, since black students are generally more dependent on such aid (*New York Times,* 30 April 1990, A10). The median income for blacks in 1987 was 57. 1 percent of that for whites, which was lower than in any year in the 1970s. Forty-five percent of black children are poor, compared with 15 percent of white children (Morton M. Kondracke, "The Two Black Americas," *New Republic,* 6 February 1989, 17–18.

32. Bercovitch, "Problem of Ideology," 636.

33. Foucault, *History of Sexuality,* 95–96.

34. Booth, *Critical Understanding,* 259.

THERON BRITT

11

Before the Law, after the Judgment: Schizophrenia in John Barth's *The Floating Opera*

Sacvan Bercovitch's concentration on the ideological work of the symbol of "America" in Puritan rhetoric and of the role of the self in that rhetoric offers a suggestive model for understanding more recent literature. Even if the terms do not, the form and function of that rhetoric may survive in contemporary literature. Bercovitch's insight is that Puritan rhetoric once connected the profane and the sacred as a means of social control; its great power was to unite apparent opposites, reconcile contradictions, and incorporate as integral to its own workings a process of endless self-critique based in part on the self's distance from an ideal, thereby incorporating acts of criticism as essential to its own strategy. It is this action of incorporating dissent that survives in more recent literature.

But this Puritan strategy of endless self-critique had a price. If Puritan rhetoric incorporated dissent through endless self-questioning in order to maintain a form of cultural consensus, it did so at the price of endless self-doubt. Bercovitch has shown, moreover, that this doubt continues in the tension in this Puritan legacy through the conflicting terms of the Emersonian faith that "'America' wed the ideals of individualism, community, and continuing revolution" in a representative American self, and thus that self-interest paradoxically always flowed into the common good.[1] In this century the trace of Emersonian faith in the social good as attached to the self-reliant individual must contend with an increasing sense of that individual's isolation and alienation. Now it is clearer that the idea of "America" and the characteristic American self was, and has been from the beginning, composed of elements that produce what Bercovitch has called a "cultural schizophrenia" (*AJ*, 191). Yet he claims in *The Puritan Origins of the American Self*[2] that "the [Puritan] rhetoric survived, finally, not by chance but by merit, because it was compelling enough in content and flexible enough in form to invite adaptation" (186). Indeed, it is most likely that this "cultural schizophrenia," or split between the ideal and lived social reality that Bercovitch finds as the engine in the Puritan jeremiad and again in adapted form in Emersonian self-reliance or Hawthorne's ambiguity, is the element that has invited adaptation and survives in contemporary American fiction. But the interesting question is what new form of adaptation this management of dissent may have taken.

Bercovitch has mentioned, but not developed, in his work on *The Scarlet Letter* how the process of "American" ideology he outlines would "also include contemporary American culture, insofar as it may be said to build on ideological continuities from Hawthorne's time."[3] The terms, of course, will be quite changed, but one key area of investigation that might show the adaptation and continuities of the ideological engine Bercovitch has outlined would be the presentation of the self in fiction, for as Bercovitch asserts, "the only plausible modes of American dissent are those that center on the self: as stranger or prophet, rebel or revolutionary, lawbreaker or Truth-seeker, or any other adversarial or oppositional form of individualism" ("A-Politics," 646). And it is in the conception of the self that the most striking continuities at the level of ideology appear in contemporary American fiction, for if the Puritan suffered from what Bercovitch calls a "schizophrenic singlemindedness" (*PO*, 23) in the attempt to overcome oneself in one's reach for the ideal, the contemporary writer has a more distinctly "schizophrenic" self with which to contend in a world grown barren of ideals.

Tony Tanner has formulated a sense of this tension in contemporary American fiction, but in linguistic, ahistorical terms. Tanner's approach in *City of Words*[4] asserts a profound tension in contemporary American fiction, based on the fact that "many recent American writers are unusually aware of this quite fundamental and inescapable paradox: that to exist, a book, a vision, a system, like a person, has to have an outline—there can be no identity without contour. But contours signify arrest, they involve restraint and the acceptance of limits" (*CW*, 17), a fact that works against living "an unpatterned, unconditioned life . . . in which your movements and stillnesses, choices and repudiations are all your own" (*CW*, 15). Tanner claims that, for the contemporary American writer, this binding paradox produces a dread or "paranoid" "nightmare of being totally controlled" (*CW*, 16), and that American writers resist this control as much as they can, though when they write they inevitably enter into a system that entails some form of limit or arrest, and so they must endlessly struggle against themselves, making one system in order to escape another. Tanner's focus on paranoia as the privileged trope of postwar American fiction, however, tends to overlook the social function of this fiction and to obscure the effect of the breakdown of the systems paranoids construct, a breakdown better modeled on the concept of schizophrenia. Bercovitch's analysis of the social aspect of American literature, on the other hand, can help us see the continuities of this fiction with an American tradition, and as well the ideological work of this fiction to transmute apparent radicalism into forms of cultural consensus.

Jean Baudrillard argues in "The Ecstasy of Communication"[5] that our world situation has changed, and with it our characteristic illnesses. Marking the shift from a modernist sensibility, Baudrillard asserts that "if paranoia was the pathology of organization, of the structuration of a rigid and jealous world; then with communication and information, with the immanent promiscuity of all these networks, with their continual connections, we are now in a new form of schizophrenia" ("Ecstasy of Communication," 132). In other words, the changed historical situation of post-World War II America's emerging information economy, coupled to the enlarged effects of capital, destabilizes even the paranoid drive for order. The ideals that once helped the engine of the Puritan jeremiad are now difficult to find; so, lacking one of its key terms, the conflict between the ideal and lived social reality fueling the jeremiad must find a new form.

This new form is perhaps best conceived not as paranoid but as schizophrenic, a term that designates the loss of distance and collapse of interiority proper to an older modernist conception of the self. Instead of the paranoid who constructs systems as a defense against the chaos of experience, the schizophrenic rather is that figure who undoes the possibility of system. More extreme than any Puritan, the schizophrenic questions fundamental assumptions of a discrete break between subject and object and its attendant conception of truth.[6] Consequently, it is possible that the strategies of containment Bercovitch has labeled a "cultural schizophrenia" still may link our cultural past to our present, though we must account for the fact that the new lived social reality of communication and information has evaporated the concept of the ideal upon which previous modes of social stability depended. What remains, nonetheless, is a new form of the self whose final *effects* are remarkably similar to those Bercovitch has found in Puritan and classic American literature.

This trope of the schizophrenic suggests a new relationship for the postmodern writer to a world different from that of those immediate precursors, the modernists. "Splitting" is the fundamental symptom of schizophrenia[7] and should not be confused with the problems associated with so-called multiple personalities or split personalities. The ultimate narcissism of the clinical schizophrenic, the inward turning, leaves the patient pursuing an endlessly retreating hall of mirrors within the self, but we should not be fooled by this apparent singularity of a "self," since one does not create alternative selves. In fact, this point cannot be stressed overmuch, because of the danger of seeing schizophrenia as a disease that produces a series of discrete self-images. Such a view of a simple split could not be farther from the clinical record. This is a disease of a mind's grappling with its own processes, its own "events." In one important sense—the ability to yoke together sense data—schizophrenia can be thought of as a meaning disorder, an inability to make the world make sense. The schizophrenic cannot link up the disparate bits of experience into meaningful wholes, but instead feels them as discrete units that resist appropriation, categorization, and "understanding." These experiences constitute, in other words, a breakdown in the signifying chain. Considered as a meaning disorder, the schizophrenic experience is similar to what many artists experience in post-World War II industrial society. Governed in part by a series of narratives, society must be able to resist the breakdown of those narratives, but in large part in our recent past it has not, and it is this potential for rupturing narrative order that begins to suggest the ideological function of a "schizophrenic" aesthetic and to link it to Bercovitch's analysis of a peculiarly American self. The values of "Adamic innocence, agrarian harmony, personal freedom, the unbounded frontiers of thought and language" are all "rooted in the rhetoric of American identity,"[8] but what happens to that Adamic innocence when the frontiers of thought and language really are "unbounded" by normalizing constraints of an implied coherent self? What happens of course can be called "schizophrenia," and its effects are rather more conservative than disruptive.

On the personal level, this breakdown is so disquieting because it leaves the individual living in a perpetual present moment. What has broken at the individual level is the tie to the movement of time. The faculty (located, researchers believe, in the hippocampus region of the brain) that allows us each a personal history—a past and a future—is lost. Utilizing the work of Lacan, Fredric Jameson notes that "with the breakdown of the signifying chain, therefore, the schizophrenic is reduced to an experience of pure material Signifiers, or in other words of a series of pure and unrelated presents in time."[9] If at the individual level schizophrenia shows a self frozen in a perpetual present, at the cultural level it names an example of what Jameson calls a disabling "pastiche," the breakdown of history brought about by the leveling of all signification to the same plane of meaning.

The breakdown in temporality—the loss of the sense of a coherent past and link to the future—lets the individual in for an orgy of sensory overload and breaks the links to those around one that a social praxis demands, so the radical or utopian potential of such a self is limited. And thus the ideological function of what might be called a "schizophrenic" literary aesthetic becomes clearer: Aimless isolation is all that is available to the schizophrenic, for in order to ascribe meaning to one's experiences and escape from the eternal present, one must be able to impose a narrative code to structure and order perception into categories of before and after, greater and lesser, in a binary chain. Jameson, among others, points out the link between a concept of schizophrenia and culture by showing that such a master code is what has been thrown into question by postmodernism's endless interrogation of absolutes. And though this questioning would appear to subvert social order, the paradoxical result of apparently undermining cultural codes is a species of social paralysis whose effect is to contain dissent by dissolving motives for action. This is not, of course, an entirely new possibility for American fiction. In his reading of Hawthorne, for instance, Bercovitch notes a pattern of pluralism that converts the prospects of many truths into one strategy. Hawthorne's pluralism produces "a mystifying *sense* of multiplicity—through which each set of questions and answers is turned toward the same solution: All meanings are partly true; hence interpreters must choose as many parts of the truth, and/or as many truths as they can possibly find in the symbol" ("A-Politics," 639). And of course this inclusive strategy turns criticism to its own account as part of its dynamic engine.

A similar strategy can be found in John Barth's first novel, *The Floating Opera* (1956);[10] it is among the first in post-world War II American fiction to explore an apparently new "schizophrenic" way of writing. Barth's approach grows not directly out of classic American fiction, but more out of a confrontation with post-World War II existential modernism's undermining of absolutes (e.g., in Sartre, Camus). Barth can hardly be said to be *directly* influenced by classic American texts, nor particularly concerned with social issues. But what is interesting for us to see is that his largely aesthetic concerns not only respond to a moment of modernism but also perform a familiar type of cultural work through manipulation of the idea of the self. His revision works through his novel's linkage of two seemingly unrelated topics, the law and schizophrenia, topics that have never been adequately examined together by the critics.[11] Specifically, in this novel Barth links authority to a peculiar psychology to reveal the schizophrenic moment in the law, but we can read further to see that cultural work being done in the paradoxical moment of law in Barth's own "cultural schizophrenia" as a method that both legitimates the social role of his fiction and acts, as Bercovitch has shown concerning Puritan and classic American literature, to contain dissent.

Ostensibly *The Floating Opera* focuses on the ethical problem of suicide and hence on the familiar modernist problems of the individual confronting his or her own existential predicament, but Barth's novel marks a turn away from the modernism of his precursors and pursues a path marked by the loss of interiority and the breakdown of temporality characteristic of the postmodern. Much post-World War II existential fiction, such as Camus's *The Fall*, stresses the homelessness, alienation, and struggle of the self in opposition to society (familiar modernist themes); but the question that Barth takes up is the extent to which the critique of bourgeois certainties by existential modernism not only undid the bourgeois unity of the subject but also simultaneously reaffirmed in a displaced form the status of the individual as the locus of meaning and value.

In *The Floating Opera* Barth's critique of the existential self begins with the law. The central plot device of a court case, which narrator Todd Andrews (a lawyer) is shepherding through the halls of justice, eventually reveals Barth's narrator as an ironic figure for the law. Like the law, Todd suffers from a type of drifting movement; like the law, he appears to be above the petty squabbles of those around him, particularly his close friends (involved with him in a love triangle) Jane and Harrison Mack; and, like the law, he only *pretends* to an impassive and impartial curiosity in things around him. He proclaims an objective neutrality and identifies with the law, asserting, "The law and I are uncommitted" (*FO*, 83). But as a consequence that should make us pause over the "neutrality" of the law, he further maintains, "I insist upon my basic and ultimate irresponsibility" (*FO*, 83). Like the law, Todd is neither neutral nor impassive; he is double, never speaking in a single voice, a fact graphically symbolized in chapter 20, "Calliope Music," which is a "chapter in two voices" (*FO*, 168) of text printed side-by-side in two columns rather than in one longer one as is usual; the columns begin in the same voice, then modulate back and forth, changing slightly as they go along, following parallel tracks of self-negation and self-creation—suicide and the law. In the "starboard" column, we learn that "those who would live reasonably should have reasons for remaining alive. Reasonable enough?" Juxtaposed next to this on the same page in the "port" column is similar material in which, in passing, Todd tells us, "Never did there exist such an unparalleled floating opera as the law in its less efficient moments" (*FO*, 169). This juxtaposition of a tale of the law as unmoored "floating opera" with a reasonable person's recourse to suicide is no accident, for it shows the law as itself a double-voiced, schizophrenic operation, a work in two voices that are simultaneously the "one" voice of reason. The fact that Todd can vacillate between equally tenable possibilities because nothing has intrinsic value exposes the emptiness of the law's narrative. He must look elsewhere for his "law," as in the situation of the Mack inheritance case: there the "law" is legitimated by the rhetorical power of "poetry" and a judge's prejudice. What the scene of the law played out on Barth's floating stage calls up is a picture of a self-reflexive fiction, but one that oscillates, like the many oscillations within the Mack inheritance case, between equally tenable alternatives. And the result is that the law is, like Todd, at least in part unstable and itself in search of a principle of order, a victim of the reason on which it rests. Todd is in the position Bercovitch has attributed to Hawthorne: "to interpret (in Hawthorne's fiction) is to acknowledge a priori that reality is meaning fragmented by plural points of view" ("A-Politics," 640). But Todd does not have Hawthorne's faith in process, in the self that would choose to keep interpreting, for that very gesture to continue is one that his drive toward suicide puts into question.

If Todd is a figure for the law in this novel, then the law is troubled indeed, for his "self" offers no alternative ground on which to anchor one's choices. Initially Barth's confrontation with his literary precursors begins not with the "values" of the free individual (a problem from classic American fiction), but rather with their lack (a problem of twentieth-century fiction). Todd Andrews asserts the commonplace of twentieth-century philosophy that "nothing has intrinsic value" (*FO*, 165). And since nothing is valuable in itself, the conclusion is that "the value of everything is attributed to it, from outside, by people" (*FO*, 167), a position that brings up the question of the sign's arbitrary linkage to the world; but in this case the plurality of signification is a problem of consciousness—the choice of the free individual. Like the existentialist he eventually parodies, Todd, for instance, "can usually interpret a number of possible significances, often conflicting, sometimes contradictory" (*FO*, 139) in anything, making rational choice impossible. Ironically echoing Emerson, Todd can insouciantly claim that "assenting even simultaneously to contradictory propositions has never especially troubled me. I was not and am not interested in the truth or falsehood of" statements (*FO*, 35); or that "everything, I'm afraid, is significant, and nothing finally is important" (*FO*, 6). If conflicting and contradictory statements can simultaneously circulate in his system, then the principles of reason (hierarchy and order)—ruled by the necessity for noncontradiction—cannot govern it. Since for Todd "any arrangement of things at all is an order" (*FO*, 9), any order works as well as another. But this is exactly his main problem. As a figure for the law, he dispenses with external stable values, thus producing as a side effect a hyperbolic image of the recourse one is forced upon—individual freedom. Unhinged from the constraints of objective law and contradiction, one is free to interpret and do as one pleases, "absolutely." Here Todd appears to push the limits of, and hence parody, individualism.

However, lest we settle for this rather familiar existentialist position, we should note that this logic is the beginning of Todd's apparent schizophrenia.

Barth makes evident that Todd, as an "absolutely" free subject, is in fact caught in a bind familiar to existential fiction in which one is free to choose but without any clear criteria for judgment. In this gesture Barth is a step beyond Hawthorne's ambiguity, though it should be clear that one could follow Hawthorne's path to this particular abyss. As a symptom of this situation, Todd becomes obsessed with control, and though the narrative wanders metonymically, associatively, there is a pattern centered on Todd's need for control. In his narrative Todd moves from one "mask" to another, from "rake" to "saint" to "cynic," each one a failure, each one explicitly a device to rationalize his existence in the face of impending death, and each one forced on him by circumstances. Nevertheless, the fact that these masks are imposed from the *outside* should remind us that Todd's inner workings are a function of something beyond himself. His "self" seems to be a series of "pure accidents," no matter how hard he strives for control. Crucially different from his existential cousins, he does not have the luxury of even the empty shell of the self to fall back on. Todd's problem consequently is, in the end, an artistic one of how to manage his multiplying "selves." This is to say that Barth concentrates on Todd's masks as signs of a need for control in order to explore the refuge of the self in a world without absolutes.

Todd's drive to control is everywhere in the narrative; he breaks his habits so nothing will make him its "vassal" (*FO*, 122); he won't allow himself, "a free agent, to be dictated to by a miserable nickel" (*FO*, 212) when he flips a coin to determine if the Macks should or should not get their inheritance—he would rather control their future and judge them himself; he is even willing to bribe Mrs. Mack, Sr.'s black house servant, Eustacia Callader, in order to win the law case. Moreover, in law school, he begins the "long process of assuming hard control over" himself (*FO*, 134), but it is to no avail, since he realizes that "all my masks were half conscious attempts to master the fact with which I had to live; that none had made me master of that fact; that where cynicism had failed, no future mask could succeed; that, in short, my heart was the master of all the rest of me, even of my will" (*FO*, 222). However, Todd is resourceful, and so there is one more turn to the logic: "There was no mastering the fact with which I lived, but I could master the fact of my living with it by destroying myself, and the result was the same—I was the master" (*FO*, 223). Since reason and logic are his game, his mastery through self-destruction is linked to all rational mastery and to reason as a tool or repression: to control is to kill. In effect, Barth shows that Todd is not the hero of existential fiction who creates through his own choice a unique alternative world against bourgeois conformism. Rather he is an exemplar of the schizophrenic confusion that flows from that turn to the self. For though he attempts his "mastery" by blowing up self, friends, and the whole town, when his scheme fails for unknown reasons, his narrative takes a turn uncharacteristic of existential fiction, and he simply resumes the life he had attempted to leave, happy with the realization that there is no more reason to die than to live. His various "masks" fail him, but his actions reveal his movement from one mask to another as a schizophrenic sign of the collapse of his "interiority."

Todd's attempts at mastery push to the fore a question beyond Hawthorne's ambiguity but that haunts existential fiction. If the ultimate act is to choose, knowing the absurdity of choice, what is to be done when the choosing agency—the self—cannot choose, is paralyzed, is as "weatherless" as Jacob Horner from Barth's novel *The End of the Road* (written in the same year as the *Opera*)? We can see the fragmentation such a position creates in the fact that the characters that Todd Andrews as author presents have a decidedly unhealthy resemblance to himself. He takes on, for instance, both the fastidious habits and profession of his father, a lawyer and suicide. Another of his doubles is Harrison, Jr., who seems to see Todd as a kind of role model. And then there is Colonel Henry Morton, thriving capitalist of Cambridge, Maryland,whose attempts to avoid indebtedness reflect Todd's own desire to avoid obligation (mastery by another). Yet his most obvious double is Harrison Mack, Sr., the pickle king, whose insanity produces the symptoms of saving and preserving all his wastes, both wills and feces—129 pickle jars full. Like Todd, Mack, Sr., has a fear of letting anything of himself go; and like Todd, the writer who wants to be master, he seems to want power over others, through threatening to inherit and disinherit his heirs. Like the elder Mack, Todd, through his plan centering on Mack's feces, decides to let Harrison, Jr., inherit or not. And so, like the elder Mack, Todd shows signs of being a control-obsessed paranoid, but one who looks on, detached and impassive, at what his body is doing or what is being done to his body, unwilling or unable to make the paranoid leap into certainty. Impassive about destroying a little girl who might be his daughter (or might not—the text resists any such easy closure), his close friends the Macks, and of course the townspeople of Cambridge, Todd is finally less a paranoid than a detached observer, a schizophrenic voyeur at his own experience. As detached from his body as he can be, Todd is a literally sick man possessed of a myocardial infarction, prostate trouble and impotence. Encased in a body whose next heartbeat may be its last, he is obsessed with mastering death, but there is nothing heroic nor even anti-heroic in this stance. Rather, the existential "individual" is here ironically figured as a series of fragments unhealthily combined in random order.

As long as critics try to understand the novel in individual psychological terms, they repeat the isolation and fragmentation common to existential thematics and miss Barth's critique of these themes. The type of schizophrenia that Todd suffers from figures a meaning disorder that undercuts an individual's ability to legislate a coherent self. As Todd moves from rake to saint to cynic, his sense of personal identity undergoes a series of breaks ("masks"), because the underlying signifying chain of meaning by which he structured each identity, or "mask," of his existence breaks down until all the "masks" lose their ability to mask over anything and begin to function in precisely the opposite way from which they began—not as masks, but as signs that there is in fact nothing to mask over, nothing but surfaces. His "character" begins to function as a discursive formation. So instead of exposing individual alienation, Todd Andrews's personal torments mirror the destruction of those structures of meaning and value by which the normative constraints of culture allow personal identity to function. Through Todd, Barth accomplishes the destruction of representational "character" and attacks a conception of will or choice as being "inside" a consistent self.

As Barth critiques his immediate precursors' bastion of the self, he at the same time offers an alternative to the isolation of the existential modernist self. In all cases of his confrontation with death, Todd's rationality survives to produce new masks, an action that may explain the driving force of this narrative. The novel explicitly attempts to classify and understand what remains a mystery; it is "an attempt to learn why my father hanged himself, no more" (*FO*, 217). His enfeebled emotional experience, counted and classified, his affair with Jane Mack, duly listed and categorized in his *Inquiry*; and the whole narrative itself of *The Floating Opera*, only a chapter in the larger *Inquiry* into the reasons for his father's suicide and its relation to him (*FO*, 215)—all these are signs not only of his attempt at rational control but also of its failure. However, what may have been a sign of despair for an earlier novelist is not so here, for Barth turns this failure to name or explain into the very engine of his narrative, and so repeats a gesture that Bercovitch has noted is the motive power in much American literature from the Puritans through to classic nineteenth-century texts. Like Hawthorne's strategy of pluralism, the alternative Barth produces has less to do with masks than it has to do with *movement* from one mask to another. As readers of Barth's own relation as writer to the world, we can see that the destruction of "character" is itself part of a larger aesthetic strategy of control and legitimation designed to create a valid place for his fiction.

With each failure to name his experience Todd moves on to another mask, not the least of which is that of "Author"; yet his urge to classify and thus understand experience is endlessly deferred, because "there is no will-o'-the-wisp so elusive as the cause of any human act"; moreover, he reminds us of the emptiness of epistemological justification by citing Hume to the effect that "causation is never more than an inference; and any inference involves at some point the leap from what we see to what we can't see" (*FO*, 214). Yet within this emptiness, for him "it is enough for me to do an hour's work, or two hours' work, on my *Inquiry* every night after supper, to make me feel just a little bit outside of time and heartbeats" (*FO*, 50). Writing keeps death at bay by ordering and imposing meaning on the facts of his life; it provides him with a repertory of evasions, digressions, and masks, and, as he says, takes on an end in itself, and so becomes a reason for living. Apparently through his *Inquiry* language becomes the tool by which Todd controls an intransigent reality, and this we can recognize as the stance of modernism—the Author imposing self-generated order on the world. Or at least it seems to serve as such; Todd notes himself the interminable nature of his writing, and of his control over the reader he is not completely satisfied, for he tells the reader, "You are freer, perhaps, than you'd be comfortable knowing" (*FO*, 98). Todd's "freedom" in its existential guise is an illusion in terms of what it frees the "self" to do. It unfortunately frees him to enter into the essentially shizophrenic movement between choices. And this reveals the limits to the existential model and the control open to an artist through language—a virtual collapse of the will and potential paralysis (which Barth calls "cosmopsis" in *The End of the Road*).

But more importantly, Todd's schizophrenic self seems to be linked to the infinite production of narrative. His loss of control of his "masks" links the law and his psychology to both the infinite regression of meaning within language, which runs throughout the novel through the theme of "imperfect communication," and to the problem of artistic production. In simple terms, he seems unable successfully to stage his personality. The only time Todd does have a "perfect communication," it is in sign language in a bomb crater during the First World War with a German sergeant whom Todd ends up later killing. Although he begins his *Inquiry* as a letter telling his father about his heart condition, he continues it in order to find out why his father committed suicide, but of course his father will never receive it, and their communication will remain imperfect, cut short by death. Most importantly, between him and his reader, too, there is imperfect communication (*FO*, 218), and so his *Inquiry*, he knows, is part of a process whose task is endless (*FO*, 247); to the reader he asserts, "You understand, do you, that the nature of my purpose—to make as short as possible the gap between fact and opinion—renders the *Inquiry* interminable?" (*FO*, 215). The narrative exists quite explicitly, then, within a gap in knowing, a gap he is trying to fill up, ostensibly to explain his father's suicide (the absent father, lost origin, empty place of authority), but more to the point to generate a "mask" that will function to explain his own reasons for living.

However, though his failure to communicate may trouble Todd, we cannot but see that it helps out Barth. That "imperfect communication" seems to keep Todd going, keep him writing, but always reminding him of his lack, his failing heart, his father's death, the inexplicable nature to experience and the void beyond his attempts at mastery. And so he must keep going in his endless writing of new fictions in his drive toward mastery, apparently in harmony with Hawthorne's strategy of pluralism. As the self implied within existential modernist fiction seems to be coming apart under the stress of self-definition, a new yet familiar role for the writer is emerging, a role that is to create ever new masks. But the key to this treasure is that Barth's aesthetic works against Todd's aims toward mastery in a gesture that in effect ironically allows Barth a form of mastery over the problem of his own artistic materials, a form of mastery constituted by an endless narrative machine founded on the death of the existential subject. And this of course is what we must begin to suspect is both the dominant "mask" of the novel and the law of Barth's fiction.

If Todd's schizophrenic shift from one mask to another is the literalization of the strain involved in legitimating any law, we can understand his narrative function more fully if we see that he is that figure who in this text nevertheless ironically "writes the law" for those around him. To the townspeople he is a lawgiver, not a Moses but a sort of passive and unacknowledged Zarathustra who is willing and able to dictate not only to the old men of the Dorchester Explorers' Club, but also to the entire town. He dictates the most primal law of who should live and who should die when he decides to blow up *The Original and Unparalleled Floating Opera*. Todd's actions *seem* to make law through the assertion of his will (i.e., the gesture of the Modernist Author) not just for himself but for others, because, like Hawthorne's Hester, he lives in what Bercovitch calls the "landscape of misguided rebellion: a wild, self-vaunting independence leading by a ghastly logic of its own to the brink of murder and suicide" ("A-Politics," 633). Yet unlike Hester, Todd rejects *any* guide, sees suicide at novel's end as simply another possibility, and does not, as Hester eventually does, give up his "ghastly logic." But like Hawthorne in relation to Hester, Barth apparently pulls back from his narrator and the ghastly logic of his drive toward mastery, because of course *nothing happens* because of Todd's actions. No one is killed, the central law case remains unsettled, and any resolution stemming from his decisions remains deferred. The assertion of his will can only be an ironic one, his "self" clear by novel's end to be just another mask, another role, another fiction.

Like the modernist works Barth parodies, his fiction continues to pose the question of self-reflexivity, but now through the displacement of the self into the indeterminate "play" of the production of texts. On the one hand the "advance" of Barth's technique exposes the modernist "choice" of existential individualism as itself a ruse, a "mask" that covers over the fiction of producing the self as a harbor within the "void" of meaning. But on the other hand, this criticism has left Barth in a more difficult position than that of his modernist and existential precursors. What his own methodology forces him to now confront is a literary world in which even the tenuous certainty of existential isolation is no longer a given. What his own fiction thus stages at the level of its aesthetics is the dimunition of the real and erasure of the referent—that is, the place of the schizophrenic.[12] The danger for Barth is that it leaves him with one place to go and one thing to say again and again. It pushes his fiction further away from the social world and into its own aesthetic processes.

The "advance" he has gained through a critique of his own literary context brings with it a new problem perhaps best thought of in his work through the role and function of the artist, a theme he pursues again and again in later work. For the question inevitably arises that if the law depends on a fiction, then what does fiction depend on? It is easy to see how Barth exposes the fiction of the law, but perhaps more important is to follow the path he lays down for the law of his fiction. From first novel to latest essay, Barth is consistent on a few points. In a revisionary headnote (*The Friday Book* [1984])[13] appended to his first essay on literary art ("How to Make A Universe" [1960]), Barth says he continues to "believe the main thing it [the essay] says" (*F*, 15). What it says is that, on the one hand, like the modernists he explicitly follows, he institutes a vision of the Author as God the Artist, who creates a cosmos by "transforming the apparently blank givens of existence "in the smithy of his soul" to something ordered and fine and pregnant with human significance" (*F*, 21). This Joycean allusion seems to indicate the cosmos of the modernist artist who imposes meaning on the chaos of experience and thus institutes a new order of the subject. But on the other hand, this novelist, who has "an immodest and subversive resemblance to God" (*F*, 22), makes fictions in which "the ideas are never the main thing" (*F*, 23); in other words, like the universe, for Barth a novel finally is "beyond philosophy, theology, literary criticism, and the sometimes torturing attempts of its inhabitants to understand it and their place in it" (*F*, 24), and, like God's incomprehensible universe, a novel simply exists, its meaning is displaced into the mere fact of existence, and the "order" a novelist generates is finally subject only to its own logic and constraints—that is, a formalist order of textuality.

In 1960 Barth could make fun of the image of the modernist artist, asking the rhetorical question, "Aren't artist types supposed to stay up all night, grow beards, take lovers, get cirrhosis of the liver, and generally astonish the bourgeoisie?" (*F*, 15). Perhaps because no one in the bourgeoisie was seriously astonished anymore, the artist's task by the mid fifties had been irreversibly changed and made more difficult. Like the fiction of the modernists he claims as heirs, fiction in Barth's vision depends on the Artist, but the Artist is only an Author who is in turn a fiction displaced into a text whose "law" is never absolute.

Yet the displacement of the Author into the text is not without its own moment of authority. What the scene of the law in Barth's novel calls up finally is the role of literature in relation to the motivation of action. Kafka's modernist parable of the nature of authority, "Before the Law,"[14] is instructive here. In this parable, a man from the country comes before the law and asks to be let in, but the doorkeeper tells him that he cannot enter, and though he waits for years and entreats the doorkeeper with everything he has, he waits in vain. In order to enter the door of the law, which Kafka tells us we all want to do, he would have to break the prohibition laid down by the doorkeeper. He never tries to get by the doorkeeper, and instead merely peers into the receding hallway and the many doors of the law, each more fearsome and difficult than the next, each guarded by a terrible doorkeeper. The man stands paralyzed and eventually dies without entering into the law. This outcome sets up a paradox of authority: for the man standing before the law, in order to be in the law he must break it. In this sense, we, too, are "before the law," waiting for its arrival in the sense of being in the gap separating us from the law's truth, but after the judgment in the sense of being subject to the workings of a law we cannot justify. If we wait all our days, like the man before the law, we will die having done nothing, for, at least if we follow Kafka, the law is not found but made. The man before the law cannot act "lawfully," since he is "before the law" attempting to "enter into it," but can only do so after making his own law. In other words, he is caught in a trap of self-reflexive self-legitimation.[15] Like Kafka's man before the law, Todd's play with logic in the courts marks the law's need to write itself without residue or excess and cover over its nakedness. What the law must cover over is that it is at best a self-reflexive fiction, but one that produces force and binding consequences (at least temporarily) as its distinguishing mark. Law must resolve its own inner contradictions in ways that minimize its fictional aspect in order to maintain its status as law, since it is under the burden of writing the authority of authority itself.[16] So anything that exposes its fictionality is a threat, and Barth's treatment of the law—that the law might be "schizophrenic"—seems to be a blow at law's foundations. And yet it is not the law of courts at which Barth is aiming.

Questioning reason's limits leads Barth to the contradictory moment of authority, for law must found itself on the concept of the objective application of rational precepts, but whenever reason is questioned, as in Barth's novel, or one tries to found reason's own "law" of priority, one comes up against a moment of textual indeterminacy that requires a "mask." This double bind of the law produces a movement from one position to another without escape *except* through the founding gesture of the artist; this figure is the (modernist) one who writes the law by resolving the play of indeterminacy in the act of making. This artist writes the imposition of the law, but through Barth's questioning of the subjectivity accorded to the artist's act of choice—Todd's schizophrenia—this law is itself always in question, is dispersed into the text's many layers and in effect into a new level of indeterminacy beyond modernist alienation, into a new level based on the endless production of narrative. So finally *The Floating Opera* does write a paradoxical and self-reflexive form of law—the law of indeterminacy.

What it legislates is the postmodern denial of depth, and it replaces depth with a fascination for a series of surfaces themselves unhinged from motive, cause, or verification. Authenticity is here no longer at issue, since the origin a work would look to for validation, whether it be the Author or History, is always a self-created myth. The result is that this "law" in Barth's aesthetic of schizophrenia, much like Hawthorne's strategy of pluralism, contains dissent by allowing all alternatives within that space it opens up, a space that is simultaneously before the law yet after judgment. Much like the Puritans and Hawthorne before him, Barth has found a strategy of pluralism that requires perpetual movement, but one that moves through a complex refiguring of the self. While the terms of consensus have changed, the strategy is in fact quite familiar.

Bercovitch's analysis of *The Scarlet Letter* could apply here, for, like Hawthorne's, Barth's novel is a complex "story of socialization, where the point of socialization is not to conform, but to consent. Anyone can submit; the socialized *believe*. . . . And that involves the total self—past, present, and future, private and public, thought and action, or if necessary inaction" ("A-Politics," 630). An echo of Hawthorne's ambiguity, Barth's "law" of narrative is displaced into the authorial self, but that "self" ironically becomes a marker for the death of the subject, a death or "inaction" that finally is the novel's guiding problematic. As such, the novel marks a significant shift from the strategies of modernism to the indeterminate play of postmodernism. By embracing a new level of indeterminacy, Barth seemingly ungrounds fiction from its last vestige of relation to representation in order to carve out a space for new artistic work, letting his fiction float instead in a space of its own production. However, this schizophrenic "liberation" of fiction from the constraints of mimesis brings with it its own troubling "law," for with the destruction of the referent, when the map precedes the territory, the critical dissent of fiction appears able only to question the power of its own workings, and thus indirectly legislate for the status quo and disarm its potential to motivate social change.

NOTES

1. Sacvan Bercovitch, *The American Jeremiad* (Madison: University of Wisconsin Press, 1978), 183. Hereafter cited as *AJ*.

2. Sacvan Bercovitch, *The Puritan Origins of the American Self* (New Haven: Yale University Press, 1975). Hereafter cited as *PO*.

3. Sacvan Bercovitch, "The A-Politics of Ambiguity in *The Scarlet Letter*," *New Literary History* 19, no. 3 (1988): 629–54. Bercovitch extends his reading of Hawthorne's fiction in"Hawthorne's A-Morality of Compromise," *Representations* 24 (Fall 1988): 1–27.

4. Tony Tanner, *City of Words: American Fiction 1950–1970* (New York: Harper & Row, 1971). Hereafter cited as *CW*.

5. Jean Baudrillard, "The Ecstasy of Communication," in *The Anti-Aesthetic: Essays on Postmodern Culture*, ed. Hal Foster, (Port Townsend, Wash.: Bay Press, 1983) 126–33.

6. See Louis A. Sass, "Introspection, Schizophrenia, and the Fragmentation of Self," *Representations* 19 (Summer 1987): 1–34.

7. J. Laplanche and J.-B. Pontalis, *The Language of Psycho-Analysis*, trans. Donald Nicholson-Smith, (New York: Norton, 1973), 35–36. See also their listings for *fixation, paraphrenia* (Freud's favored term), and *paranoia*. See also Sigmund Freud, "The Unconscious" (1915e), ed. and trans. James Strachey, *Standard Edition of the Complete Psychological Works of Sigmund Freud*, XIV, chap. 7: 159–209.

8. Sacvan Bercovitch, "Afterword," in *Ideology and Classic American Literature* (New York, London: Cambridge University Press, 1986), 420.

9. Fredric Jameson, "Postmodernism, or the Cultural Logic of Late Capitalism," *New Left Review* 146 (July/August 1984): 72.

10. John Barth, *The Floating Opera* (1967; reprint, New York: Bantam Books, 1972). The first edition (with alternate ending) is *The Floating Opera* (New York: Appleton-Century-Crosts, 1956). Citation is to the 1972 edition, hereafter noted as *FO*.

11. The critical response has mapped the thematics of the novel quite well, linking Barth to his existential precursors. See Richard

Schickel, "*The Floating Opera*," *Critique* 6, no. 2 (1963): 53–67; Tanner, *City of Words*; Jac Tharpe, *John Barth: The Comic Sublimity of Paradox* (Carbondale: Southern Illinois University Press, 1974); David Morrell, *John Barth, An Introduction* (University Park and London: Pennsylvania State University Press, 1976). On the psychology of the novel, see Charles Harris, "Todd Andrews, Ontological Insecurity, and *The Floating Opera*," *Critique* 18, no. 2 (1977): 34–50; Dennis M. Martin, "Desire and Disease: The Psychological Pattern of *The Floating Opera*," *Critique* 18, no. 2 (1977): 17–33; E. P. Walkiewicz, *John Barth* (Boston: Twayne, 1986). On the complex relation of father to son in the novel, see Heide Ziegler, *John Barth* (London and New York: Methuen, 1987), 19–25.

12. See Jean Baudrillard, "The Precession of Simulacra," in *Art after Modernism: Rethinking Representation*, ed. Brian Wallis, (Boston: Godine, 1984), 254.

13. John Barth, "How to Make a Universe," *The Friday Book: Essays and Other Nonfiction* (New York: Putnam, 1984), 15. Hereafter cited as *F.*

14. Franz Kafka, "Before the Law," in *Franz Kafka: The Complete Stories*, trans. Willa and Edwin Muir, ed. Nahum N. Glatzer, (1946; reprint, New York: Schocken Books, 1976), 3–4.

15. For a critique of how literature inhabits the law, see Jacques Derrida, "The Law of Genre," trans. Avital Ronell, *Glyph* 7 (Baltimore: Johns Hopkins University Press, 1980): 202–29. Perhaps the most extensive and perceptive reading of Kafka's text is Jacques Derrida, "Devant la loi," trans. Avital Ronell, in *Kafka and the Contemporary Critical Performance*, ed. Alan Udoff, (Bloomington: Indiana University Press, 1987).

16. On the need for and lack of impartiality in the law, see Morton J. Horwitz, *The Transformation of American Law, 1780–1860* (Cambridge: Harvard University Press, 1977), 256–57. See also Stanley Fish, "Anti-Professionalism," *Cardozo Law Review* 7 (1986): 645–77. See also Peter Gabel, "Reification in Legal Reasoning," *Research in Law and Sociology* 3:25–51. Gabel notes that "through the law we tell ourselves, through the collective terror and coercion that I have described, that what is, ought to be—that the system follows a law. This profound tautology expresses what I mean when I say that the function of law is legitimation" (29). And for a legal scholar's perspective on the novel, see Robin L. West, "Adjudication Is Not Interpretation: Some Reservations about the Law-as-Literature Movement," *Tennessee Law Review* 54 (1987): 203–78. West gives an extensive critique of *The Floating Opera* and the problem of the choice between finding or making law. And finally, see David Kairys, "Legal Reasoning," in *The Politics of Law: A Progressive Critique* (New York: Pantheon, 1982): "Law is simply politics by other means" (17).

CAROL COLATRELLA

12

Bercovitch's Paradox: Critical Dissent, Marginality, and the Example of Melville

In an essay surveying the practices of New Americanist critics, Donald Pease uses the term *field-Imaginary* to describe how these critics imagine their subject field and to indicate how their ideological interests reconfigure American literature and culture.[1] Pease's essay reviews Frederick Crews's recent attack on New Americanist criticism, demonstrates how New Americanists deny the separation of public questions from aesthetic study, and explains how their ideological criticism offers the possibility of political change. In describing the pivotal role played by Sacvan Bercovitch, whom Pease represents as a mediating figure between older historicist approaches and the more explicitly political approaches of the New Americanists, Pease develops what I will refer to as "Bercovitch's paradox": Bercovitch's explanation of how dissensus is incorporated as an affirmation of culture itself becomes an ideology privileging consensus and negating the possibility that dissenters are truly able to effect change in society.[2]

For Pease, Bercovitch's claim that dissensus cannot radically change culture does not take into account the highly charged political effects of today's scholarship. Bercovitch argues that literary analysis should not be confused with social action, but Pease counters by noting that New Americanists affect society by "revisionist interventions into the canon" ("New Americanists," 32).[3] Pease asserts that academic culture, and therefore culture at large, has been revolutionized and continues to change as a result of ideological and political innovations inaugurated by New Americanists using New Historicist approaches that incorporate historical, anthropological, sociological, and linguistic disciplinary interests. Because New Americanist critics/scholars broaden the field-Imaginary of American literature beyond the aesthetic, they resist separating public from cultural discourse. By drawing on cultural explanations to contextualize literary texts or by using literary methods to explicate cultural documents, New Americanist critics are "*liaisons between* cultural and public realms, they are at once within the field yet external to it" ("New Americanists," 31). Pease claims that their roles as mediators and as "representatives of subjects excluded from the field-Imaginary by the previous political unconscious" enable them to "overcome oppositional containment" by inserting previously omitted subjects into literary and historical discourses ("New Americanists," 31, 29).[4]

In criticizing Bercovitch's metanarrative of dissent and cohesion as enshrining the oppositional discourse of cold-war ideology, Pease marginalizes Bercovitch's view of ideology and culture as out of step with work by New Americanists that demonstrates how politics and culture are enmeshed in academic practice. Yet Pease's argument works by distinguishing not how critics oppose Bercovitch's cultural model, but how they extrapolate from it and extend its significance into a broader political realm. The *boundary 2* essays by New Americanists demonstrate that the rhetoric of dissent and its assimilation by culture remains a valid account despite Pease's concern that it is itself an ideologically driven narrative. Bercovitch's model of dissensus has not been superseded, only enacted, in another anthology that explores diverse points of view under an umbrella topic. While Pease discounts whether dissensus serves as a viable model explaining the cultural force of literary studies, he introduces a collection offering "counter-hegemonic" essays as authoritatively transforming the discipline of American Studies.

Pease assumes the progressivist nature of critical studies and assures us that the revisionist interventions of the New Americanists in the *boundary 2* collection represent an advance on Bercovitch's theory. Responding to Crews, Pease optimistically sees recent criticism as changing culture, but he does not discuss the considerable resistance outside the academy to New Americanist criticism; re-forming the canon, becoming more interdisciplinary, and analyzing ideology in aesthetic practice are supported by some academics but not the culture at large. Instead of revitalizing the general culture's attitude toward American literature and changing political views, new critical discourses have generated conservative responses that contain new academic programs by marking them as oppositional and unrelated to mainstream thinking; so-called "political correctness" is represented as an ideology working against what most Americans believe.[5] Academic change has been represented in the media as dissent from accepted social principles, and many Americans react negatively to what they perceive as a liberal agenda arbitrarily changing university curricula.

Although Pease cites canon formation as a case demonstrating that Bercovitch's model of dissensus is not an adequate explanation of how New Americanist criticism can affect practical change, he ends his essay by noting that so far only academia has changed and that the rest of the culture will follow. The field of American studies, and therefore the university curriculum, now includes W. E. B. Du Bois, but, as Pease indicates, "such inclusion speak powerfully to what changes still need to be effected in U.S. culture" ("New Americanists," 37). By acknowledging the limited changes effected by the New Americanists, Pease's explanation of the political power of ideological criticism demonstrates how dissenting views are gradually incorporated into the larger cultural narrative. Although New Americanist criticism offers hope for effective political change, a hope missing from the metanarrative of dissensus, so far that political change is held off as a promise even in Pease's essay. Pease views Bercovitch's metanarrative of how dissent reaffirms culture as a theory that impedes the progress of American studies if it is universally applied, but Pease himself follows the model of cohesion and dissent to describe how New Americanist revisions affect the stories we tell our students.

Pease's optimistic rejoinder to Crews's review claims that the critic has the potential to transform society through pedagogical practices, but even this power cannot forestall another hegemonic order that will be countered. Indeed, the conservative claim that political correctness has become a fascism of the Left arises as a dissenting view reacting against what are perceived as already accepted principles of multiculturalism and diversity. Pease suggests that the New Americanists can potentially become the hegemonic order dominating the academy. Because it is difficult to transcend Bercovitch's formulation of how the marginal is incorporated by dominant social forces if we use that model to describe how the academy is changing, it might be more useful to consider why the reaffirmation of culture through dissensus is an attractive concept for him.

Bercovitch has devoted much attention to the question of how ideology "pretends to truth." He asserts that "to criticize a piece of ideology is to see through it, to expose its historical functions, necessarily from an extrinsic, and usually from a hostile, perspective."[6] While this method of ideological criticism has inspired critics studying how exclusions based on race, class, and gender have affected American studies, Bercovitch's work remains centered on the construction of value systems and their symbolization rather than interrogating how a particular ideology affects women, ethnic minorities, or the poor. His continuing interest remains investigating how the marginal point of view is initially opposed but eventually subsumed by a dominant social order.

Any analysis of Bercovitch's theory must consider how his seemingly pessimistic outlook concerning the efficacy of dissent is deeply affected by his recognition of his own marginal status in relation to American culture. This marginality is profoundly demonstrated by his validation of American Renaissance authors who felt alienated from their culture—Herman Melville in particular. It is no surprise that Melville is an author Bercovitch acknowledges as difficult to write about, for his own critical position resembles Melville's self-determined position as a writer whose alienation from the world of his father led him to disdain systems and system making.

What is most striking in comparing the critic to the writer is their shared prevailing attitude toward social change, an attitude that suggests that although change is very much needed, it is unlikely to occur, because authorities routinely resist it. H. Bruce Franklin and Michael Rogin have convincingly demonstrated how in its attack on class interest Melville's fiction offers powerful social criticism.[7] Bercovitch, in *The American Jeremiad,* considers Melville's early writings as "the great mid-nineteenth-century example of . . . cultural schizophrenia," and he judges Melville's ambivalence as locked in a "symbolic structure" of promoting and denouncing America.[8] In *Pierre* and *Redburn* Melville reveals a static system of social class at work through the failure of the individual to exercise social mobility; Bercovitch discusses the novels in an article relating individual and national identity.[9] In other fictions, including *White-Jacket, Moby-Dick, Mardi, The Confidence-Man,* and the short stories, Melville describes more generally how tyrannical authority tramples individual rights; Bercovitch has carefully analyzed this theme in relation to *The Scarlet Letter.* As a social critic conscious of the ideological role of historical narrative, Bercovitch revises our understanding of the Puritans and Revolutionary myth making, a subject Melville considered in *Pierre* and explicitly developed in *Israel Potter.*

Most significantly, both writers rely on cross-cultural comparisons as a means of enunciating social criticism. In his essay "Discovering America," Bercovitch relates how his status as a Canadian Jew has encouraged him to approach the study of American literature as an exercise in cross-cultural or comparative cultural criticism. Melville's own career began with the publication of *Typee,* a travel narrative that offers comparative cultural criticism in the form of a South Seas romance. While I would not want to claim that Bercovitch has modeled his scholarly career on Melville's artistic one, I note that Melville's work as a critic of culture has served as a touchstone for Bercovitch's development of a comparative critical perspective analyzing cultural rituals.

Accordingly, I adopt Bercovitch's perspective to discuss *Typee,* a text demonstrating how in the interest of continuity a community demands the absorption of dissent and resists true social change. In particular I focus on Melville's response to the nineteenth-century prison reformers' philosophies of human behavior, philosophies that demanded the acculturation of the individual into the normative community. The rehabilitation process, as acculturation, required the criminal to enter into a liminal state in prison in order to reenter the community as a normal citizen. By looking at issues of liminality and marginality, I show how Melville utilizes the image of a captive in society to refer to the artist or any social critic; the narrator of *Typee* becomes further marginalized in the telling of his story, for he recognizes how acculturation can sometimes fail. In order to put my reading of the novel in an appropriate historical context, I summarize nineteenth-century views regarding transgression and criminal behavior as examples of dissidence similar to those represented in Melville's fictions.

AUTHORITY, TRANSGRESSION, AND LIMINALITY

The nineteenth-century prison reform movement was typical of American reform movements of the period in offering the possibility of improving an inherited technology deemed outmoded for a rapidly industrializing society. According to reformers, industrial progress could be matched by improvements in criminal justice, most notably in the construction and maintenance of penitentiaries built to conform to modern ideas of incarceration developed in the late eighteenth century.[10] Reformers attempted to rehabilitate transgressive individuals by subjecting them to schedules and environments organized to instill discipline. In the 1840s and 1850s there was a "growing conviction that crime was a disease of the finer sensibilities, to be prevented by education and social reform."[11] Inmates learned discipline through education, one dominated by religious principles and practices, rather than punishment; the whip was meant for only the most hardened cases.

The prisoner was redeemed from the power of past actions, habits, attitudes, and companions as a way of stabilizing society; institutional reform represented "an effort to insure the cohesion of the community in new and changing circumstances."[12] The views shared by prison reformers, often embodied in narratives by ministers or criminals, emphasized a Puritan code that invested redemptive status in what Bercovitch terms "the symbol of America" and associated individual redemption with this national symbol. Anyone could be redeemed with the right combination of habit and encouragement. The conjunction of individual and national myths predicated on the always evolving and maturing American character provided a powerful motivation for enforcing penitentiary rules as a way of forming good citizens. Ironically, a myth enshrining the value of the Puritans' or colony's right to dissent from an unrighteous authority began to serve as support for a repressive and authoritarian system to control individual impulses perceived as deviant.

In the 1830s and 1840s prison reform societies in New York, Boston, and Philadelphia monitored the penitentiaries located in their vicinities, and their members debated rehabilitation techniques and philosophies in society and popular journals. Promoted as the most suitable means of instilling discipline in the individual, the solitary (Philadelphia) and silent (Auburn) systems of punishment advocated by prison reformers provided a target for Melville's fictional criticism of social injustice, while the philosophical statements published by the reformers served as rhetorical models that he parodied in his novels and short stories.[13]

Sensitive to the social ills of his culture, Melville sold his fiction to journals that also published essays on rehabilitation, and he prided himself on the contemporary relevance of his works, often alluding to historical criminals and reformers in his conversations, letters, and fiction. He joked with Evert Duyckinck about women inmates of Sing Sing, received an introduction to meet the French prison reformer Gustave de Beaumont, and visited the Auburn penitentiary during a lecture tour in upstate New York.[14] What is even more striking than biographical anecdotes linking Melville to the subject of prison reform is the preponderance of prison references in the novels and short stories. His fiction describes punishment and discipline as social acts that brutalize an underclass of working men and women; each work documents abuses that authority engenders, abuses that should be eliminated after being called to the reader's attention. For example, Melville noted with satisfaction how the graphic description of flogging in *White Jacket* had encouraged the United States Navy to abolish this practice.[15]

COMPARING WICKEDNESS: THE VOICE OF THE PARTICIPANT-OBSERVER IN *TYPEE*

Typee (1846) was originally published as an "authentic" travel narrative presenting cogent social criticism in the guise of a romance describing the idyllic lives of South Seas natives. In order to appear in John Murray's series the Colonial and Home Library, the manuscript was amended by Melville to satisfy his publisher's wish that the book edify as well as entertain its readers. As Leon Howard explains, Melville

> had told a story which appealed to John Murray and which contained enough out-of-the-way information to make it adaptable to the publisher's new project. But it was too good—and too predominantly—a story, and he was required to add more material about the manners and customs of a strange people in order to fulfill his publisher's promise to contribute to the "intellectual advancement" of his readers.[16]

Presented to the public as a partially fictional ethnography, *Typee* presents the participant-observer's point of view as the product of a consciousness confronting another culture and demonstrates how observing a different culture creates a new voice, that of a traveler who is forever changed by his experience.

Somewhat inspired by the European romantic's nostalgia for the primitive, Melville develops a distinctively American comparison of the civilized and the primitive by constructing a narrator whose voice mediates between cultures.[17] The participant-observer's voice in *Typee* describes the development of an individual consciousness as it recognizes the values that limit and enhance both cultures. In acknowledging how culture both constrains and enables the individual, the novel represents a significant model for Bercovitch's criticism.

It is Tommo's nostalgia for two homes that sets him apart from other literary voyagers who have commented on cultural differences.[18] As a travel narrative, *Typee* is different from European Enlightenment works that describe what the primitive might teach the civilized, not only because it presents an American vision, but because it demonstrates the inefficacy of national and cultural bias.[19] Understanding that each culture enables and constrains individual and social freedoms, Tommo resembles no one so much as he does a twentieth-century poststructuralist anthropological critic who accepts cultural differences as inevitable and often overwhelming for the individual.

Structured as a romantic adventure story, *Typee* presents a personalized ethnography of tribal customs. It includes descriptions of family and kinship structures, food, religious observances, clothing and body ornamentation, language, leisure activities, and the influence of Europeans on the Typees that mark the novel as an anthropological investigation into another culture; but it also contains self-reflective commentary that makes it a metaethnography.[20] The narrator, a young sailor who takes on the name *Tommo* when he meets the Typees, blends romantic revery and vitriolic social criticism as he changes his appearance, outlook, and philosophy of life in responding to his hosts.[21] Tommo's reactions to another culture represent what a contemporary critic of anthropology calls "the paradoxical nature of ethnographic knowledge."[22]

The conflicting aims of ethnographic practice create the paradox. James Clifford argues that modern ethnographic practice depends on two attitudes—anthropological humanism and ethnographic surrealism. Both perspectives are "elements within a complex process that generates cultural meanings, definitions of self and other." These ways of seeing are contrasted by the anthropologist as interdependent aspects of the process of cultural knowledge. "To state the contrast schematically," Clifford explains,

> anthropological humanism begins with the different and renders it—through naming, classifying, describing, interpreting—comprehensible. It familiarizes. An ethnographic surrealist practice, by contrast, attacks the familiar, provoking the irruption of otherness—the unexpected. (*Predicament of Culture,* 145–46)

Clifford distinguishes these two strands of ethnographic practice, the familiarizing of a different culture and the attacking of the familiar in a culture, but he acknowledges that both characteristics identify the modern global perspective valued by twentieth-century ethnographers. The conflicting impulses of humanism and surrealism appear as stylistic modes in twentieth-century anthropology and in *Typee.* In Melville's novel the first-person narrator ambivalently swings between both modes in describing an adventure that relies upon his fundamental inability to decide whether the Typee represent the familiar or the unexpected. When Clifford refers to "the paradoxical nature of ethnographic knowledge," he reminds us that anthropology as a discipline assumes the cultural incorporation of difference and that an anthropological attitude necessitates a difficult relation between observer and observed culture.

The ambivalent voice of the participant-observer in *Typee* combines the paradoxical impulses of the ethnographer who struggles to see another culture in order to offer a global perspective of culture in general. In reading cultural rituals of the Typees as different from the "Christian" practices of contemporary Americans, Tommo takes up a critical posture that makes him a marginalized, yet friendly, observer of both cultures. Like anthropological critics encountering an other that becomes familiar, Melville creates a cultural criticism that redefines narrative conventions of travel literature by placing Tommo between America and Typee. Bercovitch's cross-cultural approach to literature similarly depends upon adopting a position at the edge of a cultural system. The ethnographer's role as observer, the critical posture described by Bercovitch, is what allows Tommo to compare cultures without evaluating them according to any hierarchical status and to explain how one culture affects the development of another.

The American title of *Typee—Typee, a Peep at Polynesian Life—*reveals Melville's ambivalence as a reader whose fascination with island culture verges on voyeuristic observation of an exotically different realm. *Typee* describes the first-person narrator's adventures that brought the novelist into the public eye as "the man who lived among cannibals," a reputation that he complained, in a letter to Hawthorne, might never leave him, but which on occasion he used to his advantage. A decade after the publication of *Typee,* Melville presented himself to audiences in the Northeast and Midwest as a lecturer qualified to speak on "travel" and "the South Seas." "Going primitive" became a marketable commodity for him.

The participant-observer's point of view in *Typee* creates the persona of Tommo, who takes shape as the melancholy American seeking relief in a tropical paradise. Until our first-person narrator introduces himself to the Typees, we do not know his name. Only when the name *Tommo* is offered up as the least objectionable name that the Typee chief can pronounce do we learn who is speaking. It is significant that Tommo appears nameless until he confronts the Typees. Throughout the narrative we learn about the first-person narrator only as we hear about the Typees; we find out Tommo's identity by observing his interactions with the tribe. His preferences regarding food, clothing, and friendship emerge only as a result of contact with the natives, just as the character of the tribe develops only in reference to his point of view.

The anthropologist, or the critic who takes up an anthropological point of view, acts as participant-observer and creates an identity based on observations of others. In "Discovering America," Bercovitch describes how his methodology arose out of his experience of being an outsider in American culture, permitting him to examine critically the values held by that culture. The critic must be willing to be transformed, to enter into a liminal state that will only partly satisfy the desire for knowledge and/or belonging. Tommo's point of view, his character, and his methodology develop similarly as he reacts to the Typees, whose way of life is very different from that which he has left behind.

Tommo observes Typee culture and presents his views in a seemingly detached way, but he also partially enters into the culture and creates an identity motivated by the desire to flee. He seems particularly driven to escape by a need to change his surroundings. The narrator is initially defined only by his longing to satisfy his hunger and leave his dreary life aboard ship. The island paradise he seeks further characterizes him as a idealistic dreamer who might find a home in the South Seas. Because he does come upon the idyllic and harmonious existence he has yearned for, we might assume that Tommo would remain in Typee. But a fear that he is being kept captive only to be consumed haunts the narrator and encourages him to give up his Polynesian life and escape his native captors. Throughout the course of his narrative, Tommo struggles to balance relaxed happiness with his ominous dread of some gruesome fate. His state of tension is never resolved, for he appears to be in a permanent liminal condition.[23]

The narrator's ambivalence toward the Typees is most clearly demonstrated by his difficulty in accepting his captivity among cannibals. The Typees are virtuously domestic except in their tendency toward cannibalism, evidence of which Tommo stumbles on accidentally. The antitheses that frame Tommo's dilemma of being unhappy in paradise (civilization versus savagery, attraction to the Typees versus revulsion from the Typees, being part of the community versus being a stranger in it or a potential victim of its cannibalism) demonstrate that ambivalences are not resolved in the course of the narrative. The narrator's state of tension as he confronts and struggles with Typee culture does not produce transcendent wisdom that he can take away when he escapes. His experience of Typee life permits him instead to compare two cultures and to represent the chaotic and bewildering effects of doing ethnography as well as experiencing the confusion of acculturation.[24]

By understanding oppression and marginalization in the context of Typee culture, Tommo becomes more like the Typees, who suffer in their interactions with the Christian missionaries, as he becomes more of a stranger to his own society. It is ironic that Tommo views his mostly friendly stay among the natives as a kind of imprisonment, held by the Typees because he has jumped ship and entered their community, but his captivity does not make him hostile to the Typees. Unlike other Westerners described in the novel, he presents a more understanding vision of their way of life, because he recognizes that he has more freedom as a prisoner among cannibals than he does as a free man in Western society.[25]

Waxing eloquent about the "primitive" virtues of Fayaway and her people, *Typee* criticizes the United States as a society dominated by the harsh dicta of a capitalist order. But neither culture emerges as superior, for Tommo carefully distinguishes the benefits and disadvantages of both. The centerpiece of comparative cultural criticism occurs in chapter 17 of *Typee,* entitled "Comparative Wickedness of Civilized and Unenlightened People," which claims that the Typees live in peace and harmony because their society abjures money. Tommo reflects on the evils of money, and he considers that the benefits of life in Polynesian society depend on its lack of a capitalist economy:

> There were none of those thousand sources of irritation that the ingenuity of civilized man has created to mar his own felicity. There were no foreclosures of mortgages, no protested notes, no bills payable, no debts of honor in Typee; no unreasonable tailors and shoemakers, perversely bent on being paid; no duns of any description; no assault and battery attorneys, to foment discord, backing their clients up to a quarrel, and then knocking their heads together; no poor relations, everlastingly occupying the spare bed-chamber, and diminishing the elbow room at the family table; no destitute widows with their children starving on the cold charities of the world; no beggars; no debtors' prisons; no proud and hard-hearted nabobs in Typee; or to sum up all in one word—no Money! That 'root of all evil' was not to be found in the valley (126).

Evil, justice, and punishment appear as inevitably constructed by cultural values, for Tommo describes dissident behavior within the context of a particular culture. According to his reasoning, prisons are necessary only in hierarchical societies that punish those who are unable to beat the system. Melville, who was well-informed about penitentiary practices, knew that prison laborers often supported the state institutions that held them.[26]

In general, Melville's fictions offer intense responses to criminality and the criminal justice system, sometimes sympathetic toward those who are abused by authority and, more rarely, critical of those who transgress.[27] In *Typee* he associates criminality with capitalism.[28] For the natives, crime does not exist; without much private property and without needs engendered by capitalist production, the only transgressions appear to be those enacted against cultural taboos. Tommo must receive special dispensation to take Fayaway on a boat, but the Typees adjust to this innovation with the same equanimity that permits Mehevi to adopt Tommo's cast-off shoes as a badge of honor. These innovations don't upset the system; they are incorporated as minor additions to already accepted ritual.

Similarly, Tommo accepts certain aspects of Typee culture and adjusts his diet, dress, and attitude. Compared with the demanding life of "civilization," Typee seems a welcome relief to Tommo. He develops a taste for *poee-poee* (73) and learns to discriminate his preferences for certain preparations of breadfruit, calling one particular recipe "luscious" (114). He wears native dress, a yellow tappa for indoor wear, and supplements it with a robe when he ventures outside (121). As his mysterious leg wound improves, he becomes more comfortable in rambling around the valley with the natives and describes a lifting of the melancholy that set in after his companion Toby's departure: "I began to experience an elasticity of mind which placed me beyond the reach of those dismal forebodings to which I had so lately been a prey" (123). This "elasticity of mind" permits him to appreciate the advantages of living in Typee, called by him the "Happy Valley" secluded from "a world of care and anxiety." Tommo appreciates that the Polynesian "enjoyed an infinitely happier, though certainly a less intellectual existence, than the self-complacent European" (124). By the time he decides to wear a gala costume for a ritual festival, he looks more like a Polynesian than any other American or European in the text, and Mehevi, among others, is "delighted" by his appearance (165).

Although Tommo doesn't see any prisons holding Polynesians in Typee, he does come to regard the narrowly defined existence he is permitted by his hosts as a kind of captivity. He is forbidden to travel freely, and he is always watched by Kory-Kory, who reports his activities to the chiefs. The ostensible reason the Typees give for keeping close watch on Tommo is that his injured leg requires that others protect him from dangerous tribes unfriendly to theirs. Toby's report of being attacked by the Happars would seem to support the Typees (101), but Tommo remains suspicious of the natives. After Fayaway reports that Toby has left on a boat, Tommo fears that Toby's disappearance could mean he has already fallen victim to the seemingly friendly Typees. Tommo distrusts the Typees, despite their care, because he does not understand why they welcome his company; fattening up their captive seems a possible explanation.[29] As close as Tommo feels to Fayaway and Kory-Kory, he cannot completely trust them; after all they are, he thinks, still cannibals.

Another characteristic of life in Typee that reminds Tommo of prison is the elaborate tattooing that most young men eagerly wear. Kory-Kory's tattoos are explicitly described as a kind of imprisonment because he

> had seen fit to embellish his face with three broad longitudinal stripes of tattooing, which . . . crossed his nasal organ,

> descended into the hollow of his eyes, and even skirted the borders of his mouth. Each completely spanned his physiognomy; one extending in a line with his eyes, another crossing the face in the vicinity of the nose, and the third sweeping along his lips from ear to ear. His countenance thus triply hooped, as it were, with tattooing, always reminded me of those unhappy wretches whom I have sometimes observed gazing out sentimentally from behind the grated bars of a prison window. (83)

Although pursued vigorously by the Typees, Tommo rejects being tattooed, because he wants to be able to leave the tribe and reenter American society much as he left it. A prominently worn tattoo would make it more difficult for him to live outside of Typee, and he resists the persistent attempts of the natives to convince him to submit to this adornment. Accepting a tattoo would mean being absorbed by the culture, although it is a less violent form of absorption than cannibalism.

In chapter 32, Tommo notes, after meeting Karky the tattoo artist, "My life was one of absolute wretchedness" (231). Tommo fears tattooing as the outward sign of cannibalism, a sign that would mark complete conversion to the Typee way of life and a harbinger of the "painful malady" that mysteriously afflicts his leg (232). Fear of tattooing appears, and the medical ailment reappears, in the narrative just before Tommo glimpses three heads, one of which is a white man's, that serve during his few moments of panic as tangible proof of Typee viciousness. Once again his fear of cannibalism returns, and he resolves to escape from imprisonment.[30]

After Tommo escapes from another culture he has come to regard as his prison, he heads for the ocean (which has come to represent "Home" and "Mother") as eagerly as he had previously jumped ship and headed for Polynesian land. His leave-taking of the Typees reveals his bonds with both cultures, the "primitive" and the "civilized." Although eager to escape the wrath of young warriors who pursue him, he is sad to say good-bye to Fayaway and Kory-Kory. The first chapter of *Omoo* confirms this ambivalence by acknowledging that Tommo misses the Typees almost as soon as he leaves them:

> But how far short of our expectations is oftentimes the fulfillment of the most ardent hopes. Safe aboard a ship—so long my earnest prayer—with home and friends once more in

> prospect, I nevertheless felt weighed down by a melancholy that could not be shaken off. It was the thought of never more seeing those, who, notwithstanding their desire to retain me a captive, had, upon the whole, treated me so kindly. I was leaving them forever.[31]

Torn between the desire to stay and the desire to leave, when he feels he has been captured and held, Tommo always swings back toward the other choice. He wants to be wherever he isn't, and he seeks out marginality as preferential to being part of any system.

In *Typee* the attractions of being outside culture while being able to dip into it are also demonstrated in the characters of Toby, the author's shipmate who escapes from the rigors of shipboard life and sojourns briefly among the Typees, and Marnoo, the outcast who serves as a go-between for the Typees and their neighboring tribes. Marnoo is welcome to visit the various tribes, but none takes him in as a member; his role as a mediator permits news to travel between tribes. Because he is able to speak a number of dialects as well as English, he can talk to members of other tribes and Europeans, but all remain suspicious of these abilities. The narrator similarly describes Toby as "one of those class of rovers you sometimes meet at sea, who never reveal their origin, never allude to home, and go rambling over the world as if pursued by some mysterious fate they cannot possible elude (32). Like Marnoo and Toby, Tommo fails to find happiness in a particular society, for he prefers to be able to shuttle between cultures.[32]

By interacting with the Typees, Tommo constructs a persona and a narrative that he might not have otherwise produced. By living among the tribe he becomes less American and more Typee and creates an identity as a mediator between the two cultures that recognizes the failure of any system to satisfy individual desires.[33] Although Tommo leaves paradise, he cannot be satisfied, for his development as a thinking individual and his very sense of self become inextricably entwined with his observation of Typee culture.

Of course, Tommo is not the only Melvillean protagonist who reaches the conclusion that his fate is to wander. We do not know what happens to Ishmael at the end of *Moby-Dick,* except that he survives, and we know that the narrators of *Omoo, Redburn,* and *White-Jacket* also survive, but for what end we are not told. As Redburn learns when he returns to his native shore, the sailor's inability to find a home anywhere is an example of how anyone who tries to escape the strictures of society feels alienated, alone, and friendless in a bustling city where each individual seems entrenched in an unhappy position. The sailor is a jack-of-all-trades and master of none who is at home neither on land nor at sea. Melville poignantly writes that "sailors only go *round* the world, without going *into* it; and their reminiscences of travel are only a dim recollection of a chain of tap-rooms surrounding the globe."[34]

The sailor's position as a marginalized anthropological observer of two cultures resembles the posture advocated by current theorists of culture, including Bercovitch. Sailors travel the world, but they resist being enmeshed in a particular culture, offering a lesson to anthropologists and literary critics. Cultural criticism requires adopting a position removed from the observed area. As Myra Jehlen asserts in an important directive to feminists, the critic must, like Archimedes, "find a standpoint off this world altogether."[35] The critic's perpetual search for a better place that is always a promise deferred describes participation in what Bercovitch calls a myth of "American selfhood," "an identity in progress, advancing from prophecies performed toward paradise to be regained."[36]

Holding marginality as a positive vantage point puts Bercovitch in the company of other cultural critics whose personal crossing of national borders influences their work.[37] In a chapter on modern Anglo-French orientalism in *Orientalism,* Edward Said notes that Erich Auerbach reproduced in a late essay a poignant quotation from Hugo of St. Victor's *Didascalicon:* "The man who finds his homeland sweet is still a tender beginner; he to whom every soil is as his native one is already strong; but he is perfect to whom the entire world is as a foreign land." Said remarks that

> the more one is able to leave one's cultural home, the more easily is one able to judge it, and the whole world as well, with the spiritual detachment *and* generosity necessary for true vision. The more easily, too, does one assess oneself and alien cultures with the same combination of intimacy and distance.[38]

This statement marks Said's "critical posture," according to Clifford, as "humanist," because his "stance seems to presuppose a particularist, even individualist attitude combined with cosmopolitanism and a general valorization of creative process" (Clifford, *Predicament of Culture,* 263).[39]

The charge of humanism might also be directed at Bercovitch, for, like Said, Bercovitch assumes that both writers and symbols can affect history.[40] Analyzing the rhetoric of the jeremiad as a representation constructed by individuals and communities, one that in turn influences them, he indicates that one can endorse or resist cultural symbols. His discussion of the symbol of America acknowledges that "all our classic writers (to varying degrees) labored against the myth as well as within it" and "all of them, however captivated by the national dream, also *used* the dream to reach beyond the categories of their culture."[41] Pease argues that dissensus according to the Bercovitchean formulation results in a consensus of fragmentation, but Bercovitch's model of cohesion offers a way of dealing with cultural confrontation that respects individual differences by assessing how cultures resist and yet incline toward change. Bercovitch has contributed to the field of American studies by offering the metanarrative of dissensus as a powerful tool for unpacking cultural interaction. Although its universality has been challenged, the model of dissent reaffirming American culture has not been superseded as an explanation of cultural change and remains a cogent formulation of the particularly American process of familiarizing marginality by incorporation.

NOTES

1. Pease, "New Americanists: Revisionist Interventions into the Canon," *boundary 2* 17, no. 1 (Spring 1990): 1–37.

2. Myra Jehlen notes Clifford Geertz's similar description of Mannheim's Paradox in *Ideology and Classic American Literature,* ed. Sacvan Bercovitch and Myra Jehlen (Cambridge: Cambridge University Press, 1986), 12.

3. Bercovitch, "Discovering America: A Cross-Cultural Perspective" this volume.

4. In his introduction to volume 2 of New Americanist essays, "National Identities, Postmodern Artifacts, and Postnational Narratives," *boundary 2* 19, (Spring 1992): 1–13, Pease corrects his earlier criticism of Crews (2), offers an extended explanation of how critics are mediators, and indicates that the 1992 essays "configure individually and collectively *post*national narratives as the surfaces on which New Americanists have constructed their identities" (3). Because Pease does not comment on Sacvan Bercovitch's work in the 1992 introduction, my discussion here responds only to Pease's 1990 essay.

5. I am thinking of the debate over the Stanford curriculum and the

backlash against multiculturalism described in Dinesh D'Souza's *Illiberal Education* (New York: Free Press, 1991) as well as recent battles that pit the NEH as a defender of traditional American scholarship against the fashionable and seemingly dangerous "political correctness" of the MLA.

6. Sacvan Bercovitch, "Afterword," in *Ideology and Classic American Literature* (Cambridge: Cambridge University Press, 1986), 421.

7. See H. Bruce Franklin, *Prison Literature in America: The Victim as Criminal and Artist* (Westport, Conn.: Lawrence Hill, 1978), and Michael Rogin, *Subversive Genealogy: The Politics and Art of Herman Melville* (Berkeley: University of California Press, 1983).

8. Sacvan Bercovitch, *The American Jeremiad* (Madison: University of Wisconsin Press, 1978), 191, 194.

9. Sacvan Bercovitch, "Melville's Search for National Identity: Son and Father in *Redburn, Pierre,* and *Billy Budd,*" *College Language Association Journal* 10 (March 1967): 217–28.

10. A contemporary survey of the reforms is given in Gustave de Beaumont and Alexis de Tocqueville, *On the Penitentiary System in the United States and Its Application in France,* trans. Francis Lieber (Philadelphia: Carey, Lea, & Blanchard, 1833). Also see Orlando F. Lewis, *The Development of American Prisons and Prison Customs, 1776–1845* (Prison Association of New York, 1922), and W. David Lewis, *From Newgate to Dannemora: The Rise of the Penitentiary in New York, 1776–1848* (Ithaca: Cornell University Press, 1965). A history of English penitentiaries is given in Michael Ignatieff, *A Just Measure of Pain: The Penitentiary in the Industrial Revolution, 1750–1850* (New York: Pantheon, 1978). Michel Foucault documents the shift from prison to penitentiary in France in *Discipline and Punish,* trans. Alan Sheridan (New York: Vintage, 1979).

11. David Brion Davis, *Homicide in American Fiction, 1798–1860* (Ithaca: Cornell University Press, 1957), 22.

12. From David Rothman, *The Discovery of the Asylum: Social Order and Disorder in the New Republic* (Boston and Toronto: Little, Brown, 1971), xviii. Rothman has noted regarding reform that penitentiaries were only one means of effecting social change: "Americans in the Jacksonian era began to construct and support institutions for deviant and dependent members of the community" (xii).

13. See Michael C. Berthold's 1987 Harvard dissertation on prison reform and Melville, "Who Ain't a Slave?"

14. Duyckinck's journal is held in the New York Public Library. Edward Everett's letter of introduction to Beaumont was evidently never used by Melville; it is reproduced in Melville, *Journals,* ed. Howard C.

Horsford with Lynn Horth (Evanston and Chicago: Northwestern University-Newberry Library, 1989), 612. Merton Sealts, *Melville as Lecturer* (Cambridge: Harvard University Press, 1957), 28–30, indicates that an article on page 3, column 1 of the 6 January 1858 issue of the Auburn *Daily American* documented Melville's visit to the prison on the previous day.

15. See his letter of 6 October 1850 to Evert Duyckinck, reproduced in *The Letters of Herman Melville,* ed. Merrell R. Davis and William H. Gilman (New Haven: Yale University Press, 1960), 114–15. On issues of authority, see Nicholas Canaday, Jr. *Melville and Authority* (Gainesville: University of Florida Press, 1968).

16. Leon Howard, "Historical Note," in Melville, *Typee* (Evanston and Chicago: Northwestern University-Newberry Library, 1968), 280.

17. Vernon Parrington claims that *Typee* offers an American response to an exotic culture because it is Melville's "answer to the French romantic Utopia of man in a state of nature. That the rankling wounds in man's heart are poisoned, if not originally inflicted, by social institutions, he was partly convinced, and he felt a lively concern lest western civilization should bring its futile restlessness to the simple island people." See Parrington, *Main Currents in American Literature,* vol. 2 (New York: Harcourt, Brace, & Company, 1927), 261–62.

18. The closest comparison can be made with Gulliver, whose experience with the Houyhnhnms convinces him that their emissaries might teach "the first principles of honour, justice, truth, temperance, public spirit, fortitude, chastity, friendship, benevolence, and fidelity" to civilized Europeans. See Jonathan Swift, *Gulliver's Travels,* chap. 12.

19. According to Merton Sealts (*Melville's Reading* [Columbia: University of South Carolina Press, 1988], later in life Melville read Montaigne and Rousseau and might have even read Montesquieu, all of whom addressed the question of how "civilized" people might respond to "primitive" cultures, but the primary sources for *Typee* remain travel narratives, especially those by William Ellis, Charles Stewart, and David Porter. Montaigne valued travel and saw it is as a means of extending the individual's perspective on life. He also noted that "each man calls barbarism whatever is not his own practice; for indeed it seems we have no other test of truth and reason than the example and pattern of the opinions and customs of the country we live in " (Montaigne, "Of cannibals," *The Complete Essays of Montaigne,* trans. Donald Frame [Stanford: Stanford University Press, 1943], 152). Similar relativistic claims appear in *La Nouvelle Hélöise,* where Rousseau describes Saint-Preux's observations of villagers, and in *The Persian Letters,* where Montesquieu discusses the Troglodytes.

20. Charles Anderson, *Melville in the South Seas* (New York: Columbia University Press, 1949), and T. Walter Herbert, *Marquesan Encounters:*

Melville and the Meaning of Civilization (Cambridge: Harvard University Press, 1980), offer two views of how Melville's observations document the cultures of the islands.

21. Note the parallel between Kevin Costner's *Dances with Wolves* and *Typee* discerned by David Arthur in his letter to the editor of the Arts and Leisure section of the *New York Times*, 17 February 1991.

22. James Clifford, *The Predicament of Culture: Twentieth-Century Ethnography, Literature, and Art* (Cambridge: Harvard University Press, 1988), 145.

23. For a definition of liminality as a cultural ritual, see Victor Turner, *Dramas, Fields, and Metaphors* (Ithaca: Cornell University Press, 1974), 13.

24. As Clifford remarks, "The surrealist moment in ethnography is that moment in which the possibility of comparison exists in unmediated tension with sheer incongruity" (*Predicament of Culture*, 146).

25. On the mixed meanings of Typee culture, see Toni H. Oliviero, "Ambiguous Utopia: Savagery and Civilization in *Typee* and *Omoo*," *Modern Language Studies* 13, (Winter 1983): 39–46.

26. The factory, the city, and the ship appear elsewhere in Melville's fiction as institutions predicated on authoritarian discipline and punishment associated with European and American penitentiaries. Jails and/or prisons are settings in *Pierre*, "Bartleby," *Israel Potter*, and *Billy Budd*; as Michael C. Berthold writes, "In the social contracts at work in Herman Melville's fiction, man is born in chains and is everywhere in chains" ("'Portentous Somethings': Melville's *Typee* and the Language of Captivity," *New England Quarterly* 60, (December 1987): 549.

27. David Reynolds claims Melville demonstrates an ambivalence toward criminal behavior that reproduces contemporary cultural values toward criminality (*Beneath the American Renaissance: The Subversive Imagination in the Age of Emerson and Melville* [Cambridge: Harvard University Press, 1988], esp. chap. 6).

28. As Melville demonstrated in other works, the economic injustice of class relations in Western cultures enslaved particular groups in society for the benefit of others. For example, the women who work in the paper mills described in "A Tartarus of Maids" are imprisoned in order to support the bachelors described in the paired sketch about lawyers. This portrait of captive labor eerily resembles the morally suspect project of enforced convict labor that provided prisons with a lucrative source of revenue.

29. I think John Samson overstates Tommo's distrust as his inability to abandon cultural stereotypes because he cannot "perceive the natives in

a culturally relative way" ("The Dynamics of History and Fiction in Melville's *Typee,*" *American Quarterly* 36 [Spring 1984]: 282).

30. Janet Giltrow ("Speaking Out: Travel and Structure in Herman Melville's Early Narratives," *American Literature* 52 [1980–81]: 31) links cannibalism in the text to the narrator's fear of being absorbed by a foreign place.

31. *Omoo* (Evanston and Chicago: Northwestern University-Newberry Library, 1968) 7.

32. Robert K. Martin ("Enviable Isles: Melville's South Seas," *Modern Language Studies* 12, no. 1 [Winter 1982]: 74) sees Marnoo and Toby as Melville's ideal, "somewhere between civilization and savagery." Toby's rescuer, who is described in the sequel as living as a kind of mercenary with a number of native wives, also serves as an example of a mediating marginal figure.

33. Wai-chee Dimock argues that it is unclear why Tommo leaves Typee, for both Typee society and American society are flawed communities ("*Typee:* Melville's Critique of Community," (*ESQ* 30 [October 1984]: 27–39).

34. Melville, *Redburn* (Evanston and Chicago: Northwestern University-Newberry Library, 1969), 133.

35. Myra Jehlen, "Archimedes and the Paradox of Feminist Criticism," *The Signs Reader* (Chicago: University of Chicago Press, 1983), 70.

36. Sacvan Bercovitch, *Puritan Origins of the American Self* (New Haven: Yale University Press, 1975), 143.

37. I disagree with Paul Bové, who argues that "Bercovitch's institutional power and scholarly, critical decorum . . . make him 'representative' within American studies"; Bové overlooks Bercovitch's biographical origin, religion, and move to America as determining factors in his critical perspective. See Bové, "A Politics of 'American' Criticism," in *In the Wake of Theory* (Middletown, Conn.: Wesleyan University Press, 1992), 56.

38. Edward Said, *Orientalism* (New York: Random House, 1978), 259. Bové also glosses this passage but comes to a different conclusion from mine. Bove notes that Said's suggestion admonishing the cultural critic to emulate the experience of exile applies more appropriately to the theories of postcolonialism advanced by Gayatri Spivak than it does to the critical practices of Bercovitch. See Bové, "A Politics of 'American' Criticism," 62–63.

39. Clifford indicates that "Said's humanist perspectives do not harmonize with his use of methods derived from Foucault, who is of course a

radical critic of humanism" but notes that certain inconsistencies demonstrated in *Orientalism* should not work against our appreciation of Said's "pioneering attempt to use Foucault systematically in an extended cultural analysis. Its difficulties and successes should thus be of interest to historians, critics, and anthropologists" (*Predicament of Culture,* 264).

40. In *Orientalism* 23, Said represents his difference from Foucault by indicating that he believes "in the determining imprint of individual writers."

41. Bercovitch, *American Jeremiad,* 179–80.

Contributors

JOSEPH ALKANA is assistant professor of English at the University of Miami. He has published articles on Hawthorne and on the American Enlightenment in *Philological Quarterly* and *Texas Studies in Literature and Language.* He is currently working on a study of nineteenth-century American psychology and literature.

BARRY ALLEN teaches philosophy at McMaster University in Hamilton, Ontario. His book, *Truth in Philosophy,* is forthcoming from Harvard University Press.

SACVAN BERCOVITCH is Charles H. Carswell Professor of English and American Literature at Harvard University. He is the author of many articles and books on American literature and culture, most recently *The Office of The Scarlet Letter,* which won the 1992 James Russell Lowell Prize of the MLA, and *The Rites of Assent: Transformations in the Symbolic Construction of America.* He is general editor of the forthcoming multivolume Cambridge History of American Literature.

THERON BRITT is assistant professor of English at Memphis State University. He has contributed essays on medical discourse to *The Journal of Health and Social Behavior, The Journal of Health Services,* and *Sociomedical Perspectives on Patient Care* (1992). He is currently writing a book on contemporary American fiction.

EMILY MILLER BUDICK is associate professor of American studies at the Hebrew University of Jerusalem. In addition to numerous essays on American literary figures, she has published *Emily Dickinson and the Life of Language and Fiction* and *Historical Consciousness: The American Romance Tradition.*

HELEN BURKE is assistant professor of English at Florida State University. Her essays have appeared in *ELH, Genre, Tulsa Studies in*

Women's Literature, and *The Eighteenth Century: Theory and Interpretation.* She is currently working on a study of eighteenth-century Irish drama.

DONALD J. CHILDS is assistant professor of English at the University of Ottawa. He has published essays in *ELH, American Literature, Essays in Criticism,* and *The Journal of Modern Literature* and is working on a study of T. S. Eliot.

CAROL COLATRELLA teaches literature at Rensselaer Polytechnic Institute. Her publications include *Evolution, Sacrifice, and Narrative: Balzac, Zola, and Faulkner* (1990). She is writing a book on Melville's rhetoric and nineteenth-century prison reform.

KATHLEEN FLANAGAN is assistant professor of English at Longwood College. She has published articles on modern American poetry and the Orient, and on postcolonial literature in English. She is currently at work on a study of colonialism in women's writing about Africa.

RAEL MEYEROWITZ teaches in the Literature and History Program at Harvard. He has published on Wallace Stevens and is currently completing a book on Jewish-American critics.

JOSÉ DAVID SALDÍVAR is associate professor of American literature at the University of California at Santa Cruz. He has published essays in *American Literary History, Dispositio,* and *Latin American Literary Review.* His book *The Dialectics of Our America: Genealogy, Cultural Critique, and Literary History* appeared in 1991.

KATHY SMITH is assistant director of the New Hampshire Humanities Council. She is a published poet who has taught writing at the University of Massachusetts at Amherst, St. Lawrence University, and the University of New Hampshire. Her essay on John McPhee appears in *Literary Journalism in the Twentieth Century.*

PRISCILLA WALD is assistant professor of American literature at Columbia University. She has published essays in *American Literary History, boundary 2,* and *Prospects.* She is currently completing a manuscript entitled *Constituting Americans.*